Mitchell Symons was born in 1957 in London and educated at Mill Hill School and the LSE where he studied Law. Since leaving BBC TV, where he was a researcher and then a director, he has worked as a writer, broadcaster and journalist. He was a principal writer of early editions of the board game Trivial Pursuit and has devised many television formats. Currently, he writes a weekly column for the *Sunday Express*. As for that difficult third novel he mentioned in *That Book* and *This Book*, he's no closer to finishing it.

www.**books**at**trans**world.co.uk

Also by Mitchell Symons

Non-fiction
Forfeit!
The Equation Book of Sports Crosswords
The Equation Book of Movie Crosswords
The You Magazine Book of Journolists
    (four books, co-author)
Movielists (co-author)
The Sunday Magazine Book of Crosswords
The Hello! Magazine Book of Crosswords
    (three books)
How To Be Fat: The Chip And Fry Diet (co-author)
The Book of Criminal Records
The Book of Lists
The Book of Celebrity Lists
The Book of Celebrity Sex Lists
The Bill Clinton Joke Book
National Lottery Big Draw 2000 (co-author)
That Book
This Book
Why Girls Can't Throw

Fiction
All In
The Lot

THE
OTHER
BOOK

THE OTHER BOOK

MITCHELL SYMONS

BANTAM PRESS

LONDON · TORONTO · SYDNEY · AUCKLAND · JOHANNESBURG

TRANSWORLD PUBLISHERS
61–63 Uxbridge Road, London W5 5SA
a division of The Random House Group Ltd

RANDOM HOUSE AUSTRALIA (PTY) LTD
20 Alfred Street, Milsons Point, Sydney,
New South Wales 2061, Australia

RANDOM HOUSE NEW ZEALAND LTD
18 Poland Road, Glenfield, Auckland 10, New Zealand

RANDOM HOUSE SOUTH AFRICA (PTY) LTD
Endulini, 5a Jubilee Road, Parktown 2193, South Africa

Published 2005 by Bantam Press
a division of Transworld Publishers

A catalogue record for this book is available from the British Library.
ISBN 0593 054806

Printed by Mackays of Chatham plc, Chatham, Kent

10 9 8 7 6 5 4 3 2 1

Papers used by Transworld Publishers are natural, recyclable products made
from wood grown in sustainable forests. The manufacturing
processes conform to the environmental regulations
of the country of origin.

To Penny, Jack and Charlie
with all my love

"More appealing than knowledge itself is the feeling of knowledge"
(Daniel J. Boorstin)

FIRSTS

Orville Wright was involved in the **first** aircraft accident (his passenger was killed).

Thomas Jefferson grew the **first** tomatoes in the United States. He wanted to prove to Americans that they were not poisonous (which people believed them to be).

The **first** female guest host of *Saturday Night Live* was Candice Bergen.

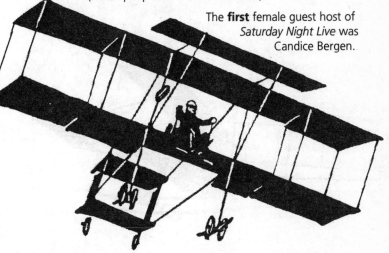

The **first** photograph of the moon was taken in 1839 (by Louis Daguerre).

The **first** electric Christmas lights were put together by a telephone switchboard installer. Candles were deemed to be too dangerous near a telephone switchboard so the installer took some lights from an old switchboard, connected them together, hooked them up to a battery and put them round a Christmas tree.

The **first** process of colour photography – using three colours – was patented (by William Morgan-Brown) in 1876.

Sunglasses **first** became popular in the 1920s when movie stars began wearing them to counteract the photographers' bright lights.

Pickled herrings were **first** eaten in the 14th century.

Jim Morrison of The Doors was the **first** rock star to be arrested on stage.

The world's **first** cash dispenser was opened by Reg Varney at Barclays Bank, Enfield, London in 1967.

Everton were the **first** British football club to introduce a stripe down the side of their shorts.

The **first** heart pacemaker (external) was fitted in 1952. The first *internal* pacemaker was fitted in 1958. The **first** successful heart operation had been carried out in 1896 by Louis Rehn in Frankfurt, Germany.

The duplicating machine was **first** patented by James Watt in 1780. The photocopier was invented in 1938 by Chester Carlson of New York.

Linoleum, the floor covering used in many kitchens, was **first** patented in 1863 by Frederick Walton of London.

The London Underground system was **first** used in 1863.

The typewriter was **first** patented by Henry Mill in 1714, but he never managed to market his invention.

The world's **first** scheduled passenger air service started in Florida in 1914.

The **first** toothbrush was invented in China in 1498.

The **first** supermarket in the world was in France.

In 1840 Henry Wadsworth Longfellow became the **first** American to have plumbing installed in his house.

Ties were **first** worn in Croatia (which is why they were called cravats, from *à la croate*).

The **first** British telephone directory was published by the London Telephone Company in 1880. It listed in excess of 250 names and numbers.

Lee Montague presented the **first** edition of *Jackanory* in 1964.

Sir Jimmy Savile presented the **first** edition of *Top Of The Pops* in 1964.

Jackie Rae presented the **first** edition of *The Golden Shot* in 1967.

The **first** word spoken by an ape in the movie *Planet of The Apes* was 'Smile'.

Sylvia Peters presented the **first** edition of *Come Dancing* in 1950.

Sir Alastair Burnet presented the **first** edition of *News At Ten* in 1967.

The **first** electric burglar alarm was installed in 1858 by one Edwin T. Holmes of Boston, Massachusetts. It is not recorded whether or not it worked.

Marilyn Monroe's **first** modelling agency had offices in the Ambassador Hotel – the same hotel in which Robert F. Kennedy was assassinated.

The **first** commercially successful escalator was patented in 1892 by Jesse Reno of New York.

Mark Knopfler wrote the **first** ever CD single ('Brothers In Arms').

The **first** ever organized Christmas Day swim in the freezing cold Serpentine in London's Hyde Park took place in 1864.

The **first** police force was established in Paris in 1667.

The **first** taxis with metered fares were operational in 1907.

The **first** British Christmas card showed people drinking and so the temperance societies tried to get it banned.

The **first** Harley Davidson motorcycle was built in 1903 and used a tomato can as a carburettor.

The **first** fax machine was patented in 1843, 33 years before Alexander Graham Bell demonstrated the telephone.

The **first** city in the world to have a population of over one million was London.

Construction workers' hard hats were **first** used in the building of the Hoover Dam in 1933.

The **first** episode of *Joanie Loves Chachi* was the highest-rated American programme in the history of Korean television. 'Chachi' is Korean for 'penis'.

Pitcairn Airlines was the **first** airline to provide sick bags (in 1922).

The **first** ever Royal Christmas broadcast was made by King George V on radio in 1932.

PEOPLE BORN ON SIGNIFICANT DAYS IN HISTORY

Fiona Phillips – the day the farthing coin ceased to be legal tender in the UK

Michael Imperioli – the day Colonel Jean-Bédel Bokassa took over the Central African Republic after a coup

Bridget Fonda – the day France and China announced their decision to establish diplomatic relations

Bonjour

Nicolas Cage – the day the Leyland Motor Company challenged the US blockade of Cuba by selling 450 buses to Cuba

Steven Soderbergh – the day George Wallace became Governor of Alabama

Aaliyah – the day the Shah of Iran fled the country

Dr Dre – the day The Gambia gained independence from the UK

Queen Latifah – the day Prince Sihanouk of Cambodia was deposed

Sarah Jessica Parker – the day Martin Luther King led civil rights activists on a march from Selma to Montgomery

Quentin Tarantino – the day Dr Beeching issued his report calling for huge cuts in Britain's rail network

Roger Black – the day the USSR launched Luna 10, which became the first spaceprobe to enter orbit around the moon

Uma Thurman – the day the US invaded Cambodia

Mike Myers – the day the Organization of African Unity was established

Heidi Klum – the day the Greek military junta overthrew the monarchy and proclaimed a republic

Alanis Morissette – the day there was an explosion at the Flixborough chemical plant

Anna Kournikova – the day Israel destroyed Iraq's nuclear reactor

Elizabeth Hurley – the day of the Battle of Dong Xoai in the Vietnam War

Joanne Harris – the day that President Johnson signed the Civil Rights Act into law

Lleyton Hewitt – the day that Jean Harris was convicted of murdering Dr Herman Tarnower, creator of the Scarsdale diet

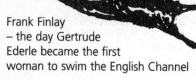

Frank Finlay
– the day Gertrude
Ederle became the first
woman to swim the English Channel

Maria Von Trapp – the day the Cullinan Diamond was found

Hughie Green – the day Estonia was declared independent

John Grisham – the day Malenkov resigned in the USSR

Jean-Jacques Burnel – the day identity cards were abolished in Britain

Dame Kiri Te Kanawa – the day the US Air Force began daylight bombing raids on Berlin

Marti Pellow – the day an archbishop of Canterbury and a pope met for the first time in 400 years

Harold Robbins – the day British Summer Time began

Patsy Palmer – the day Thomas Cook was denationalized

Joe McGann – the day the first life peers were named

Christian Slater – the final day of Woodstock

Ken Norton – the day the atomic bomb was dropped on Nagasaki

José Feliciano – the day Vidkun Quisling was sentenced to death

Margaret Lockwood – the day the British army used tanks for the first time

Barnes Wallis – the day the gramophone was patented

Elie Wiesel – the day the discovery of penicillin was announced

Rick Parfitt – the day the first Morris Minor was produced

Dame Anita Roddick – the day the Battle of Alamein started

Spiro Agnew – the day the Kaiser abdicated

Peter Schmeichel – the day the Dartford Tunnel was opened

Calvin Klein – the day the Russians counterattacked at Stalingrad

Joe Walsh – the day Princess Elizabeth married Prince Philip

Jimi Hendrix – the day the French fleet was sunk at Toulon

Randy Newman – the day the Tehran Conference took place

Joanna Trollope – the day Tito formed a government in Yugoslavia

PEOPLE WHO WERE BORN/GREW UP IN POVERTY

Roman Abramovich, Michael Barrymore, Clara Bow, Kenneth Branagh, Robert Burns, Sir Michael Caine, Mariah Carey, Miguel de Cervantes, Coco Chanel, Ray Charles, Sir Arthur Conan Doyle, Billy Connolly, Joan Crawford, Kirk Douglas, Chris Eubank, Eusebio, Marty Feldman, Sir Tom Finney, Cary Grant, Alex Harvey, Susan Hayward, Jools Holland, Ken Hom, Harry Houdini, Jesse Jackson, Brian Kennedy, Nikita Khrushchev, Lennox Lewis, Sonny Liston, Harold Lloyd, Sophia Loren, John Lydon, Anna Magnani, Diego Maradona, Walter Matthau, Martine McCutcheon, Marilyn Monroe, Sir V.S. Naipaul, Makhaya Ntini, Dolly Parton, Pele, Sidney Poitier, Elvis Presley, Rene Russo, Gerhard Schröder, Maria Sharapova, Hilary Swank, Phil Taylor, Billy Bob Thornton, Mao Tse-tung, Shania Twain, Pancho Villa, Elisabeth Welch, Oprah Winfrey

PURE TRIVIA

Eskimos never gamble.

More than half the world's people have never made or received a telephone call.

The buzz generated by an electric razor in Britain is in the key of G. In America it is in the key of B flat.

Henry Ford never had a driving licence.

Popeye's friend Wimpy's full name is J. Wellington Wimpy.

Popeye's girlfriend Olive had a brother called Castor Oyl.

Tomato ketchup was once sold as a medicine.

Buenos Aires has more psychoanalysts per head than any other place in the world.

The original name of Pac-Man was going to be PUCK MAN, until executives saw the obvious potential for parody.

97 per cent of Canadians would not borrow a toothbrush if they forgot to pack their own.

The Snickers bar was named after a horse the Mars family owned.

Frank Baum got the name Oz in *The Wizard of Oz* from one of his alphabetized filing cabinets (O–Z).

Al Capone's older brother was a policeman in Nebraska.

There is enough lead in the average pencil to draw a line 35 miles long.

Humans have 46 chromosomes, peas have 14 and crayfish have 200.

***Dracula* is the most filmed story of all time. *Dr Jekyll and Mr Hyde* comes second and *Oliver Twist* third.**

Cabbage is 91 per cent water.

The straw was invented by Egyptian brewers to taste beer during brewing without disturbing the fermenting matter floating on the top.

Coca-Cola has a pH of 2.8.

65 per cent of Elvis impersonators are of Asian descent.

Donald Duck has a sister called Dumbella.

Oscars given out during World War Two were made of wood because metal was in short supply.

Siamese twins Chang and Eng Bunker once had a punch-up over alcohol.

George W. Bush was the 17th US state governor to become president.

Snow White's sister is called Rose Red.

Good Friday once fell on Boxing Day. (It was a horse named Good Friday and it fell in a race on 26 December 1899.)

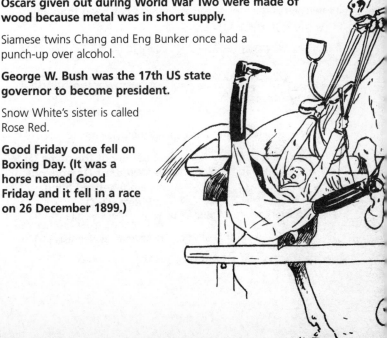

35 per cent of people who use personal ads for dating are already married.

In 1933, Mickey Mouse got 800,000 fan letters.

Sigmund Freud had a morbid fear of ferns.

A 'pen knife' was originally used to trim the tip of a quill.

In Alcatraz, Al Capone was inmate number 85.

California has issued driving licences to six people called Jesus Christ.

There are 22 stars in the Paramount logo.

Watermelon is a vegetable.

Kleenex tissues were originally used as filters in gas masks.

A 12-ounce (340g) jar of peanut butter contains about 548 peanuts.

More people use blue toothbrushes than red ones.

PEOPLE AND THEIR FAVOURITE CHILDREN'S BOOK

Magnus Magnusson, Barry Unsworth: *The Wind In The Willows*

Victoria Wood: *The Swish of The Curtain*

Emma Forbes: *Charlie And The Chocolate Factory*

Dawn French, Will Carling: *The Hobbit*

Joanna Lumley: *Tom Sawyer*

Tony Blair, Lord Melvyn Bragg: *Kidnapped*

Antoine De Caunes,
Sir Alex Ferguson:
Treasure Island

**Richard Wilson:
*Andersonville***

Lorraine Kelly: *Just So
Stories*

**Paddy Ashdown:
*Kim***

Keith Floyd:
*Swallows And
Amazons*

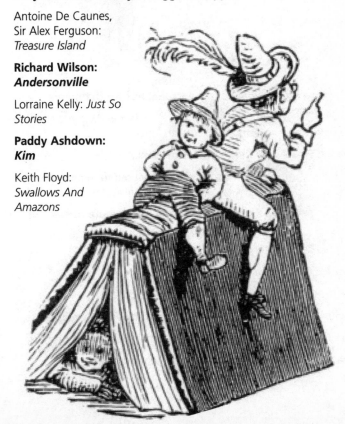

Anthea Turner, Eamonn Holmes, Carol Smillie: *The Lion, The Witch And The Wardrobe*

Chris Evans: *Black Beauty*

Loyd Grossman: The Horatio Hornblower novels

Professor Stephen Hawking: *She*

Sir David Attenborough: *The Bird of Paradise*

Gary Oldman: *Gulliver's Travels*

Natalie Appleton: *Amelia Bedelia And The Surprise Shower*

Philippa Forrester: *The Talking Parcel*

Harold Pinter: *Ulysses*

V.I. Lenin: *Uncle Tom's Cabin*

Ian Rankin: *Fox in Socks*

Ed McBain: *The Cat In The Hat*

PLACES THAT HAVE BEEN CALLED THE VENICE OF THE NORTH

Hamburg

Stockholm

Amsterdam

Manchester

Bruges

Edinburgh

Amiens

St Petersburg

Birmingham

Giethoorn

Ottawa

PLACES THAT HAVE BEEN CALLED THE VENICE OF THE SOUTH

Fort Lauderdale

Mykonos

Zakynthos

Tarpon Springs

Sitangkai

Sète

PLACES THAT HAVE BEEN CALLED THE VENICE OF THE EAST

Bangkok

Udaipur

Alappuzha

Alleppey

Lijiang

Suzhou

Shan, Myanmar

Pii Mai

PLACES THAT HAVE BEEN CALLED THE VENICE OF THE WEST

Nantes

Galway

San Antonio, Texas

Seattle

Onlys

John Laurie was the **only** member of the cast of *Dad's Army* to have served in the Home Guard.

The Ganges river in India has the **only** genuine freshwater sharks in the world.

Bill Clinton sent **only** two emails during his eight-year presidency. One was to John Glenn aboard the space shuttle, and the other was to test the email system.

Venus is the **only** planet that rotates clockwise.

Canada is the **only** country not to win a gold medal in the summer Olympic Games while hosting the event.

Madrid and Valletta are the **only** European capital cities that are not on a river.

The **only** living tissue in the human body that contains no blood vessels is the transparent cornea of the eye.

Salt is the **only** rock humans can eat.

Diane Keaton was the **only** cast member of the original production of *Hair* to refuse to take her clothes off.

Honey is the **only** food that doesn't spoil.

The Aleutian islands of Alaska are the **only** part of the United States invaded by the Japanese during World War Two.

The San Francisco cable cars are the **only** mobile national monuments in the US.

Texas is the **only** US state that permits residents to vote from space.

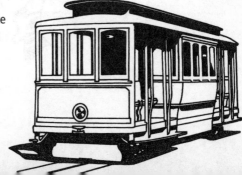

THE ONLY PEOPLE TO HAVE WON THE TONY AND THE OSCAR FOR THE SAME ROLE

José Ferrer for *Cyrano De Bergerac* (Tony: 1947/ Oscar: 1950)

Shirley Booth for *Come Back, Little Sheba* (1950/1953)

Yul Brynner for *The King And I* (1952/1956)

Rex Harrison for *My Fair Lady* (1957/1964)

Anne Bancroft for *The Miracle Worker* (1960/1962)

Paul Scofield for *A Man for All Seasons* (1962/1966)

Jack Albertson for *The Subject Was Roses* (1965/1968)

Joel Grey for *Cabaret* (1967/1973)

NB. Lila Kedrova did it the other way around. She won a 1964 Oscar for *Zorba the Greek*, and 20 years later won a Tony for the same role in *Zorba*.

THINGS INVENTED BY ITALIANS (AND NOT ALL OF THEM BY LEONARDO DA VINCI)

The parachute, the camera obscura, the piano, the pretzel, the radio, the espresso machine, spectacles, the mariner compass, the thermometer, the barometer, magnets, the telescope, the condom, scissors, the mechanical calculator, the pedometer, the wind vane, Fibonacci numbers, natural plastic, the ice cream cone

Everest firsts

First ascent: 29 May 1953 by Edmund Hillary and Tenzing Norgay.

First recorded deaths: 7 Sherpas in an avalanche in 1922.

First person to reach the summit twice: Nawang Gombu Sherpa on 20 May 1965.

First woman to reach the summit: Junko Tabei on 16 May 1975.

First ascent without bottled oxygen: Peter Habeler and Reinhold Messner on 8 May 1978.

First winter ascent: Krzysztof Wielicki on 17 February 1980.

First blind person to reach the summit: Erik Weihenmayer on 25 May 2001.

ALL THE WINNERS OF THE 'OLDIE OF THE YEAR' AWARD

2005: Sir David Attenborough

2004: Sir Ranulph Fiennes

2003: Tony Blackburn

2002: Eric Sykes

2001: Sir John Mortimer

2000: Peter O'Toole

1999: Dame Thora Hird

1998: No Award

1997: Baroness Barbara Castle of Blackburn

1996: Richard Wilson

1995: Spike Milligan

1994: Judge Stephen Tumim

1993: David Gower

FAMILY

Ms Dynamite is one of 11 children.

Celine Dion is one of 14 children.

After divorcing Penelope Wilton, Daniel Massey married her sister Lindy.

Dame Catherine Cookson's 'sister' turned out to be her mother.

Pancho Gonzales was married to Andre Agassi's sister.

Kevin Spacey's older brother is a professional Rod Stewart impersonator.

COUSINS

Glenn Close & Brooke Shields

Cyrille Regis & John Regis

Imogen Stubbs & Alexander Armstrong

Brian Littrell & Kevin Richardson (both Backstreet Boys)

Andy Bell & Giant Haystacks

Alan Napier (Alfred in the *Batman* TV series) & Neville Chamberlain

Robert Aldrich & Nelson Rockefeller

Clive Allen & Paul Allen

Jack Cardiff & Kay Kendall

Russell Crowe & Martin Crowe

Olympia Dukakis & Michael Dukakis

Clive Dunn & Gretchen Franklin

Les Ferdinand & Rio Ferdinand

Joseph Fiennes & Sir Ranulph Fiennes

Ben Warriss & Jimmy Jewel

Tommy Lee Jones & Boxcar Willie

Mike Love & Brian Wilson

James Joyce & Adolphe Menjou

Michael Tilson Thomas & Paul Muni

Ramon Navarro & Dolores Del Rio

Bill Pertwee & Jon Pertwee

McLean Stevenson & Adlai Stevenson

Diane Ladd & Tennessee Williams

Marla Maples & Heather Locklear

Kate Robbins & Sir Paul McCartney

Dame Margaret Rutherford & Tony Benn

Gloria Vanderbilt & Beatrice Straight

Maryam D'Abo & Mike D'Abo

People with famous godparents

Crispian Mills (Hywel Bennett)

Anna Massey (John Ford)

Zak Starkey (Keith Moon)

Angelina Jolie (Maximilian Schell)

Skyler Shaye (Jon Voight)

Sheridan Morley (Alexander Wollcott)

Bryce Dallas Howard (Henry Winkler)

Patsy Kensit (Reggie Kray)

Juliet Mills (Vivien Leigh)

Bijou Phillips (Andy Warhol)

Phoebe Cates (Jacqueline Susann)

Henry Dent-Brocklehurst (Camilla, Duchess of Cornwall)

Joel Cadbury (Douglas Bader)

Scott Quinnell (Mervyn Davies)

Daniel Massey (Sir Noel Coward)

Chris Cowdrey (Peter May)

Kara Noble (Shelley Winters)

Sean Lennon (Sir Elton John)

Santa Palmer-Tomkinson (Prince Charles)

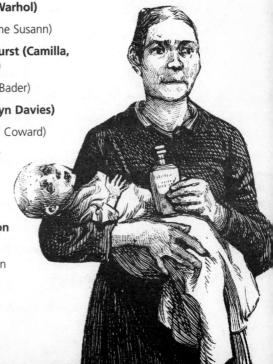

PEOPLE WITH FAMOUS ANCESTORS

Issy Van Rendwick – William of Orange

Sir John Gielgud – Ellen Terry

Matthew Fleming – Ian Fleming

Queen Sofia of Spain – Queen Victoria

Joanna Trollope – Anthony Trollope

Jason Patric – Jackie Gleason (grandfather)

Pat Boone – Daniel Boone

Nelson Eddy – President Martin Van Buren

Sophie Dahl (Roald Dahl & Stanley Holloway – her grandfathers)

Holly Valance and Benny Hill are related: Benny was Holly's grandfather's cousin

Al Murray's great-great-great-great-grandfather was William Makepeace Thackeray

Christopher Plummer is the great-grandson of former Canadian Prime Minister Sir John Abbott

Jodie Kidd's great-grandfather was the first Lord Beaverbrook

Adam Hart-Davis's great-great-great-grandfather was King William IV

Wayne Rooney – Bob Fitzsimmons

John Kerry – King Henry III

PEOPLE AND WHAT THEIR FATHERS DID FOR A LIVING

Sean Penn (Film director – but was out of work after being blacklisted as a Communist)

Amanda Burton (Headmaster)

Colin Farrell (Stockbroker)

Anna Kournikova (Wrestler)

Hugh Grant (Carpet salesman)

Ben Affleck (Social worker)

Damon Albarn (Art school lecturer)

Christian Bale (Airline pilot)

Ioan Gruffudd (Teacher)

Nicky Campbell (Map publisher)

Ryan Giggs (Rugby League professional)

Julia Ormond (Software designer)

Gareth Gates (Postman)

Sacha Baron Cohen (Menswear shop owner)

Jennifer Lopez (Computer specialist at Guardian Insurance in NYC)

Leonardo DiCaprio (Comic book dealer)

Teri Hatcher (Nuclear physicist)

Tom Cruise (Electrical engineer)

Peter Bowles (Chauffeur)

Francesca Annis (Banker)

John Cleese (Insurance salesman)

Vanessa Feltz (Knicker manufacturer)

Anthony Andrews (BBC musical arranger)

Freddie Starr (Carpenter)

Greta Scacchi (Artist)

Mike Read (Publican)

Lord Andrew Lloyd Webber (Organist)

Dame Elizabeth Taylor (Art dealer)

Neil Young (Journalist)

Bob Geldof (Commercial traveller)

Morrissey (Hospital porter)

Mark Knopfler (Architect)

Paul Daniels (Cinema projectionist)

Simon Le Bon (Foreign Office civil servant)

Rik Mayall (Teacher)

Will Smith (Refrigeration engineer)

Oliver Stone (Stockbroker)

Peter Stringfellow (Steelworker)

Michael Jackson (Crane driver)

Ruby Wax (Sausage-skin manufacturer)

Fiona Bruce (Managing director of Unilever)

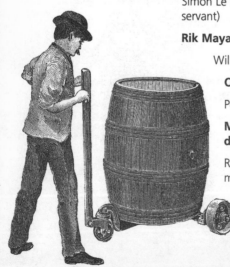

Julia Somerville (Senior civil servant at GCHQ)

Gloria Estefan (Soldier in dictator Batista's bodyguard)

Keith Allen (Navy submariner)

J.K. Rowling (Engineer)

Delia Smith (Printer)

Jon Bon Jovi (Hairdresser)

Brendan Fraser (Tourism executive)

Leslie Nielsen (Royal Canadian Mountie)

Richard Briers (Bookmaker)

PEOPLE WHOSE FATHERS WERE POLICEMEN

Siân Phillips, Adam Woodyatt, Paul Nicholls, Darren Day, Hywel Bennett, Ilie Nastase, Kevin Lloyd, Gordon Sherry, David May, Jacques Santer, Liz Robertson, Simon Gregson, Lord George Robertson, Fred MacAulay, Alice Faye, Pam Ferris, Christian Gross, Nicola Stephenson, Screaming Lord Sutch

People whose fathers were clergymen

John Motson, Virginia Wade, Lord David Steel, Pearl Bailey, Ingmar Bergman, Hugh Dennis, Erskine Caldwell, Alistair Cooke, George McGovern, Walter Mondale, Agnes Moorehead, Dean Rusk, Albert Schweitzer, Anna Richardson, Me-One, Jonathan Edwards, D'Angelo, David Tennant

People whose fathers were rabbis

Lord Victor Mishcon, Mickey Duff, Josh Salzmann, Isaac Bashevis Singer, Michael Fabricant

People whose fathers were professional footballers

Jason Weaver, Donald Houston, Robin Cousins

People whose fathers were MPs

Baroness Sarah Hogg, Jeremy Thorpe, Baroness Ann Mallalieu (and her grandfather too)

PEOPLE WHOSE FATHERS WERE DOCTORS

Lisa Kudrow, Reese Witherspoon, Frances Edmonds, Baroness Tessa Jowell, Sister Wendy Beckett, Sandra Bernhard, John Dunlop, Mary Killen, Adnan Khashoggi, Paul Bradley, Fred Zinnemann

PEOPLE WHOSE FATHERS WERE BOXERS

Freddie Starr, Bruce Oldfield, Wayne Rooney, Rudy Giuliani, Jennifer Capriati, Frank Sinatra, Steve Jones, Mikey Graham, Andre Agassi, Paul Weller, Brian Glover, Craig Raine

BROUGHT UP BY A SINGLE PARENT

Mick Hucknall, Barry Manilow, Clive James, Susan Hampshire, Billy Connolly, Fay Weldon, Keanu Reeves, Drew Barrymore, Dina Carroll, Ulrika Jonsson, Michael Crawford, Jamie Bell

PEOPLE WITH TWIN BROTHERS/SISTERS

Scarlett Johansson (Hunter)

Gisele Bundchen (Patricia)

Plum Sykes (Lucy)

Ashton Kutcher (Michael)

Simon Cowell (Nicholas)

Janel Moloney (Carey)

Felipe Contepomi (Manuel)

GIRLS WHO EMANCIPATED THEMSELVES FROM THEIR PARENTS

Bijou Phillips (at 14)

Alicia Silverstone (at 15. When she was a child, her overactive imagination led her to claim that her parents were aliens and that her mother, an airline stewardess, was Olivia Newton-John)

Michelle Williams (at 16)

Skyler Shaye (at 15)

Juliette Lewis (at 14)

PEOPLE WITH FAMOUS FATHERS

Helen Storey (David Storey)

Lucy Briers (Richard Briers)

Sophie Ward (Simon Ward)

Damon Hill (Graham Hill)

Abigail McKern (Leo McKern)

Jason Connery (Sean Connery)

Kiefer Sutherland (Donald Sutherland)

Julian Lennon (John Lennon)

Stella McCartney (Sir Paul McCartney)

Jacques Villeneuve (Gilles Villeneuve)

Kim Wilde (Marty Wilde)

Andrea Boardman (Stan Boardman)

Suzanne Charlton (Sir Bobby Charlton)

Kirsty MacColl (Ewan MacColl)

Julia Sawalha (Nadim Sawalha)

Linus Roache (William Roache)

Paula Yates (Hughie Green)

Liza Tarbuck (Jimmy Tarbuck)

Hannah Waterman (Dennis Waterman)

Jack Ryder (Jack Hues)

Bijou Phillips (John Phillips)

Kate Beckinsale (Richard Beckinsale)

WOMEN WHOSE FAMOUS MOTHERS HAVE A DIFFERENT SURNAME

Rudi Davies (Beryl Bainbridge)

Beatie Edney (Sylvia Syms)

Susannah Harker (Polly Adams)

Finty Williams (Dame Judi Dench)

Wynonna (Naomi Judd)

Keira Knightley (Sharman Macdonald)

PARENTS OF TWINS

Julia Roberts, Oliver Letwin, Dougray Scott, Geena Davis (at age 47), Dickie Davies, Madeleine Albright, Nigel Spackman, David Batty, Willie Thorne, Corbin Bernsen, David Coleman, Roy Boulting (himself a twin), Chris Cowdrey, Charles Moore, Ronald Searle, Desmond Wilcox, Fred Winter, Lou Diamond Phillips, Michael Aspel, Dr Hilary Jones, Jayne Irving, Lord Geoffrey Howe, Ed Asner, Henry Mancini, Rick Nelson, Meredith Baxter-Birney, Jim Brown, Andy Gibb (himself the brother of twins), Susan Hayward, Loretta Lynn, Otto Preminger, Nelson Rockefeller, Alice Beer, Graham Cowdrey, Rip Torn

GRANDPARENTS OF TWINS

Sir Alex Ferguson, Tammy Wynette, Tony Britton, Frances Shand-Kydd, George Bush, Arthur Scargill, Richard Stilgoe, Lady Antonia Fraser, Lord Michael Heseltine, Lord Colin Cowdrey

FAMOUS PEOPLE WHO WERE BORN 'ILLEGITIMATE'

T.E. Lawrence, William the Conqueror, Richard Wagner, Sophia Loren, Willy Brandt, Sir Alec Guinness, Sarah Bernhardt, Leonardo da Vinci, Demi Moore, Macaulay Culkin, Ella Fitzgerald, Oprah Winfrey, Ryan Giggs, Naomi Campbell, Coco Chanel, Dame Catherine Cookson, Sir Cyril Smith, Ruud Gullit, Samantha Janus, Fidel Castro, Franco Zeffirelli, The Duchess of Windsor, Tony O'Reilly, Marilyn Monroe, Eric Clapton, Bruce Oldfield, Gary Glitter, Billie Holiday, Mike Tyson, Saddam Hussein, Paul Cézanne, Jesse Jackson, Maria Montessori, August Strindberg, Juan Perón, Sadie Frost

PEOPLE WHO NEVER KNEW THEIR FATHERS

Kerry Katona, Kelly Holmes, David Blaine, Denise Lewis, Alan Milburn, Charlene Tilton, Gary Glitter, Gregor Fisher, Rodney Bickerstaffe, Shaun Scott, Prince Michael of Kent, Natalia Makarova, Lee Trevino, Rod Steiger, Marilyn Monroe, Gerhard Schröder, Peter Ackroyd, Fidel Edwards, Riddick Bowe, Sir Alec Guinness, Lee Harvey Oswald, Pat Barker, Lord Byron

PEOPLE WHO NEVER KNEW THEIR MOTHERS

Sir Laurence Olivier, Helen Suzman, Eric Sykes

PEOPLE WITH A GERMAN PARENT

Eric Bana (Mother)

Leonardo DiCaprio (Mother)

Dennis Franz (Father)

PEOPLE WITH A FRENCH PARENT

Joanne Harris (Mother)

John Hegley (Father – half-French)

Melanie Blatt (Mother)

Claire Tomalin (Father)

Davina McCall (Mother)

Alison Moyet (Father)

Brian Capron (Father)

Sir James Goldsmith (Mother)

Peter De Savary (Father)

Mary Pierce (Mother)

Kevin Maxwell (Mother)

Raymond 'Teasy-Weasy' Bessone (Mother)

Melissa Bell (Mother)

Irene Handl (Mother)

Francesca Annis (Mother – half-French)

Jane Lapotaire (Mother – half-French)

Jodie Foster (Mother)

Cardinal Basil Hume (Mother)

Claire Trevor (Father)

THINGS SAID ABOUT FRANCE AND THE FRENCH

'When God created France, He realized that He had gone overboard in creating the most perfect place on Earth. So to balance it out, he created the French people.' (Anon)

'Somewhere between the Angels and the French lies the rest of humanity' (Mark Twain)

'The French are just useless. They can't organize a piss-up in a brewery.' (Sir Elton John)

'We always have been, we are, and I hope that we always shall be detested in France.' (The Duke of Wellington)

'France was a long despotism tempered by epigrams.' (Thomas Carlyle)

'Going to war without France is like going deer hunting without an accordion. You just leave a lot of useless, noisy baggage behind.' (Jed Babbin)

'The reason French streets have trees planted down both sides is that the Germans like to march in the shade.' (Anon)

'If you want to visit Paris, the best time to go is during August, when there aren't any French people there.' (Kenneth Stilling)

PEOPLE AND THE SUBJECTS THEY STUDIED AT UNIVERSITY

J.K. Rowling – French and Classics

Mira Sorvino – East Asian Studies

Robin Williams – Political Science

Martin Short – Social Work

Thandie Newton – Anthropology

Alistair McGowan – English

Cate Blanchett – Economics and Fine Arts

John Cleese – Law

Richard Blackwood – Business Studies

Glenn Close – Anthropology

Hugh Grant – English

Brian May – Physics

Sanjeev Bhaskar – Marketing

Lucy Liu – Asian Languages and Culture

Brooke Shields – French

Hugh Bonneville – Theology

Rory Bremner – French and German

Brad Pitt – Journalism

Rowan Atkinson – Electrical Engineering

Paul Simon – English

Chris Lowe – Architecture

Jonathan Ross – East European Modern History

Donald Fagen – English

Victoria Principal – Law

Harry Enfield – Politics

Cindy Crawford – Chemical Engineering (on a full scholarship)

Lisa Kudrow – Sociobiology (originally wanted to be a doctor like her father, a headache expert)

NUMBERS

Multiply 37,037 by any single number (1–9), then multiply that number by 3. Every digit in the answer will be the same as that first single number.

In the US, a centillion is the number 1 followed by 300 zeros. In Britain it has 600 zeros.

The number 17 is considered unlucky in Italy.

There are 318,979,564,000 possible combinations of the first four moves in chess.

One year contains 31,557,600 seconds.

'Eleven plus two' is an anagram of 'Twelve plus one'.

Any number squared is equal to 4 (2 squared) more than the product of the numbers two either side of it:
5 squared is 25 (3 x 7 is 21)
8 squared is 64 (6 x 10 is 60)

Any number squared is equal to 9 (3 squared) more than the product of the numbers three either side of it:
5 squared is 25 (2 x 8 is 16)
8 squared is 64 (5 x 11 is 55), and so on.

HISTORY

People didn't always say hello when they answered the phone. When the first regular phone service was established in 1878 in the US, people said 'Ahoy'.

Of the 266 men who have been Pope, 33 have died violently.

In 18th-century Britain, you could take out insurance against going to hell.

In 1915, William Wrigley Jr sent chewing gum to everyone in the phone book.

Olive oil was once used for washing the body in Mediterranean countries.

Bagpipes were invented in Iran, then brought to Scotland by the Romans.

The world's youngest parents were eight and nine, and lived in China in 1910.

In England in the 17th century, married women had, on average, 13 children.

India was the richest country in the world until the time of British invasion in the early 17th century.

Ahoy!

Benito Mussolini would ward off the evil eye by touching his testicles.

Stalin's left foot had webbed toes.

Between 1947 and 1959, 42 nuclear devices were detonated in the Marshall Islands in the Pacific Ocean.

Playing cards that were issued to British pilots in World War Two could be soaked in water and unfolded to reveal a map in the event of capture.

In Egypt in the late 19th century, mummies were used as fuel for locomotives, since wood and coal were scarce but mummies were plentiful.

Louis IV of France had a stomach the size of two regular stomachs.

Paul Gauguin was a labourer on the Panama Canal.

In the middle ages, the highest court in France ordered the execution of a cow for injuring someone.

Moby Dick sold 50 copies during its writer Herman Melville's lifetime.

King Louis XIX ruled France for 15 minutes.

Japan did not send an ambassador to another nation until 1860.

In 16th-century Turkey, drinking coffee was punishable by death.

Leprosy is the world's oldest known disease, dating back to 1350BC.

Stone wheels several feet in diameter were once used as currency by the Yap Islanders of Micronesia.

It cost $7 million to build the *Titanic* and $200 million to make a film about it.

Two dogs survived the sinking of the *Titanic*.

The passion fruit was named by Spanish missionaries to whom the plant suggested the nails and thorns of Christ's suffering (or Passion) at the crucifixion.

Charles Dickens earned as much for his lectures as he did for his twenty novels.

In medieval Japan, it was fashionable for women to have black teeth.

When the *Mayflower* was no longer needed, it was taken apart and rebuilt as a barn.

Russia's Peter the Great taxed men who wore a beard.

In the 19th century, in an attempt to debunk the myth that Friday was an unlucky day for mariners, the British Navy named a new ship HMS *Friday*, found a Captain Friday to command it, and sent it to sea on a Friday. Neither ship nor crew were heard of again.

Apollo 11 had 20 seconds of fuel left when it landed.

In 18th-century English gambling dens, there was an employee whose only job it was to swallow the dice in the event of a police raid.

The formal name for the Pony Express was the Central Overland California & Pike's Peak Express Company.

In 1930, Grace Robin, a model, demonstrated contact lenses for the first time.

The streets of ancient Mesopotamia were literally knee deep in rubbish, since there was no effective way of getting rid of it.

In ancient Egypt, noblewomen were given a few days to ripen after death in order not to provide temptation for the embalmers.

George Washington's false teeth were carved from hippopotamus ivory and cow's teeth and fixed together with metal springs.

In ancient Rome, a crooked nose was considered to indicate leadership potential.

The gold earrings many sailors wore were to pay for a decent burial on their death.

St Patrick, the patron saint of Ireland, was not Irish.

The world's oldest active parliamentary body is the Icelandic Althing, which met first before the year 1000.

The Chinese used fingerprints as a method of identification as far back as AD700.

ALL THE UN SECRETARY-GENERALS SINCE ITS FORMATION

Trygve Lie (Norway) 1946–53

Dag Hammarskjöld (Sweden) 1953–61

U Thant (Burma) 1962–71

Kurt Waldheim (Austria) 1972–81

Javier Pérez de Cuéllar (Peru) 1982–91

Boutros Boutros-Ghali (Egypt) 1992–96

Kofi Annan (Ghana) 1997–

BIRDS ETC.

Pigeons can fly 600 miles in a day.

Flamingos get their colour from their food, tiny green algae which turn pink during digestion.

There are giant bats in Indonesia with a wingspan of nearly 1.8 metres (6 feet).

The common little brown bat of North America is, for its size, the world's longest-lived mammal. It can live to the age of 32.

Percentage of bird species that are monogamous: 90. Percentage of mammal species that are monogamous: 3.

Baby robins eat 4.25 metres (14 feet) of earthworms per day.

A duck has three eyelids.

Chickens, ducks and ostriches are eaten before they're born and after they're dead.

A robin's egg is blue, but if you put it in vinegar it turns yellow after 30 days.

Penguins have sex twice a year.

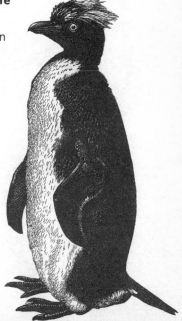

Big Ben lost five minutes one day when a flock of starlings perched on the minute hand.

Crows have the biggest brains of any bird, relative to body size.

Birds need gravity in order to swallow.

A parrot's beak can exert a force of 350 pounds per square inch as it snaps shut.

Many species of bird mate on the wing. They fly high and then mate on the descent.

Chickens that lay brown eggs have red ear lobes.

White cockatoos can be sexed by eye colour. The males have black irises and an invisible pupil; the females have a paler iris with a visible pupil.

The ostrich yolk is the largest single cell in the world.

To keep cool, ostriches urinate on their legs.

The Pallid Bat has immunity
to the poison of the scorpions upon which it feeds.

Some birds have eyes that weigh more than their brains.

Frog-eating bats find and identify edible frogs by listening to the
mating calls. Frogs counter this by hiding and using short calls that
are hard to locate.

**Fishing bats use echolocation so well they can detect a hair's
breadth of minnow fin above a pond surface.**

Vampire bats adopt orphans and have been known to risk their lives
to share food with less fortunate roost-mates.

BIRD NAMES

Jackass Penguin, Wandering Albatross, Red-faced Shag, Blue-footed Booby, Intermediate Egret, Short-toed Lark, Ovenbird, Solitary Sandpiper, Least Bittern, Adjutant Stork, Sacred Ibis, Horned Screamer, Smew, Killdeer, Turnstone, Beach Thick-knee, Laughing Gull, Fairy Tern, Masked Lovebird, Roadrunner, Screech Owl, Large Frogmouth, Chimney Swift, Train-bearing Hermit, Turquoise-browed Motmot, Toco Toucan, Barred Woodcreeper, Spotted Antbird, Cock-of-the-Rock, Ornate Umbrellabird, Vermilion Flycatcher, Reddish Plantcutter, Superb Lyrebird, Racquet-tailed Drongo, Crestless Gardener, Satin Bowerbird, Magnificent Riflebird, Spotted Creeper, Striped Jungle Babbler, Fairy Bluebird, Noisy Friarbird, Bananaquit, Painted Bunting, Social Weaver, Red-legged Honeycreeper, Junglefowl, Northern Shoveler, Wrinkled Hornbill, Blue-bearded Bee-eater, Dollarbird, Edible-nest Swiftlet, Buffy Fish Owl, Little Stint, Changeable Hawk Eagle, Straw-headed Bulbul, Spectacled Spiderhunter

PATRONS

Anthea Turner – Born Free Foundation

Stephen Fry – Norwich Playhouse

Lord Richard Attenborough – Kingsley Hall Community Centre

**Brian Blessed – Dearne Community Miners'
Welfare Scheme**

Jean Boht – British Homoeopathic Association

Sue Cook – Parents At Work

John Craven – Rainforest Action Fund

Elizabeth Dawn – Manchester Taxi Drivers Association

Chris Tarrant – Phoenix Centre For The Physically Handicapped

Martyn Lewis – Youth For Britain

Patsy Palmer – Action On Addiction

Davina McCall – Focus (a drink and drugs rehabilitation charity)

Catherine Zeta-Jones – Wales's Longfields Association

**Amanda Holden – Emmaus (a community project
for the homeless)**

Emma Forbes – Great Ormond Street
Children's Hospital

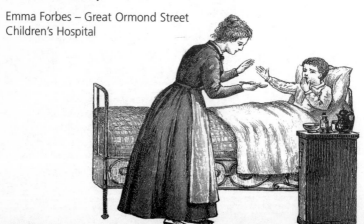

PATRONS OF PIPEDOWN
(THE CAMPAIGN AGAINST PIPED MUSIC)

George Melly, Stephen Fry, Joanna Lumley, Tony Parsons, Julian
Lloyd Webber, A.N. Wilson, Claire Tomalin, Richard
Baker, Lesley Garrett, Alfred Brendel, Tom
Conti, Lady Antonia Fraser, John Humphrys,
Miriam Margolyes, Sir Simon Rattle,
Prunella Scales, Keith Waterhouse

PEOPLE WHO FAILED THE 11-PLUS

Sir Michael Gambon, Paul Merton, Delia Smith, David Essex ('on purpose because the secondary modern was a great sports school'), Zandra Rhodes, Alan Titchmarsh, Barbara Dickson, Susan Penhaligon, Bruce Robinson, Sue Townsend, Dame Anita Roddick, John Sullivan, Sir Bernard Ingham, Ken Livingstone, Brian Clough, Sir Alan Walters, Geoffrey Boycott, Ann Widdecombe (after getting whooping cough with complications), Magnus Mills, Elaine Paige, Sir Alan Sugar, Phil Redmond, Paula Hamilton, Colin Firth, Philip Gould, Martin McGuinness, Kay Mellor, John Prescott, Robert Lindsay, Trevor Baylis, Charles Dance, Chris Boardman, Robert Kilroy-Silk, Max Clifford, Carla Lane, Nigella Lawson (she refused to take a maths paper: 'I put my hand up, gave it back and said, "I'm sorry, I don't do this".')

GENUINE SIMILES TAKEN FROM GENUINE GCSE ENGLISH ESSAYS

The plan was simple, like my brother Phil. But unlike Phil, this plan just might work.

The little boat gently drifted across the pond exactly the way a bowling ball wouldn't.

His thoughts tumbled in his head, making and breaking alliances like underpants in a tumble dryer.

The young fighter had a hungry look, the kind you get from not eating for a while.

Her hair glistened in the rain like nose hair after a sneeze.

Her eyes were like two brown circles with big black dots in the centre.

Her vocabulary was as bad as, like, whatever.

He was as tall as a six-foot-three-inch tree.

Long separated by cruel fate, the star-crossed lovers raced across the grassy field towards each other like two freight trains, one having left York at 6.36 p.m. travelling at 55mph, the other from Peterborough at 4.19 p.m. at a speed of 35mph.

She had a deep, throaty, genuine laugh, like that sound a dog makes just before it throws up.

John and Mary had never met. They were like two hummingbirds who had also never met.

The thunder was ominous-sounding, much like the sound of a thin sheet of metal being shaken backstage during the storm scene in a play.

The red brick wall was the colour of a brick-red crayon.

The door had been forced, as forced as the dialogue during the interview portion of *Family Fortunes*.

Shots rang out, as shots are wont to do.

Her artistic sense was exquisitely refined, like someone who can tell butter from 'I Can't Believe It's Not Butter'.

The politician was gone but unnoticed, like the full stop after the Dr on a Dr Pepper can.

The knife was as sharp as the tone used by Glenda Jackson MP in her first several points of parliamentary procedure made to Robin Cook MP, Leader of the House of Commons, in the House Judiciary Committee hearings on the suspension of Keith Vaz MP.

The ballerina rose gracefully *en pointe* and extended one slender leg behind her, like a dog at a lamppost.

The revelation that his marriage of 30 years had disintegrated because of his wife's infidelity came as a rude shock, like a surcharge at a formerly surcharge-free cashpoint.

It was a working class tradition, like fathers chasing kids around with their power tools.

He was deeply in love. When she spoke, he thought he heard bells, as if she were a dustcart reversing.

She was as easy as the *Daily Star* crossword.

 She grew on him like she was a colony of E. coli and he was room-temperature British beef.

She walked into my office like a centipede with 98 missing legs.

Her voice had that tense, grating quality, like a first-generation thermal paper fax machine that needed a band tightened.

It hurt the way your tongue hurts after you accidentally staple it to the wall.

HEAD BOYS AT SCHOOL

Henry Olonga, Stephen Leahy, Terry Waite,
Liam Neeson, Lord John Taylor, Tim Pigott-
Smith, Chris Woodhead, Michael Grade,
Edward Stourton, Chris Barrie

HEAD GIRLS AT SCHOOL

**Clare Balding, Victoria Smurfit, Jennifer James, Chief
Constable Pauline Clare, Selina Scott, Glenys Kinnock,
Marcelle d'Argy Smith**

DEPUTY HEAD BOYS

Phil Neville, Jack Straw,
Dudley Moore, Euan Blair

DEPUTY HEAD GIRLS

**Santa Palmer-Tomkinson, Antonia Okonma,
Coleen McLoughlin (Wayne Rooney's
girlfriend)**

GENUINE THINGS WRITTEN BY SCHOOL STUDENTS IN HISTORY ESSAYS

In midevil times most people were alliterate.

The greatest writer of the Renaissance was William Shakespeare. He was born in the year 1564, supposedly on his birthday. He never made much money and is famous only because of his plays. He wrote tragedies, comedies and hysterectomies, all in Islamic pentameter. Romeo and Juliet are an example of a heroic couplet. Romeo's last wish was to be laid by Juliet.

The Bible is full of interesting caricatures. In the first book of the Bible, Guinessis, Adam and Eve were created from an apple tree. One of their children, Cain, asked, 'Am I my brother's son?'

Julius Caesar extinguished himself on the battlefields of Gaul. The Ides of March murdered him because they thought he was going to be made king. Dying, he gasped out: 'Tee hee, Brutus.'

Actually, Homer was not written by Homer but by another man of that name.

Socrates was a famous Greek teacher who went around giving people advice. They killed him. Socrates died from an overdose of wedlock. After his death, his career suffered a dramatic decline.

Moses led the Hebrew slaves to the Red Sea, where they made unleavened bread which is bread made without any ingredients. Moses went up on Mount Cyanide to get the ten commandments. He died before he ever reached Canada.

In the Olympic games, Greeks ran races

Solomon had three hundred wives and seven hundred porcupines.

Nero was a cruel tyranny who would torture his subjects by playing the fiddle to them.

Ancient Egypt was inhabited by mummies and they all wrote in hydraulics. They lived in the Sarah Dessert and traveled by Camelot. The climate of the Sarah is such that the inhabitants have to live elsewhere.

Joan of Arc was burnt to a steak and was cannonized by Bernard Shaw.

Finally Magna Carta provided that no man should be hanged twice for the same offence.

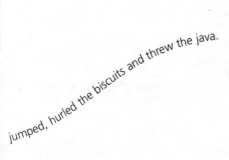

jumped, hurled the biscuits and threw the java.

It was an age of great inventions and discoveries. Gutenberg invented removable type and the Bible. Another important invention was the circulation of blood.

Sir Walter Raleigh is a historical figure because he invented cigarettes and started smoking. And Sir Francis Drake circumcised the world with a 100-foot clipper.

Delegates from the original 13 states formed the Contented Congress. Thomas Jefferson, a Virgin, and Benjamin Franklin were two singers of the Declaration of Independence. Franklin discovered electricity by rubbing two cats backwards and declared, 'A horse divided against itself cannot stand.' Franklin died in 1790 and is still dead.

Queen Elizabeth was the 'Virgin Queen'. As a queen she was a success. When she exposed herself before her troops they all shouted 'hurrah'.

Writing at the same time as Shakespeare was Miguel Cervantes. He wrote Donkey Hote. The next great author was John Milton. Milton wrote Paradise Lost. Then his wife died and he wrote Paradise Regained.

Eventually, the Romans conquered the Greeks. History calls people Romans because they never stayed in one place for very long.

During the Renaissance America began. Christopher Columbus was a great navigator who discovered America while cursing about the Atlantic. Later, the Pilgrims crossed the ocean, and this was called Pilgrim's Progress. The winter of 1620 was a hard one for the settlers. Many people died and many babies were born. Captain John Smith was responsible for all this.

Another story was William Tell, who shot an arrow through an apple while standing on his son's head.

The First World War, caused by the assignation of the Arch-Duck by an anahist, ushered in a new error in the anals of human history.

One of the causes of the Revolutionary War was the English putting tacks in their tea. Also, the colonists would send their parcels through the post without stamps. Finally the colonists won the war and no longer had to pay for taxis.

Soon the Constitution of the United States was adopted to secure domestic hostility. Under the constitution the people enjoyed the right to keep bare arms.

Meanwhile in Europe, the enlightenment was a reasonable time. Voltaire invented electricity and also wrote a book called Candy. Gravity was invented by Issac Walton. It is chiefly noticeable in the autumn when the apples are falling off the trees.

Abraham Lincoln became America's greatest Precedent. Lincoln's mother died in infancy, and he was born in a log cabin which he built with his own hands. Abraham Lincoln freed the slaves by signing the Emasculation Proclamation. On the night of April 14, 1865, Lincoln went to the theatre

A myth is a female moth

and got shot in his seat by one of the actors in a moving picture show. The believed assinator was John Wilkes Booth, a supposingly insane actor. This ruined Booth's career.

Johann Bach wrote a great many musical compositions and had a large number of children. In between he practised on an old spinster which he kept up in his attic. Bach died from 1750 to the present. Bach was the most famous composer in the world and so was Handel. Handel was half German, half Italian and half English. He was very large.

The Greeks were a highly sculptured people, and without them we wouldn't have history. The Greeks also had myths. A myth is a female moth.

The sun never set on the British Empire because the British Empire is in the East and the sun sets in the West. Queen Victoria was the longest queen. She sat on a thorn for 63 years. She was a moral woman who practised virtue. Her death was the final event which ended her reign.

The nineteenth century was a time of a great many thoughts and inventions. People stopped reproducing by hand and started reproducing by machine. The invention of the steamboat caused a network of rivers to spring up. Cyrus McCormick invented the McCormick raper, which did the work of a hundred men. Louis Pasteur discovered a cure for rabbis. Charles Darwin was a naturalist who wrote the Organ of the Species. Madman Curie discovered radio. And Karl Marx became one of the Marx brothers.

The French Revolution was accomplished before it happened and catapulted into Napoleon. Napoleon wanted an heir to inherit his power, but since Josephine was a baroness, she couldn't have any children.

Beethoven wrote music even though he was deaf. He was so deaf he wrote loud music. He took long walks in the forest even when everyone was calling for him. Beethoven expired in 1827 and later died for this.

PEOPLE WHO LEFT SCHOOL AT 15

Archbishop George Carey, Paul Shane, David Bailey, Debbie Moore, Jeremy Beadle, Kevin Keegan, Twiggy, Dame Shirley Bassey, Sir Michael Gambon, Sir Jackie Stewart, Delia Smith

AMERICANS AND THEIR CLASSMATES' RATINGS

Billy Crystal – voted Best Personality

Lorraine Bracco – voted Ugliest Girl

Sally Field – voted Class Clown

Heather Graham – voted Most Talented

James Gandolfini – voted Best Looking

VALEDICTORIANS

Cindy Crawford

Alicia Keys

Jodie Foster

Desiree Washington

Paul Robeson

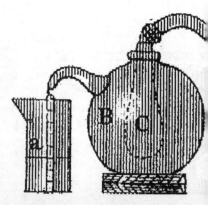

GENUINE ANSWERS GIVEN BY SCHOOL STUDENTS IN SCIENCE TESTS

The body consists of three parts: the brainium, the borax and the abominable cavity. The brainium contains the brain, the borax contains the heart and lungs, and the abominable cavity contains the bowls, of which there are five – a, e, i, o and u.

The pistol of a flower is its only protection against insects.

When you breathe, you inspire. When you do not breathe, you expire.

When you smell an odourless gas, it is probably carbon monoxide.

Dew is formed on leaves when the sun shines down on them and makes them perspire.

Nitrogen is not found in Ireland because it is not found in a free state.

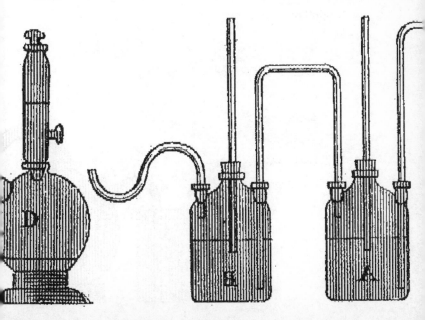

H2O is hot water, and CO2 is cold water.

To collect fumes of sulphur, hold a deacon over a flame in a test tube.

Blood flows down one leg and up the other.

Water is composed of two gins, Oxygin and Hydrogin. Oxygin is pure gin. Hydrogin is gin and water.

A fossil is an extinct animal. The older it is, the more extinct it is.

The moon is a planet just like the earth, only it is even deader.

Three kinds of blood vessels are arteries, vanes and caterpillars.

Respiration is composed of two acts, first inspiration, then expectoration.

Artificial insemination is when the farmer does it to the cow instead of the bull.

Mushrooms always grow in damp places and so they look like umbrellas.

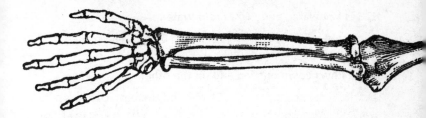

The skeleton is what is left after the insides have been taken out and the outsides have been taken off. The purpose of the skeleton is something to hitch meat to.

A supersaturated solution is one that holds more than it can hold.

Before giving a blood transfusion, find out if the blood is affirmative or negative.

A permanent set of teeth consists of eight canines, eight cuspids, two molars and eight cuspidors.

The tides are a fight between the earth and moon. All water tends towards the moon, because there is no water in the moon, and nature abhors a vacuum. I forget where the sun joins in this fight.

Many women believe that an alcoholic binge will have no ill effects on the unborn fetus, but that is a large misconception.

Germinate: To become a naturalized German.

Momentum: What you give a person when they are going away.

To remove dust from the eye, pull the eye down over the nose.

To prevent contraception, wear a condominium.

To keep milk from turning sour, keep it in the cow.

orse

Redd Foxx was

PEOPLE WHO WERE EXPELLED FROM SCHOOL

Jeff Stryker (for 'standing up for a retard')

Chevy Chase (from Haverford College for taking a cow on to the third floor of a campus building)

Adam Clayton (from a boarding school)

Alain Delon (from many schools)

xpelled on the first day for throwing a book at the teacher

Brandon Lee (for misbehaving)

Shane MacGowan (from Westminster for using drugs)

Kris Marshall (from Wells Cathedral School for 'a multitude of sins')

Rudolph Valentino (from many schools)

Harvey Keitel (for repeated truancy)

John Lydon (from a Catholic comprehensive near Pentonville prison)

Monty Don (from primary school 'for putting nettles down girls' knickers and getting more black marks in one term than anyone else in their entire school career')

THINGS SAID ABOUT SCHOOL

'I hated school. Even to this day, when I see a school bus it's just depressing to me. The poor little kids.' (Dolly Parton)

'Show me a man who has enjoyed his schooldays and I'll show you a bully and a bore.' (Robert Morley)

'The philosophy of the school room in one generation will be the philosophy of government in the next.' (Abraham Lincoln)

'You don't appreciate a lot of stuff in school until you get older. Little things like being spanked every day by a middle-aged woman: stuff you pay good money for in later life.' (Emo Phillips)

'He who opens a school door, closes a prison.' (Victor Hugo)

'Don't let schooling interfere with your education.' (Mark Twain)

'The schools ain't what they used to be and never was.' (Will Rogers)

'If there were no schools to take the children away from home part of the time, the insane asylums would be filled with mothers.' (Edward Howe)

'Education is what remains after one has forgotten what one has learned in school.' (Albert Einstein)

'A child educated only at school is an uneducated child.' (George Santayana)

'To sentence a man of true genius to the drudgery of a school is to put a racehorse on a treadmill.' (Samuel Taylor Coleridge)

'I won't say ours was a tough school, but we had our own coroner. We used to write essays like: What I'm going to be if I grow up.' (Lenny Bruce)

'Everyone is in awe of the lion tamer in a cage with half a dozen lions – everyone but a school bus driver.' (Laurence Peter)

GENUINE NOTES SENT BY PARENTS TO SCHOOL TO EXPLAIN THEIR CHILDREN'S ABSENCE

My daughter wouldn't come to school on Monday because she was tired. She spent the weekend with some Marines.

Dear school: Please exkuse John for being absent on January 28, 29, 30, 31, 32 and 33.

I kept Billie home to do Christmas shopping because I didn't know what size she wears.

Lillie was absent from school yesterday as she had a gang over.

Please excuse Johnnie for being. It was his father's fault.

Please excuse Sara for being absent. She was sick and I had her shot.

Please excuse Joey on Friday; he had loose vowels.

PEOPLE WHO WERE FAT AS CHILDREN

Brian McFadden

Gary Turner

Kate Winslet (her childhood nickname was Blubber)

**Meat Loaf (weighed more when he was
ten than he does now)**

John Malkovich (lost several stones in just a
couple of months by only eating Jell-O)

Bob Monkhouse

Martyn Lewis

Kathy Burke

Sandy Lyle (his nickname was 'Podge')

Lucy Pargeter

Maxine Carr

**Silent film star Roscoe 'Fatty' Arbuckle weighed 16 pounds
at birth**

PEOPLE WHO APPEARED IN ADVERTISEMENTS AS CHILDREN

**Reese Witherspoon (appeared in a TV commercial
when she was seven for a local Nashville florist)**

Martine McCutcheon (Kool Aid and Pears Soap)

**Lindsay Lohan (Pizza Hut, The Gap, Wendy's,
Jell-O)**

Pejorative fruits

Fruit – an old-time homosexual

Gooseberry – a third party on a date

Plum – person prone to mistakes

Prune – an elderly person

Turnip – an idiot

Lemon – a naive person

Nut – psychopath

Grapes – haemorrhoids

Limey – US slang for the English

Fig – an inconsequential person

CATCHPHRASES

'Hello, my darlings' (Charlie Drake)

'Just like that' (Tommy Cooper)

'Nick nick' (Jim Davidson)

'I thank *you*' (Arthur Askey – also 'Hello, playmates')

'I'm in charge' (Bruce Forsyth + many more including 'Nice to see you … ')

'It's the way you tell 'em' (Frank Carson)

'May your God go with you' (Dave Allen)

'Not a lot' (Paul Daniels)

'Awight?' (Michael Barrymore)

'Chase me' (Duncan Norvelle)

'Can you 'ear me, mother?' (Sandy Powell)

'You lucky people' (Tommy Trinder)

'Well, please yourselves' (Frankie Howerd)

'Aye, aye, that's your lot' (Jimmy Wheeler)

'Wotcher, cocks' (Leon Cortez)

'Can we talk?' (Joan Rivers)

'What a performance' (Sid Field)

'I'm the only gay in the village' (Matt Lucas as Dafydd in *Little Britain*)

'Lovely jubbly' (David Jason as Del Boy in *Only Fools And Horses*)

'Yeah, but no, but yeah but' (Matt Lucas as Vicky Pollard in *Little Britain*)

'Suits you, sir' (*The Fast Show*)

'Shut that door' (Larry Grayson)

'I don't believe it!' (Richard Wilson as Victor Meldrew in *One Foot In The Grave*)

'I have a cunning plan … ' (Tony Robinson as Baldrick in *Blackadder*)

'Well, here's another fine mess you've got me into' (Oliver Hardy to Stan Laurel)

'I'm a laydee' (David Walliams as Emily Howard in *Little Britain*)

'Stupid boy' (Arthur Lowe as Captain Mainwaring in *Dad's Army*)

'I'm free!' (John Inman as Mr Humphreys in *Are You Being Served?*)

'Back of the net' (Steve Coogan as Alan Partridge)

'Ooh, Betty!' (Michael Crawford as Frank Spencer in *Some Mothers Do Ave 'Em*)

'Is it coz I is black?' (Sacha Baron Cohen as Ali G)

'Yeah baby!' (Mike Myers as Austin Powers)

'You wouldn't let it lie!' (Vic Reeves)

PEOPLE WHO DID VSO

Michael Brunson, Jeremy Corbyn, Anton Lesser, David Essex (as an ambassador), Lord Bradford, Brian Hanrahan, Jon Snow, Robert Lacey, Robin Denselow

ACHIEVEMENTS AFTER THE AGE OF 80

At the age of 80, George Burns won an Oscar for his role in *The Sunshine Boys*. He died at the age of 100, having retired from live performing only three years before.

At the age of 82, Sir Winston Churchill published part one of his four-part *History Of The English Speaking Peoples*.

At the age of 84, William Gladstone was Prime Minister of Britain.

At the age of 84, W. Somerset Maugham published a collection of essays entitled *Points Of View*.

At the age of 85, Mae West starred in the film *Sextet*.

At the age of 87, Francis Rous was awarded the 1966 Nobel Prize for Medicine.

At the age of 87, Sir John Gielgud starred in the film *Prospero's Books*.

At the age of 88, Michelangelo was still sculpting.

At the age of 91, Eamon de Valera was President of Ireland.

At the age of 95, the American pianist Artur Rubinstein gave a public concert.

At the age of 95, Sir John Mills appeared in the film *Bright Young Things*.

PEOPLE WHO PUBLISHED THEIR DIARIES

Evelyn Waugh, Tony Benn, Sir Antony Sher, Sir Roger Moore, Piers Morgan, Andy Warhol, Richard Crossman, Will Carling, Barbara Castle, Sir Peter Hall, Vaslav Nijinsky, Robert Kilroy-Silk, Jeffrey Archer, Alan Clark, Claudio Ranieri, Brian Eno, Che Guevara, Samuel Pepys, Ian Hunter, Sir Alec Guinness, Anaïs Nin

ANIMALS ETC.

Sheep will not drink from running water.

Cows can smell odours six miles away.

A lion's muzzle is unique – no two lions have the same pattern of whiskers.

A Holstein's spots are unique – no two cows have the same pattern of spots.

Deer can't eat hay.

Montana mountain goats can butt heads so hard that their hooves fall off.

Cats can hear ultrasound.

The New Mexican whiptail lizard reproduces asexually, laying eggs that are clones of the mother. A courtship ritual is required between two female lizards in order to encourage the release of the eggs.

Giant pandas can eat 38 kilograms (83 pounds) of bamboo a day.

The underside of a horse's hoof is called a frog. The frog peels off several times a year with new growth.

You can tell a turtle's gender by the noise it makes: males grunt, females hiss.

The ferret was domesticated 500 years before the cat. The female ferret is a 'jill'.

Reindeer like bananas.

A rat would rather have a boiled sweet than some cheese.

Squirrels can't see red.

The tuatara lizard of New Zealand has three eyes – two that are positioned normally and an extra one on top of its head.

The woolly mammoth had tusks almost 5 metres (16 feet) long.

The sitatunga antelope is amphibious. Its water-adapted hooves are awkward on dry land.

A laboratory mouse runs 5 miles per night on its treadmill.

The world's smallest dog – the Teacup Chihuahua – weighs less than a pound when fully grown.

A bear has 42 teeth.

The Black Bear has a blue tongue.

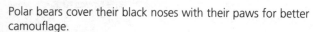

Hamsters like crickets as food.

Polar bears cover their black noses with their paws for better camouflage.

Squirrels can climb faster than they can run.

A group of twelve or more cows is called a flink.

A blind chameleon still changes colour to match his environment.

Male monkeys go bald in much

A pig sleeps on its right side.

400 quarter-pound hamburgers can be made out of one cow.

Armadillos have four babies at a time and they are always all of the same sex.

A cow gives nearly 200,000 glasses of milk in her lifetime.

A zebra is white with black stripes.

The longest snake is the Royal Python, which can grow to 10.6 metres long (35 feet).

When opossums are playing possum, they are not 'playing' – they pass out from sheer terror.

If you are chased by a crocodile, run in a serpentine fashion – a crocodile isn't good at making sharp turns.

A monkey was once tried and convicted for smoking a cigarette in Indiana.

Crocodiles never outgrow the pool in which they live. If you put a baby croc in an aquarium, it would be small for the rest of its life.

he same way that men do.

The kinkajou, which belongs to the same family as the raccoon, has a prehensile tail that is twice the length of its body. At night it wraps itself up in its tail to sleep.

The antlers of a male moose are more than 2 metres (about 7 feet) across. A moose's antlers are made up of the fastest-growing cells in the animal kingdom.

An adult hippo can bite a 3.6-metre (12-foot) adult male crocodile in half, and can open its mouth wide enough to fit a 1.2-metre (4-foot) child inside. A hippo can also outrun a man.

The world's smallest mammal (where skull size is the defining factor) is the bumblebee bat of Thailand.

A camel's backbone is as straight as a horse's.

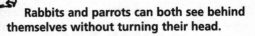

Rabbits and parrots can both see behind themselves without turning their head.

Alligators cannot move backwards.

A squirrel cannot contract or carry the rabies virus.

Camels chew in a figure-of-eight pattern.

A kangaroo can only jump when its tail is touching the ground.

At full speed, a cheetah takes 8-metre (26-foot) strides.

The honey badger in Africa can withstand bee stings that would kill another animal.

80 per cent of the noise a hippo makes is done underwater.

A cat uses its whiskers to determine if a space is big enough to squeeze through.

Koalas don't drink water, but get fluids from the eucalyptus leaves they eat. In fact, 'koala' is believed to mean 'no drink' in an Aboriginal language. Koalas have no natural predators.

There are only three types of snakes on the island of Tasmania and all three are deadly poisonous.

ANIMAL HYBRIDS

Mule: cross between a male donkey and a female horse

Hinny: cross between a male horse and a female donkey

Zeedonk: cross between a zebra and a donkey

Wolfdog: cross between a wolf and a dog

Liger: cross between a male lion and a female tiger

Cama: cross between a camel and a llama

Tigon: cross between a male tiger and a female lion

Wolphin: cross between a whale and a dolphin (only one in existence)

PEOPLE AND THEIR PETS

PERSON	PET	NAME
Reese Witherspoon	Dog: Bulldog	Frank Sinatra
Pamela Anderson	**Dog: Golden Retriever**	**Star**
Liv Tyler	Dog	Neil
Hilary Duff	**Dog: Fox Terrier/ Chihuahua**	**Little Dog**
Mariah Carey	Dogs: Shihtzus	Bing and Bong
	Jack Russell	Jack
	Yorkshire Terrier	Ginger
Paul O'Grady	**Dogs: Shihtzu Cross/Shihtzu**	**Buster and Louis**
Johnny Vaughan	Dog: British Bulldog	Harvey
Jenny Seagrove	**Dog: Springer Spaniel**	**Kizzy**
Amanda Holden	Dogs: West Highland Terriers	Nobbie and Fudge
Linda Barker	**Dog: Dachshund**	**Tiger Lilly**
Antony Worrall Thompson	Dogs: Russian Black Terrier	Jessica
	Golden Retriever	Trevor

Adrien Brody	Dog: Chihuahua	Ceelo
Vanilla Ice	Wallaroo: a kangaroo/wallaby cross	Bucky
	Goat	Pancho
Michael Stipe	Dog: Terrier	Helix
Wayne Rooney	Dog: Chow-Chow	Fizz
Natascha McElhone	Cat	Soup
Kate Bosworth	Cats	Louise and Dusty

CELEBRITIES WHO GOT DOGS FROM BATTERSEA DOGS' HOME

Simon Callow (Basil the singing dog)

Geri Halliwell (Shihtzu)

Sean Hughes

Sir Elton John (tan and white Collie cross)

Jason Connery

Samantha Robson

Kevin Spacey

Ringo Starr

Katie Boyle

Lionel Blair

Sheridan Morley

Jack Davenport

A GUIDE TO RABBITS

Rabbits are the fifth most popular pet in Britain (after goldfish, tropical fish, cats and dogs).

Rabbits are sociable creatures often found living in large groups in underground burrows or warrens. A colony of 407 rabbits was once found with a warren that had 2,080 exits.

The most popular names for British (pet) rabbits are – in order – Thumper, Flopsy and Charlie.

Most rabbits are cottontails.

A rabbit's eyes are capable of seeing in every direction, making it possible to watch predators in the air and on the ground.

Rabbits twitch their noses constantly because they depend on their sense of smell to warn them of danger.

The Ryukyu rabbit and Mexico's volcano rabbit are among the rarest mammals in the world.

The highest a rabbit has ever jumped is 46 centimetres (18 inches).

The only film Joan Rivers ever directed was entitled *Rabbit Test* (1978).

A farmer introduced 24 wild rabbits into Australia in 1859. There are now an estimated 300 million rabbits there.

Famous rabbits include: Brer Rabbit, The White Rabbit (in *Alice's Adventures in Wonderland*), Hazel, Fiver, Bigwig etc. (in *Watership Down*), Peter Rabbit, Benjamin Bunny, Bucky O'Hare, Rabbit (in A.A. Milne's Winnie the Pooh stories), Peter Cottontail, Bugs Bunny, Harvey (James Stewart's imaginary best friend in the 1950 film *Harvey*), Lola (in the film *Space Jam*), the Monster of Caer Bannog (in the film *Monty Python and the Holy Grail*), Oswald the Lucky Rabbit, Roger Rabbit, Thumper (in the film *Bambi*), Babs Bunny (in Steven Spielberg's *Tiny Toon Adventures*), Bean Bunny (in *The Muppets*), Benny Rabbit (in *Sesame Street*), the Easter Bunny.

BEFORE FAME

Lemmy used to be a roadie for Jimi Hendrix.

Tracey Ullman used to be a member of the Second Generation dance group.

Sir Elton John once auditioned for the group King Crimson.

Joseph Fiennes used to be a theatre usher and once told off Helen Mirren for not sitting down without realizing that she was one of the actresses.

Nathan Lane used to work as a singing telegram.

Stephen Sondheim once tried out as a contestant on *The $64,000 Question* (answering questions on John Ford films).

Paul Bettany used to busk on Westminster Bridge.

Errol Flynn used to work on a farm where he had to castrate sheep by biting off their testicles.

Minnie Driver attended finishing schools in Paris and Grenoble.

At one point, Jim Carrey and his family lived out of their car/trailer.

Michael Crawford took his stage name off a biscuit tin.

Stockard Channing received a substantial inheritance at the age of 15 after the death of her shipping magnate father.

Hugh Grant appeared as a contestant in the TV quiz *Top of The Form*.

Colin Farrell auditioned for Boyzone but didn't get in.

As a young woman, Lorraine Bracco was once asked to pose nude for Salvador Dalí but she refused.

Danny Kaye was sacked from his job in an insurance company after accidentally paying a claimant $40,000 instead of $4,000.

Nicole Kidman and Naomi Watts both attended North Sydney Girls' High School.

PEOPLE AND WHAT THEY DID BEFORE BECOMING FAMOUS

Delia Smith – Receptionist

Angelina Jolie – Embalmer

Jennifer Saunders – Cook in a fire station

Sonia – Collected eggs from battery chickens

Damien Hirst – Roadie for Barry Manilow

Afroman – Worked in a chicken factory

Jason Biggs – Subway sandwich maker

Ricky Gervais – Pizza delivery boy

Richard Bacon – McDonald's

Mackenzie Crook – Worked at Pizza Hut, in a chicken factory and in hospitals

Shaznay Lewis – Gardener, postman and shop assistant in Top Man

Jim Davidson – Forklift-truck driver

Rolf Harris – Postman

Alexei Sayle – Illustrator

Shane MacGowan – Worked in a record shop

Christie Brinkley – Painter

Charlie Watts – Designer in advertising

Gabriel Byrne – Plumber's assistant, apprentice chef, archaeologist, teacher

Anthony Andrews – Farm labourer

Paul Newman – Encyclopaedia salesman

John Leslie – DJ at Top Shop in Edinburgh

Edna O'Brien – Trainee pharmacist

Jon Bon Jovi – Served in Burger King

Kim Wilde – Hospital cleaner

Bernard Manning – Cigarette factory worker

Carol Smillie – Shoe shop assistant, model

Gail Porter – Shoe shop assistant; VT operator

Freddie Starr – Bricklayer

Giorgio Armani – Window dresser

Paul Young – Apprentice toolmaker at Vauxhall

Gary Kemp – Prices clerk for the *Financial Times*

Jimmy Somerville – Baker

Danny DeVito – Janitor

Helen Lederer – Social worker

Reg Presley – Bricklayer

Joan Armatrading – Accounts assistant

Richard Ashcroft – Lifeguard

FORMER LIBRARIANS

Mao Tse-tung, Sir Ludovic Kennedy, Casanova, Laurie Taylor, Anthea Turner, Philip Larkin, August Strindberg, John Braine, David Hockney, J. Edgar Hoover, Pope Pius XI, Jane Gardam, Laura Bush, Howard W. Koch, Boris Pasternak

FORMER AIR STEWARDESSES

Janice Long, Melinda Messenger, Trisha Goddard, Alex Best

EX-PONTIN'S BLUECOATS

Shane Richie, Lee Mack, Brian Conley, Vicky Entwistle, Helen Chamberlain, Shaun Williamson, Bradley Walsh, Amanda Redington, Paul Usher

FORMER PLAYBOY BUNNIES

Debbie Harry, Lauren Hutton, Fiona Richmond, Gloria Steinem (on an undercover assignment)

FORMER MINERS

Paul Shane, Sir Jimmy Savile, Dennis Skinner, Charles Bronson, Anthony Shaffer and Peter Shaffer, Fred Trueman, Jeffrey Bernard, Jocky Wilson, Harold Larwood, Ray Reardon

TRAINED AS ENGINEERS

Lord John Birt, Will Hay, Rowan Atkinson, Walter Huston, Ringo Starr, Yasser Arafat, Carol Vorderman, Kate Bellingham, Nicholas Parsons, Naim Attallah, The Bachelors, Tom Conway

FORMER DANCERS

Madonna, Jennifer Lopez, Keira Knightley, Ken Russell, Clare Francis, Toyah Willcox, Christopher Beeny, Victoria Principal, Brigitte Bardot, Suzanne Vega, Baroness Betty Boothroyd, Tina Barrett

FORMER JOURNALISTS

Frederick Forsyth, Chrissie Hynde, Evelyn Waugh, Ali MacGraw, Jilly Cooper, Mark Knopfler, Neil Tennant, Steve Harley, Patrick Stewart

FORMER EDITORS

Michael Foot: *Evening Standard*

Nina Myskow: *Jackie*

John Freeman: *New Statesman*

Libby Purves: *Tatler*

Sally Beauman: *Queen*

Anthony Holden: *Sunday Today*

Sir Richard Branson: *Student*

Sir Julian Critchley: *Town*

Sir Alastair Burnet: *The Daily Express*

Kate Thornton: *Smash Hits*

PEOPLE WHO LIVED ON A KIBBUTZ

Isla Fisher, Annie Leibovitz, Paul Kaye (aka Dennis Pennis), Jonathan Pearce, Bob Hoskins, Kit Hesketh-Harvey, Tony Hawks, Maeve Binchy, Anna Ford, Samantha Spiro, Sally Becker, Ruby Wax, Mike Leigh, Lynne Reid Banks (for nine years), Mary Tamm, Uri Geller, Dr Ruth Westheimer, Simon Le Bon, Sandra Bernhard, Jerry Seinfeld

FORMER FLATMATES

Gary Webster and Phil Middlemiss

Martin Tyler and Bob Willis

Paul Whitehouse and Harry Enfield

Taki and Peter Lawford

John Prescott and Dennis Skinner

Martin Offiah and Shaun Edwards

David Lynch and Peter Wolf

Lynda Bellingham and Julia Sawalha

Ioan Gruffudd and Matthew Rhys

Ant and Dec (then they bought houses two doors down from each other in Chiswick)

Brian McFadden and Ben Ofoedu

Rik Mayall and Rowland Rivron

Nastassja Kinski and Demi Moore

Jon Snow and Maya Angelou

Johnny Rotten and Sid Vicious

Patricia Hodge and Cheryl Campbell

MEN WHO WERE IN THE MERCHANT NAVY

Bob Mills, John Prescott, Bill Treacher, Dickie Davies, Peter Stringfellow, Gareth Hunt, Christopher Ellison, Rutger Hauer, Bob Hoskins, Jack Kerouac, Bernie Winters, Alan Weeks, Vivian Stanshall, Allen Ginsberg, Roger Scott, Ken Russell, Tommy Steele, Desmond Wilcox

PEOPLE WHO USED TO WORK IN SHOPS

Gaby Roslin (Selfridges, John Lewis and Harrods)

Katy Hill (The Body Shop and John Menzies)

Gary Numan (W.H. Smith)

Russ Abbot (Hepworths)

Mick Fleetwood (Liberty)

Betty Boo (Marks & Spencer)

Glenda Jackson (Boots)

Wendy Richard (Fortnum & Mason)

George Michael (BHS)

Annie Lennox (Mothercare)

Ted Rogers (W.H. Smith)

Bobby Davro (Bentalls)

Edwina Currie (Woolworths)

Jayne Middlemiss (Currys)

Lisa Scott-Lee (River Island: 'I used to spend hours making sure the hangers were spaced two fingers away from each other. It's quite therapeutic.')

Duncan James (Woolworths)

Charles Dance (Burton's – as a window-dresser)

PEOPLE WHO USED TO BE WAITERS/WAITRESSES

Annie Lennox, Rickie Lee Jones, Jacqueline Bisset, Dame Diana Rigg, Ellen Barkin, Paula Abdul, Alec Baldwin, Antonio Banderas, Jennifer Aniston, Ellen DeGeneres, Graham Norton, Angela Bassett (a singing waitress), Mariah Carey, Dustin Hoffman, Julianna Margulies, Edward Norton, Barbra Streisand, Russell Crowe, Kristin Davis, Julianne Moore, Robin Wright Penn, Emily Watson, Allison Janney, Julia Ormond, Monty Don, Renée Zellweger (in a topless bar – although she refused to take off her bra)

PEOPLE WHO QUALIFIED AS LAWYERS

Baroness Margaret Thatcher, Clive Anderson, Osvaldo Ardiles, Mahatma Gandhi, Sir Robin Day, Sir John Mortimer, Hoagy Carmichael, Tony Blair, Fidel Castro, Rossano Brazzi, Jerry Springer, Erle Stanley Gardner, Otto Preminger, Geraldo Rivera, Bob Mortimer

NB Bing Crosby, David Gower, Estelle Parsons and Cole Porter all studied law at university without getting their degrees.

PEOPLE WHO WORKED IN ADVERTISING

Ridley Scott (as a director – e.g. on Hovis)

Fay Weldon (as a copywriter – e.g. 'Go To Work On An Egg')

Salman Rushdie (as a copywriter – e.g. 'Cream Cakes – Naughty But Nice')

Murray Walker (as an account director. For most of his commentating career, Murray's day job was in advertising. He worked on the 'Mars A Day' campaign.)

James Herbert (as a copywriter)

Sir Alec Guinness (as a copywriter working on campaigns for Rose's Lime Juice, razors and radio valves)

Sir David Puttnam (as an account director)

Irma Kurtz (as a copywriter)

Len Deighton (as a copywriter)

Spike Lee (as a copywriter)

Martin Amis (as a copywriter)

Charlie Watts (as a designer)

Tim Allen (as a creative director)

Sela Ward (as an art director)

Hugh Grant (as an advertising account executive)

THINGS SAID ABOUT ADVERTISING

'Half the money I spend on advertising is wasted, and the trouble is, I don't know which half.' (Lord Leverhulme)

'Advertising agency: eighty-five per cent confusion and fifteen per cent commission.' (Fred Allen)

'Advertising is legalised lying.' (H.G. Wells)

'Time spent in the advertising business seems to create a permanent deformity, like the Chinese habit of foot-binding.' (Dean Acheson)

'Advertising is a racket. Its constructive contribution to humanity is exactly zero.' (F. Scott Fitzgerald)

'Advertising is the art of making whole lies out of half truths.' (Edgar A. Shoaff)

'Advertising is the rattling of a stick inside a swill bucket.' (George Orwell)

'Advertising may be described as the science of arresting the human intelligence long enough to get money from it.' (Stephen Leacock)

PEOPLE AND THE PRODUCTS THEY ADVERTISED IN JAPAN

Sting (Kirin beer)

Sir Sean Connery (Itoh sausages)

Sandy Lyle (Mizuno sportswear)

Brad Pitt (Toyota – paid $1 million per day for three days' work)

Jay Kay (Sony Walkman)

Keanu Reeves (Suntory)

Ewan McGregor (Bobson Jeans)

Arnold Schwarzenegger (Nissin Cup Noodles and DirecTV)

Brooke Shields (Aloe Mine)

Winona Ryder (Subaru Impreza)

Ringo Starr (Ringosutta apple sauce)

Dennis Hopper (Tsumura Bathclin)

Harrison Ford (Kirin beer)

Sylvester Stallone (Itoh sausages)

Charlie Sheen (Tokyo Gas)

Madonna (Jun liquor)

Gene Hackman (Kirin beer)

Richard Gere (Japan Airlines)

Bruce Willis (NTT mobile phones)

Michael Bolton (Georgia Coffee)

Jodie Foster (Honda Civic)

David Bowie (Sake)

Kevin Costner (Kirin beer)

Boy George (Shochu)

Lord Jeffrey Archer (Suntory)

Natalie Imbruglia (got her big break aged 16 as the Pineapple Princess in a Japanese chewing gum commercial)

PEOPLE WHO PROVIDED VOICES FOR THE PG TIPS CHIMPS ADS

Stanley Baxter, Arthur Lowe, Bruce Forsyth,
Pat Coombs, Kenneth Connor, Irene Handl,
Bob Monkhouse, Kenneth Williams,
Miriam Margolyes

BIZARRE PLACE NAMES

Agenda (Wisconsin, USA)

Asbestos (Canada)

Banana (Australia)

Belcher (Louisiana, USA)

Bird-in-Hand (Pennsylvania, USA)

Blubberhouses (Yorkshire)

Boom (Belgium)

Boring (Oregon, USA)

Chicken (Alaska, USA)

Chunky (Mississippi, USA)

Ding Dong (Texas, USA)

Drain (Oregon, USA)

Eye (Suffolk)

Hell (Norway)

How (Wisconsin, USA)

Howlong (Australia)

Humpty Doo (Australia)

Lower Slaughter (Gloucestershire)

Loyal (Oklahoma, USA)

Luck (Wisconsin, USA)

Mars (Pennsylvania, USA)

Matching Tye (Essex)

Medicine Hat (Canada)

Moron (Mongolia)

Nasty (Hertfordshire)

Natters (Austria)

Normal (Illinois, USA)

Parachute (Colorado, USA)

Peculiar (Missouri, USA)

Pity Me (County Durham)

Pussy (France)

Puzzletown (Pennsylvania, USA)

Rottenegg (Austria)

Rough and Ready (California, USA)

Secretary (Maryland, USA)

Silly (Belgium)

Simmering (Austria)

Siren (Wisconsin, USA)

Smackover (Arkansas, USA)

Snapfinger (Georgia, USA)

Spit Junction (Australia)

Surprise (Arizona, USA)

Tiddleywink (Wiltshire)

Tightwad (Missouri, USA)

Toast (North Carolina, USA)

Truth or Consequences (New Mexico, USA)

Useless Loop (Australia)

Vulcan (Canada)

Wham (Yorkshire)

Zig Zag (Australia)

THINGS SAID ABOUT AUSTRALIA AND THE AUSTRALIANS

'Australia has more things that will kill you than anywhere else.' (Bill Bryson)

'You don't say "cheers" when you drink a cup of tea in the bush, you say, "Christ, the flies!"' (Prince Charles)

'Australia is a huge rest home where no unwelcome news is wafted on to the pages of the worst newspapers in the world.' (Germaine Greer)

'Australians can, and do, quite readily and often in my experience, throw off all their 180 years of civilized nationhood.' (Ted Dexter)

'(Australians are) violently loud alcoholic roughnecks whose idea of fun is to throw up in your car.' (P.J. O'Rourke)

'Australia may be the only country in the world in which the word "academic" is regularly used as a term of abuse.' (Dame Leonie Kramer)

'A broad school of Australian writing has based itself on the assumption that Australia not only has a history worth bothering about but that all the history worth bothering about happened in Australia.' (Clive James)

'It's so empty and featureless – like a newspaper that has been entirely censored.' (Robert Morley)

'The Australian temper is at bottom grim: it is as though the hot sun has dried up his nature.' (Sir Neville Cardus)

'To live in Australia permanently is rather like going to a party and dancing all night with one's mother.' (Barry Humphries)

'When I look at the map and see what an ugly country Australia is, I feel that I want to go there and see if it cannot be changed into a more beautiful form.' (Oscar Wilde)

THINGS THAT COME FROM AUSTRALIA

Mimosa, emus, macadamia nuts, koala bears, kangaroos, didgeridoos, Neighbours, Aussie Rules football, acacia, bandicoots, wombats, Castlemaine XXXX, Foster's, dingoes

SOD'S LAW

In 2004, British Gas* decided to assess Sod's Law. They asked a thousand people to rate ten events according to their level of, well, soddishness.

SOD'S LAW SCORES

1. Spilling something on yourself before a date: 8.5

2. Boiler breaking down in a cold snap: 8.2

3. Traffic being worse when you're running late: 7.3

4. E-mail crashing when sending a vital document: 7.0

5. Washing machine breaking down before holidays: 6.7

6. Cooker packing up when you're expecting guests: 6.4

7. Shower running cold as you wash your hair: 6.0

8. Phone or doorbell ringing while you're in the bath: 5.3

9. Person you're gossiping about overhearing you: 4.6

10. Spare light bulbs not matching one that fails: 4.4

Meanwhile, three eminent academics (an economist, a mathematician and a psychologist) established a formula for Sod's Law: $((U+C+I) \times (10S))/20 \times A \times 1/(1-\sin(F/10))$. The letters represent five factors which can be applied to any event or action: urgency (U), complexity (C), importance (I), skill (S) and frequency (F).

* Note the frequency of gas-related mishaps.

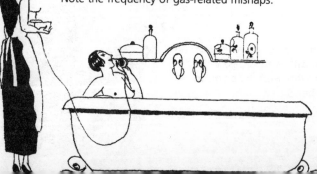

PEOPLE

Charisma Carpenter is a keen skydiver.

Sir Sean Connery appeared in a party political broadcast for the Scottish Nationalist Party.

Dick Van Dyke is ambidextrous.

William H. Macy believes that he was a Golden Retriever in a previous life.

Walt Disney's autograph bears no resemblance to the famous Disney logo.

Kirstie Alley bans anyone wearing perfume in her house (because of its destructive effect on the ozone layer).

Woody Allen eats out every day of the year.

Frank Sinatra was voted 'Worst Autograph Giver' by *Autograph Collector* magazine.

Jack Palance has never watched any of his own films.

Paul Newman stopped signing autographs 'when I was standing at a urinal at Sardi's and a guy came up with a pen and paper. I wondered: do I wash first and then shake hands?'

Before marrying his wife, Jay Leno lived (at different times) with five women who were all born on September 5.

Noah Wyle is a Civil War buff.

Wynonna took her name from the town Wynona OK, name-checked in the song *Route 66*.

Harpo Marx once tried to adopt child star Shirley Temple.

Eddie Murphy crosses himself before he enters lifts.

Matt Groening incorporated his initials into the drawing of Homer: there's an M in his hair and his ear is the letter G.

Ben Affleck's reformed alcoholic father, Tim, became Robert Downey Jr's drug counsellor.

Richie Benaud is the president of French cricket.

Lucy Liu practises the martial art of Kali-Eskrima-Silat (knife and stick fighting).

Robert Duvall has a passion for the tango and practises every day.

Maurice Chevalier had a clause in his contract with Paramount Pictures that if he ever lost his French accent, they could terminate the contract.

Sheryl Crow's front two teeth are fake – her own were knocked out when she tripped on stage.

Nick Hancock owns Sir Stanley Matthews's 1953 FA Cup Winner's medal.

Thomas Jefferson introduced ice cream to the US.

Jennifer Lopez takes along her own sheets when she stays at a hotel.

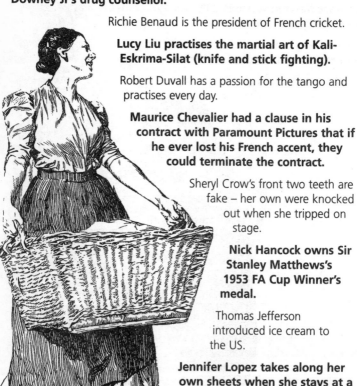

Greg Norman and Olivia Newton-John both bought vineyards.

Vincent van Gogh cut off his left ear. His 'Self-portrait with Bandaged Ear' shows the right one bandaged because he painted the mirror image.

Arnold Schoenberg suffered from triskaidecaphobia, the fear of the number 13. He died 13 minutes from midnight on Friday the 13th.

Sir Isaac Newton was just 23 years old when he discovered the law of universal gravitation.

Harrison Ford, Angelina Jolie, Patrick Swayze, Martin Shaw and Gene Hackman have all qualified as pilots.

Jordan is keen on sewing.

PEOPLE WHO WENT ON THE ORIGINAL CND MARCHES

Jeremy Beadle, Vanessa Redgrave, Humphrey Lyttelton, Rod Stewart, George Melly, Doris Lessing, Bryan Pringle, Arnold Wesker, Lindsay Anderson, Robert Bolt, Peter Vaughan, John Braine, John Arden, Michael Foot, Sheila Delaney, Dame Anita Roddick

MEMBERS OF THE DENNIS THE MENACE FAN CLUB

Joan Armatrading, Lenny Henry, Paul Gascoigne, Timmy Mallett, Suzanne Dando, Ian Woosnam, Mark Hamill, Mike Read

VEGANS

Fiona Apple, Kate Moss, Lindsay Wagner, Daryl Hannah, Martin Shaw, Yazz, Benjamin Zephaniah, Sophie Ward, Wendy Turner, Casey Affleck, Linda Blair, Julia Stiles, Tobey Maguire, Noah Wyle

CELEBRITIES WHO BOUGHT OTHER CELEBRITIES' HOUSES

Dame Elizabeth Taylor lives in a house once owned by Frank Sinatra.

Jim Davidson's home near Dorking in Surrey was Oliver Reed's.

Gangsta rapper 50 Cent bought Mike Tyson's 17-acre estate in Farmington, Connecticut.

Brittany Murphy bought Britney Spears's Hollywood Hills house.

Doris Duke bought Rudolph Valentino's house.

Dorothy Squires bought Lillie Langtry's house.

David Blaine lives in a Gothic-style manor house in the Hollywood Hills that used to belong to Harry Houdini.

Madonna and Guy Ritchie own Ashcombe House, Wiltshire – where Sir Cecil Beaton lived from 1930 to 1945.

Gwyneth Paltrow and Chris Martin bought Kate Winslet's north London home in Belsize Park.

Shane Warne bought a house in Southampton that used to belong to Matt Le Tissier.

Mackenzie Crook bought Peter Sellers's old house in Muswell Hill.

Eddie Murphy bought the house in Benedict Canyon Drive that was once owned by Cher.

Sir Paul McCartney bought Courtney Love's old house in Los Angeles.

PEOPLE AND THEIR TATTOOS

Kelis: a giant orchid on her backside

Wayne Rooney: his girlfriend Coleen's name tattooed on his shoulder

Ewan McGregor: heart-and-dagger on his right shoulder

Rachel Hunter: bee logo for her production company, Bee Knees, on her lower back

Elijah Wood: elfish symbol on his hip

Patsy Kensit: 'Liam' with shamrock on ankle

George Shultz: tiger on bottom

Lord Patrick Lichfield: seahorse on arm

Princess Stephanie of Monaco: dragon on hip

Pamela Anderson: Tommy Lee's name on wedding finger

Johnny Depp: 'Winona Forever' on arm (changed to 'Wino Forever' when he and Winona Ryder split up)

Rachel Williams: arrow on bottom

Dean Holdsworth: 'Let He Without Sin Cast The First Stone' on arm

Brian Harvey: 'Eastside' on arm

Joan Baez: flower on back

Sharron Davies: elephant on bottom

Brian Conley: No Entry sign on bottom

Kelly McGillis: red rose on ankle

Suzi Quatro: star on wrist

Brigitte Nielsen: heart on bottom

Christy Turlington: heart on ankle

Liam Gallagher: 'Patsy' on arm

Whoopi Goldberg: Woodstock on breast

Alyssa Milano: the initials 'SRW' of her ex-fiancé on her right ankle

Natasha Henstridge: intertwined male and female symbols on her coccyx; bearded lion with crown – her star sign is Leo – on her bottom

Jo O'Meara: a Chinese emblem on the bottom of her spine, a butterfly on her bum, a dolphin on her belly, a flower on her ankle and a crescent moon on her foot

Mel B.: M for 'Max' on her buttock

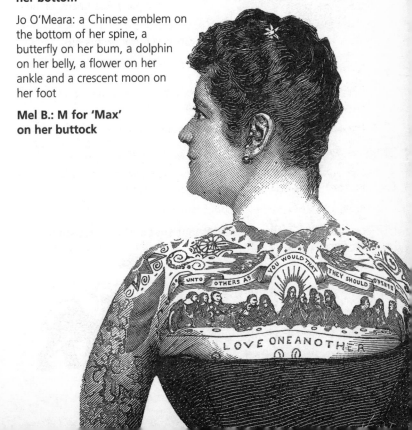

People who live/lived on houseboats

Frederick Forsyth, Nigel Planer, Imogen Stubbs, Lemmy, Sir Richard Branson, Lord David Owen, Elizabeth Emanuel, David Suchet, Dr Conor Cruise O'Brien, Lawrence Dallaglio, Alexander Armstrong, Susan Penhaligon, Leo Sayer, Mike Barson, Glynn Edwards, David Gilmour, Damien Hirst

People who made Richard Blackwell's annual 'worst-dressed women' lists

Paris Hilton (2003): 'How are you gonna keep 'em down on the farm after they've seen Paree? Grab the blinders, here comes Paris. From cyber disgrace to red carpet chills – she's the vapid Venus of Beverly Hills!'

Melanie Griffith (2003): 'Melanie defines "fatal fashion folly". A botox'd cockatoo in a painting by Dalí!'

Martha Stewart (1999): 'Dresses like the centerfold for the Farmer's Almanac. She's a 3-D girl: dull, dowdy and devastatingly dreary. Definitely not "a good thing".'

Kelly Osbourne (2002): 'A fright-wigged baby doll stuck in a goth prom gown.'

Elizabeth Hurley (2000): 'Her barely-there fashion bombs have hit a sour note – buy a coat.'

Anne Robinson (2001): 'Harry Potter in Drag … a Hogwarts horror. Anne Robinson, you are fashion's Weakest Link!'

Sarah, Duchess of York (1996): 'The bare-toed terror of London town. She looks like an unemployed barmaid in search of a crown.' Also made the list in 1988 when she was accused of looking 'like a horse that came in last'. Blackwell went on to say 'she looks terrible, like she should be making beds on the second floor of a motel'.

Geena Davis (1992): 'Big Bird in heels.'

Yoko Ono (1972): 'Oh no Yoko.'

Roseanne (1989): 'Bowling alley reject.'

David Bowie (1973): 'A cross between Joan Crawford and Marlene Dietrich doing a glitter revival of New Faces.'

Faye Dunaway (1991): 'The Depressing Diva of Designer Dreck.'

Bette Midler (1978): 'She didn't go to a rummage sale, she wore it.'

Barbra Streisand (1990): 'What can I say? Yentl's gone mental.' 1983: 'A boy version of Medusa.'

Jane Seymour (1991): 'A paisley peepshow on parade.'

Debbie Harry (1979): 'Ten cents a dance with a nickel change.'

Madonna (1992): 'The Bare-bottomed Bore of Babylon.' 1988: 'Helpless, hopeless and horrendous.'

Dennis Rodman (1996): 'The "Fashion Menace" may be the Bad Boy of basketball, but in fishnet and feathers he's a unisex wreck.'

Glenn Close (1992): 'Dracula's Daughter.'

Camilla, Duchess of Cornwall (2001): 'Packs the stylistic punch of a dilapidated Yorkshire pudding.' 1995: 'The Queen of Frump' and 'The biggest bomb to hit Britain since the Blitz'. 1994: 'Her fashion image is way off track – she looked in the mirror and watched it crack.'

The Queen (1990): 'God save the mothballs, the Stonehenge of style strikes again.'

Cher (1986): 'Popular Mechanics Playmate of the Month. Someone must have thrown a monkey wrench into her fashion taste.' 1984: 'A plucked cockatoo setting femininity back 20 years.'

Elton John (1975): 'Would be the campest spectacle in the Rose Parade.'

Demi Moore (1989): 'A Spandexed nightmare on Willis Street.'

Jodie Foster (1991): 'Her fashions would look better on Hannibal Lecter.'

Julia Roberts (1992): 'Hand out the hook for rag doll Roberts.'

Tina Turner (1985): 'Some women dress for men, some dress for women, some dress for laughs.'

Sinéad O'Connor (1992): 'No tresses, no dresses. The high priestess of pretence downright depresses.' 1990: 'Nothing compares to the bald-headed banshee of MTV.'

PEOPLE WHO CHANGED CITIZENSHIP

Warren Mitchell (from British to Australian)

Joe Bugner (from British to Australian)

Martina Navratilova (from Czech to American)

Nadia Comaneci (from Romanian to American)

Yehudi Menuhin (from American to British)

Greta Scacchi (from British to Australian)

Sheena Easton (from British to American)

Andrew Sachs (from German to British)

Zola Budd (from South African to British to South African)

Ivan Lendl (from Czech to American)

Allan Lamb (from South African to British)

John Huston (from American to Irish)

T.S. Eliot (from American to British)

Josephine Baker (from American to French)

Jane Seymour (from British to American)

Sir Anthony Hopkins (from British to American)

PEOPLE WHO NEVER, OR ALMOST NEVER, GIVE INTERVIEWS

Eric Clapton, Björn Borg, Peter Green, Nigel Twiston-Davies, Tom Bell, J.D. Salinger, Warren Beatty, Thomas Harris, Dan Aykroyd, Vangelis, Neil Armstrong, Kate Bush, Thomas Pynchon (has never even been photographed), Mutt Lange, John Deacon, Alan Rickman, David Lynch, Larry Mullen Jr, David Letterman, Syd Barrett, John Irving, Kate Moss, Chelsea Clinton, Camilla, Duchess of Cornwall, Don DeLillo, Harper Lee, Michael Kitchen, J.J. Cale, Charles Saatchi, Delia Smith, Doris Day

NON-DRIVERS

Marianne Faithfull, Stephen Byers, Barry Cryer, John McCririck, Michael Jackson, Simon Gray, Sir David Attenborough, Kathy Burke, David Copperfield, John Sessions, Marco Pierre White, Claudia Schiffer, Ken Livingstone, Gordon Brown, Wendy Richard, Anna Nicole Smith

NB Albert Einstein never learned to drive

PEOPLE WHO BOUGHT ROLLS-ROYCES

Elvis Presley, Ben Affleck (for Jennifer Lopez), Beyoncé Knowles, Gary Glitter, Zia Mahmood, Noel Gallagher, Shane Richie, Ruth Madoc, Sir Jimmy Savile, Sir Michael Caine, Donovan, Cilla Black, Vladimir Lenin, Grigori Rasputin, T.E. Lawrence, Rudyard Kipling, Idi Amin, John Lennon, Benito Mussolini, Mae West, George Bernard Shaw

PEOPLE WHO OWN(ED)/ CO-OWN(ED) RESTAURANTS

Jean-Paul Belmondo: Stressa (Paris)

Alice Cooper: Cooperstown (Phoenix)

Jennifer Lopez: Madre's (Pasadena)

William Devane: Devane's (Palm Springs)

Wayne Gretzky: Wayne Gretzky's (Toronto)

Morton Harket: Figaro (Oslo)

Timothy Hutton: P.J. Clarke's (New York City)

Sir Elton John: Le Dome (Hollywood)

Ashton Kutcher: Dolce (Los Angeles)

Moby: TeaNY (New York City)

Ricky Martin: Casa Salsa (Miami Beach)

Rob Schneider: Eleven (San Francisco)

Tom Selleck: The Black Orchid (Honolulu)

Sylvester Stallone, Bruce Willis and Arnold Schwarzenegger: the Planet Hollywood chain

Chris Kelly: Midsummer House (Cambridge)

Mariel Hemingway: Sam's Restaurant (Dallas)

Sir Michael Caine: Langan's Brasserie (London)

Mikhail Baryshnikov: Columbus (New York City)

Robert De Niro, Bill Murray, Lou Diamond Phillips and Christopher Walken: TriBeCa (New York City)

Bill Wyman: Sticky Fingers (London)

Patrick Swayze: Mulholland Drive Café (Los Angeles)

Delia Smith: The City Brasserie (Norwich)

Dan Aykroyd: House of Blues restaurant/music club chain

Whoopi Goldberg, Joe Pesci, Steven Seagal: Eclipse (Hollywood)

Steven Spielberg and Jeffrey Katzenberg: Dive! (Las Vegas)

Cameron Diaz: Bamboo (Miami)

Britney Spears: Nyla (New York City)

PEOPLE WHO ARE SUPERSTITIOUS

Kylie Minogue, Paul Dickov, Norman Cook (Fatboy Slim), Engelbert Humperdinck, Sir Elton John, Fabien Barthez, Jenni Falconer, Jelena Dokic, Michael Atherton, Henrietta Knight, Martin Bell, Huw Edwards, Mariah Carey, Diana Quick, Jilly Cooper, Michael Aspel, Tony McCoy, Goran Ivanisevic

PEOPLE WHO WERE ORDAINED DRUIDS

William Blake, William Roache, Sir Winston Churchill, John Lennon

PEOPLE AND WHAT THEY COLLECT

Patrick Stewart – *Beavis and Butthead* merchandise

George Michael (as a boy) – lizards and insects

Andre Agassi – Barry Manilow records

Clint Eastwood – jazz records

Helena Christensen – perfume bottles

Angelina Jolie – knives

Quentin Tarantino – old board games based on TV shows

Pink – stuffed frogs

Tara Palmer-Tomkinson – 'Do Not Disturb' signs from hotels around the world

Kevin Spacey – antique ashtrays

Jessica Biel – vintage glasses without lenses

Dan Aykroyd – police badges

Beau Bridges – Native American percussion instruments

George W. Bush – autographed baseballs

J.C. Chasez – Hard Rock Café menus

Bill Clinton – saxophones (real ones and miniatures)

Stephen Dorff – vintage cameras

Patrick Duffy – antique toys and children's books

Joey Fatone – Superman memorabilia

Larry Hagman – canes and flags

Mike Myers – model soldiers

Freddie Prinze – comic books

Noah Wyle – baseball cards

Philippa Forrester – first edition children's books

Jodie Foster – black & white photos

Sarah Michelle Gellar – rare books

Anna Kournikova – dolls from the countries she visits

Joan Rivers – Fabergé eggs

Roseanne – pigs

Trude Mostue – animals' testicles

Rachel Stevens – books of matches

Meat Loaf – stuffed toys

Norman Cook (Fatboy Slim) – smiley ephemera

Peter Jackson – World War One models of aeroplanes

SPORTING STARS WHO APPEARED IN FILMS

Sugar Ray Robinson – *Candy* (1968)

Muhammad Ali – *The Greatest* (1977)

Bobby Moore – *Escape To Victory* (1981)

Craig Stadler – *Tin Cup* (1996)

Ilie Nastase – *Players* (1979)

Magic Johnson – *Grand Canyon* (1991)

Pele – *Hot Shot* (1987)

Michael Johnson – *Space Jam* (1996)

Sir Henry Cooper – *Royal Flash* (1975)

Vijay Amritraj – *Octopussy* (1983)

Ken Norton – *Mandingo* (1975)

Sir Len Hutton – *The Final Test* (1953)

FICTIONAL CHARACTERS AND THEIR FIRST NAMES

Dr (John) Watson (*Sherlock Holmes*)

(Rupert) Rigsby (*Rising Damp*)

Mr (Quincy) Magoo

Inspector (Jules) Maigret

Inspector (Endeavour) Morse

Captain (George) Mainwaring (*Dad's Army*)

(Wilfred) Ivanhoe

(Hugh) Bulldog Drummond

(James) Shelley (*Shelley*)

Little Lord (Cedric) Fauntleroy

Gilligan of Gilligan's Island had a first name that was only used once, on the never-aired pilot show: Willy

NB Columbo's first name *isn't* Philip, despite claims that it is. His first name was never mentioned in the series.

DAFT LABELS

On a packet of Sainsbury's peanuts: 'Warning: Contains nuts.'

On a hairdryer: 'Do not use while sleeping.'

On a bar of Dial soap: 'Directions: Use like regular soap.'

On Marks & Spencer bread pudding: 'Product will be hot after heating.'

On Tesco's tiramisu dessert (printed on bottom of box): 'Do not turn upside down.'

On packaging for a Rowenta iron: 'Do not iron clothes on body.'

On Boots children's cough medicine: 'Do not drive a car or operate machinery after taking this medication.'

On Nytol Sleep Aid: 'Warning: May cause drowsiness.'

On a set of Christmas lights: 'For indoor or outdoor use only.'

On a Japanese food processor: 'Not to be used for the other use.'

On a child's Superman costume: 'Wearing of this garment does not enable you to fly.'

On a Swedish chainsaw: 'Do not attempt to stop chain with your hands.'

On a bottle of Palmolive dishwashing liquid: 'Do not use on food.'

MEMORABILIA SOLD AT CHRISTIE'S

Dorothy's ruby slippers from *The Wizard of Oz*: $666,000 (2000)

Paul Gascoigne's shirt from the 1990 World Cup semi-final against West Germany: £28,680 (2004)

Pele's shirt from the 1958 World Cup Final: £70,505 (2004)

Marilyn Monroe's eternity ring (given to her by Joe DiMaggio after their 1954 wedding): $772,500 (1999)

Eric Clapton's 1956 Fender Stratocaster (as used on *Layla*): $497,500 (1999)

George Harrison's 1964 Gibson SG Standard guitar: $567,000 (2004)

John Lennon's handwritten lyrics to the Beatles' song *Nowhere Man*: $455,500 (2003)

An autographed life-size picture of Marlene Dietrich used in the famous crowd scene in Peter Blake's design for the Beatles *Sergeant Pepper's Lonely Hearts Club Band* album cover: £86,250 (2003)

Britney Spears's school book report: $1,000 (2004)

The Rosebud sledge from *Citizen Kane*: $233,500 (1996)

James Bond's Aston Martin DB5: £157,750 (2001)

John Travolta's white suit from *Saturday Night Fever*: $145,500 (1995)

The Maltese Falcon icon from the 1941 film of the same name: $398,500 (1994)

Clark Gable's personal script for *Gone With The Wind*: $244,500 (1996)

Marilyn Monroe's dress when she sang *Happy Birthday* to President John F. Kennedy at Madison Square Garden, New York, in 1962: $1,267,500 (1999)

Elvis Presley's 1942 Martin D-18 acoustic guitar: £99,000 (1993)

Bob Dylan's acoustic guitar from the 1960s: $20,000 (2004)

Animation cell from Disney's 1934 *Orphan's Benefit*: $286,000 (1989)

A poster for *The Mummy* (1932): £80,750 (2001)

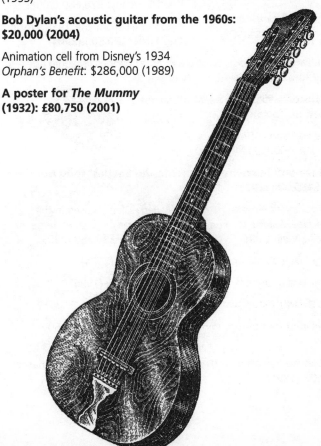

CELEBRITY ACHIEVEMENTS

Geoff Hoon and Mo Mowlam both achieved Gold in the Duke of Edinburgh's Award Scheme.

Carol Barnes and Dave Dee both became magistrates.

Gordon Brown won a *Daily Express* competition for a vision of Britain in the year 2000 when he was 21.

Sarah Michelle Gellar has a brown belt in tae kwon do.

Dame Helen Mirren was named Naturist of the Year 2004.

Of all his many talents, Leonardo da Vinci was proudest of his ability to bend iron with his bare hands.

Daryl Hannah invented a board game called Love It Or Hate It.

Paul Whitehouse won the Baby Smile of the Rhondda Valley award in 1963.

Robson Green has a category-four licence for doing professional fireworks displays.

Sir Michael Gambon and Eric Bana both became successful actors without receiving any formal acting training. The same was true for Art Carney and Beryl Reid.

PEOPLE WHO ARE FLUENT IN FOREIGN LANGUAGES

Clive James (Japanese)

Prince Philip (German)

Gary Lineker (Spanish)

Tim Roth (French and German)

Sir John Harvey-Jones (Russian)

Shirley Maclaine (Japanese)

Susannah York (French)

Lord Denis Healey (Italian)

Philip Madoc (German and Italian)

Kylie Minogue (French)

Gloria Estefan (Spanish and French)

Sandra Bullock (German)

David Soul (German and Spanish)

Salma Hayek (Arabic)

Renée Zellweger (German)

George W. Bush (Spanish)

Bill Clinton (German)

Stewart Copeland (Arabic)

Al Gore (Spanish)

William Shatner (French)

Montel Williams (Russian)

Melanie Blatt (French)

Fiona Bruce (French and Italian)

Kim Cattrall (German)

Geraldine Chaplin (Spanish)

Chelsea Clinton (German)

Jennifer Connelly (Italian and French)

Rebecca De Mornay (German and French)

Julie Dreyfus (Japanese)

Angie Everhart (French)

Molly Ringwald (French)

Sigourney Weaver (French and German)

J.K. Rowling (French)

Jennie Bond (French)

Ashley Judd (French)

Alex Kingston (German)

Donna Summer (German)

Jodie Foster (French)

Christy Turlington (Spanish)

Ted Koppel (Russian, German and French)

PARLEZ VOUS ENGLISH?

Christopher Lee (German)

Lyle Lovett (German)

Dolph Lundgren (German, French and Japanese)

Bill Paxton (German)

Famke Janssen (German and French)

Brigitte Nielsen (Italian and German)

Rosamund Pike (German and French)

Sophie Raworth (French and German)

Greta Scacchi (German)

Nastassja Kinski (French, Italian and Russian)

Greg Kinnear (Greek)

Sir Eddie George (Russian)

Prince Michael of Kent (Russian)

Michael Frayn (Russian)

Madeleine Albright (Russian)

Geoffrey Robinson (Russian)

DO YOU SPEAK FRANCAIS ?

PEOPLE WHO HAVE FLOWN HELICOPTERS

Neil Fox, Ian Botham, Sarah, Duchess of York, Prince Andrew, Adam Faith, Mark Thatcher, Kenny Jones, Noel Edmonds, Prince Charles, Barry Sheene, David Essex, Harrison Ford, Patricia Cornwell (bought a custom-painted Bell passenger helicopter, which she can legally fly alone though she prefers to hire a co-pilot)

ALL THE PEOPLE IMMORTALIZED IN WAX BY MADAME TUSSAUD'S IN 2004/5

George Clooney

Jonny Wilkinson

Michael Owen

Beyoncé Knowles

Spiderman

Colin Farrell (as Alexander and then redressed as himself)

Angelina Jolie

Jennifer Aniston

Aishwarya Rai

Justin Hawkins

Elton John (in chocolate)

PEOPLE WHO JOINED THE INSTITUTE OF ADVANCED MOTORISTS

Sir Jimmy Savile, Pam St Clement, Prince Michael of Kent, Ingrid Tarrant

AWARDED THE FREEDOM OF THE CITY OF ...

Sir Sean Connery (Edinburgh)

Sting (Newcastle)

Brigitte Bardot (Paris)

Jimmy Carter (Swansea)

Sarah, Duchess of York (York)

Nelson Mandela (Glasgow)

Jayne Torvill (Nottingham)

Christopher Dean (Nottingham)

Lord James Callaghan (Sheffield)

Lord Robert Runcie (Canterbury)

Sir David Attenborough (Leicester)

Lord Richard Attenborough (Leicester)

Jack Charlton (Dublin)

Sir Simon Rattle
(Birmingham)

Norman Wisdom (Tirana)

Brian Clough (Nottingham)

**Kenny Dalglish
(Glasgow)**

Mikhail Gorbachev (Aberdeen)

Helen Sharman (Sheffield)

Sir Paul McCartney (Liverpool)

Lisa Clayton (Birmingham)

Bill Clinton (Dublin)

Baroness Margaret Thatcher (Westminster)

John Tusa (London)

Pope John Paul II (Dublin)

Prince Charles (Swansea)

Stephen Roche (Dublin)

Gary Lineker (Leicester)

Sir Alex Ferguson (Manchester)

Kate Adie (Sunderland)

Dame Kelly Holmes (Tunbridge Wells)

AWARDED THE FREEDOM OF THE CITY OF LONDON

Billy Walker, Angela Rippon, Ernie Wise, Martyn Lewis, Sir Cliff Richard, Clare Francis, Lionel Bart, Terry Venables, Prunella Scales, Mike Oldfield, Clarissa Dickson Wright, Jimmy Tarbuck, Nelson Mandela, Sir Norman Wisdom, John Tusa, Prince Philip

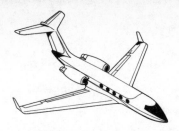

PEOPLE WHO HAD AIRPORTS NAMED AFTER THEM

John Wayne (Santa Ana)

John F. Kennedy (New York)

Charles de Gaulle (Paris)

David Ben-Gurion (Tel Aviv)

Leonardo da Vinci (Rome)

Chiang Kai Shek (Taipei)

Pierre Trudeau (Montreal)

Jan Smuts (Johannesburg)

Pope John Paul II (Krakow)

Antoine de Saint-Exupéry (Lyon)

Marco Polo (Venice)

Jomo Kenyatta (Nairobi)

Pablo Picasso (Malaga)

Konrad Adenauer (Cologne)

John Lennon (Liverpool)

Chuck Yeager (Charleston)

George Bush (Houston)

Louis Armstrong (New Orleans)

Will Rogers (Oklahoma City)

Wolfgang Mozart (Salzburg)

PEOPLE WHO HAD THEATRES NAMED AFTER THEM

Bob Hope (Eltham)

Sir John Gielgud (London)

Dame Peggy Ashcroft (Croydon)

Neil Simon (New York)

Sir Michael Redgrave (Farnham)

Sir Laurence Olivier (London)

Kenneth More (Ilford)

Dame Sybil Thorndike (Leatherhead)

Tony O'Reilly (Pittsburgh)

Dame Flora Robson (Newark)

Ivor Novello (London)

Sir Noel Coward (London)

PEOPLE AWARDED PEOPLE MAGAZINE'S ACCOLADE 'THE SEXIEST MAN ALIVE'

Jude Law (2004)

Johnny Depp (2003)

Ben Affleck (2002)

Pierce Brosnan (2001)

Brad Pitt (2000)

Richard Gere (1999)

Harrison Ford (1998)

George Clooney (1997)

Denzel Washington (1996)

Brad Pitt (1995)

Richard Gere and Cindy Crawford (in 1993, they were named 'The Sexiest Couple Alive' – in 1994 there was no award)

Nick Nolte (1992)

Patrick Swayze (1991)

Tom Cruise (1990)

Sir Sean Connery (1989)

John F. Kennedy Jr (1988)

Harry Hamlin (1987)

Mark Harmon (1986)

Mel Gibson (1985)

PEOPLE HONOURED WITH TICKER-TAPE PARADES IN NEW YORK CITY

David Lloyd George (5.10.1923)

Bobby Jones (2.7.1926 and 2.7.1930)

Charles Lindbergh (13.6.1927)

Ramsay MacDonald (4.10.1929)

Amelia Earhart (20.6.1932)

Howard Hughes (15.7.1938)

General Dwight Eisenhower (10.6.1945)

General Charles de Gaulle (27.8.1945 and 26.4.1960)

Winston Churchill (14.3.1946)

Eamon de Valera (9.3.1948)

Jawaharlal Nehru (17.10.1949)

Liaquat Ali Khan (8.5.1950)

Robert Menzies (4.8.1950)

General Douglas MacArthur (20.4.1951)

David Ben-Gurion (9.5.1951)

Ben Hogan (21.7.1953)

Emperor Haile Selassie (1.6.1954 and 4.10.1963)

Althea Gibson (11.7.1957)

Queen Elizabeth II (21.10.1957)

Willy Brandt (10.2.1959)

John F. Kennedy (19.10.1960)

John Glenn (1.3.1962)

Pope John Paul II (3.10.1979)

Nelson Mandela (20.6.1990)

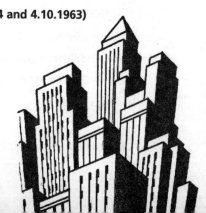

PEOPLE AWARDED HONORARY UNIVERSITY DOCTORATES

Jack Higgins (Leeds Metropolitan)

Gary Player (St Andrews)

Michael Heseltine (Liverpool)

Virginia Wade (Sussex)

Richard Wilson (Glasgow)

Jack Rowell (Bath)

Denise Robertson (Sunderland)

John Cleese (St Andrews)

Tony Blair (Northumbria)

Sir Freddie Laker (City)

Sir David Puttnam (Leicester)

Dame Cleo Laine (Open)

Sir Edward Heath (Oxford)

Johnny Ball (Sheffield Hallam)

Michael Holroyd (East Anglia)

Michael Foot (Nottingham)

Sir Peter Ustinov (Durham)

Dame Janet Baker (Bradford)

Sir Trevor Huddleston (Warwick)

Sue Lawley (Wolverhampton)

Pat Jennings (Ulster)

Richard Baker (Strathclyde)

Jack Charlton (Northumbria)

Neil Kinnock (Cardiff)

Lord Denis Healey (Bradford)

John Tusa (London)

Sir Jimmy Savile (Leeds)

Sandy Gall (Aberdeen)

Nigel Mansell (Birmingham)

Lord Brian Rix (Dundee)

Betty Boothroyd (Cambridge)

Sir Trevor McDonald (Plymouth)

Dame Iris Murdoch (Cambridge)

Sir John Gielgud (London)

Virginia Bottomley (Portsmouth)

Sir Roger Bannister (Sheffield)

Sir John Mortimer (Nottingham)

Baroness Barbara Castle (Manchester)

Placido Domingo (Georgetown)

Nigel Kennedy (Bath)

Sir Ludovic Kennedy (Strathclyde)

Terry Waite (Durham)

Margaret Drabble (East Anglia)

Sir John Harvey-Jones (Exeter)

Sue Lawley (Bristol University)

Lord Richard Attenborough (Sussex University)

Sir Patrick Moore (Birmingham)

Cilla Black (Fellowship, John Moores University)

Esther Rantzen (South Bank University)

Sir Bobby Robson (Civil Law, Newcastle)

Pierce Brosnan (Dublin Institute of Technology)

Eddie Jordan (Dublin Institute of Technology)

PEOPLE APPOINTED UNIVERSITY CHANCELLORS

Prince Philip – Edinburgh

The Duchess of York – Salford

Baroness Betty Boothroyd – Open

Bill Bryson – Durham

Jon Snow – Oxford Brookes

Prince Charles – Cardiff

Chris Patten – Oxford

Sir David Puttnam – Sunderland

Lord MacLaurin – Hertfordshire

Baroness Margaret Thatcher – Buckingham

Lord Peter Palumbo – Portsmouth

Lord Brian Rix – East London

Lord Jack Ashley – Staffordshire

Lord Richard Attenborough – Sussex

Sir Trevor McDonald – South Bank

Lord Melvyn Bragg – Leeds

Patrick Stewart – Huddersfield

ALL THE RECTORS OF THE UNIVERSITY OF ST ANDREWS SINCE 1967

As voted for by the students.

Sir Learie Constantine (1967–70)

John Cleese (1970–73)

Alan Coren (1973–76)

Frank Muir (1976–79)

Tim Brooke-Taylor (1979–82)

Katharine Whitehorn (1982–85)

Stanley Adams (1985–88)

Nicholas Parsons (1988–91)

Nicky Campbell (1991–93)

Donald Findlay (1993–99)

Andrew Neil (1999–2002)

Sir Clement Freud (2002–)

PEOPLE WHO LAUNCHED PRODUCTS

Fran Cotton and Steve Smith – sportswear (Cotton Traders)

Muhammad Ali – sportswear

Hilary Duff – canine clothing called Little Dog Duff

Sean P. Diddy Combs – Sean John, a 'tightly edited collection' of clothing

MC Hammer – a clothing range called the J. Slick Collection.

Catherine Zeta-Jones – babywear

Vinnie Jones – a clothing range called Vinnie

John Malkovich – a clothing range called Mrs Mudd

Madonna – a clothing range, the English Roses Collection

Bono – Edun ('nude' spelled backwards): socially conscious apparel

PEOPLE WHO LAUNCHED PERFUMES

Celine Dion – Belong

Stella McCartney – Stella

Paloma Picasso – Paloma Picasso

Sir Cliff Richard – Miss You Nights

Britney Spears – Curious

Paris Hilton – Paris Hilton

Jennifer Lopez – Miami Glow

HOW VALUES IN A GAME OF MONOPOLY COMPARE TO REAL LIFE

'DRUNK IN CHARGE' FINE £20 Someone found drunk in charge of a vehicle could expect a fine in the region of £500 – as well as a year's disqualification.

PAY HOSPITAL £100 At a private hospital, a basic operation such as having tonsils removed costs about £2,000.

WIN A CROSSWORD COMPETITION – COLLECT £100 Which is precisely how much *Saga* magazine, for example, gives away in its monthly crossword competition.

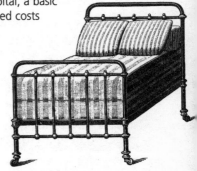

SPEEDING FINE £15 The price of a fixed speeding ticket is now £60 + 3 penalty points.

DOCTOR'S FEE £50 A Harley Street doctor will typically charge £120 for an initial consultation.

MAYFAIR In Monopoly, a house costs £200. A four-bedroom house in Mayfair would today cost a minimum of £4,000,000.

MAKE GENERAL REPAIRS ON ALL OF YOUR HOUSES. FOR EACH HOUSE PAY £25; FOR EACH HOTEL PAY £100 To make general repairs on a house – and assuming three men working for a week – would cost about £1,400; to make general repairs on a hotel – and assuming twelve men working for four weeks – would cost about £20,000.

YOU HAVE WON SECOND PRIZE IN A BEAUTY CONTEST, COLLECT £10 The runner-up in a typical small-town beauty contest could expect to win £250.

PAY SCHOOL FEES OF £150 Parents of a child boarding at a public school can expect to pay an average of £15,000 p.a.

FREE PARKING What, in Central London?

OLD SCOTTISH PROVERBS

'What may be done at any time will be done at no time.'

'False friends are worse than bitter enemies.'

'Fools look to tomorrow; wise men use tonight.'

'They talk of my drinking but never my thirst.'

'The day has eyes, the night has ears.'

'One may survive distress, but not disgrace.'

'Perfect love cannot be without equality.'

'Here's to you, as good as you are, and here's to me, as bad as I am. But as good as you are, and as bad as I am, I am as good as you are, as bad as I am.'

'Danger and delight grow on one stalk.'

'Were it not for hope, the heart would break.'

'Forsake not God till you find a better master.'

'Money is flat and meant to be piled up.'

'It's a sad house where the hen crows louder than the cock.'

'Never marry for money. Ye'll borrow it cheaper.'

'Be happy while you're living, for you're a long time dead.'

ASTRONOMY

A day on Jupiter is approximately 9 hours, 50 minutes and 30 seconds at the equator.

Average wind speed on Jupiter is 225 miles per hour.

The volume of the Moon and the volume of the Pacific Ocean are the same.

Most stars shine for at least 10 billion years.

The Earth is the densest planet in the solar system.

It takes 8 minutes 12 seconds for sunlight to reach Earth.

A manned rocket reaches the Moon in less time than it once took a stagecoach to travel the length of England.

The comic legend Will Hay was an expert astronomer who discovered the spot on the planet Saturn in 1933.

The winds on Saturn blow at 1,200 mph – 10 times faster than a strong Earth hurricane.

The number of UFO sightings increases when Mars is nearest Earth.

Every eleven years the magnetic poles of the Sun switch, in a cycle called 'Solarmax'.

Astronauts can't burp in space: there's no gravity to separate liquid from gas in their stomachs.

While astronauts might feel upset in space, lack of gravity will prevent their tears from rolling down their face.

For every extra kilogram carried on a space flight, 530 kilograms of excess fuel is needed at lift-off.

KEEN ASTRONOMERS

Sir Tom Courtenay, Kevin McNally, Robson Green, Myleene Klass, Brian May (studied for a doctorate in astronomy)

Eggs

The tradition of decorating eggs at Easter started thousands of years ago to celebrate the return of spring after a hard winter. Eggs symbolize new life.

Eggs in Britain are mostly popularly eaten boiled. Second most popular is scrambled, and third is fried.

You can tell an egg is fresh if it sinks to the bottom of a pan of water. Eggs take in air as they age, so an old egg floats more easily.

Crushed eggshells sprinkled around lettuce plants should help to stop insects nibbling the leaves.

Hens lay, in peak production, one egg a day.

In parts of France brides break an egg for luck before they enter their new home.

Paul Newman's character in *Cool Hand Luke* eats 50 hard-boiled eggs.

GENUINE THINGS WRITTEN TO TAX AND WELFARE AUTHORITIES

'I am glad to report that my husband who was reported missing is dead.'

'It is true I am a bachelor and have deducted for two children. But please believe me when I say it was an accident.'

'You have changed my little boy to a little girl. Will this make any difference?'

'I cannot pay the full amount at the moment as my husband is in hospital. As soon as I can I will send on the remains.'

'If my husband puts in a claim for a dependent named Marcia, I just want you to know that my name is Gertrude.'

'Do I have to pay taxes on the alimony my former husband is paying me? It's not as though I do anything to earn it.'

'I have to inform you that my mother-in-law passed away after receiving your form on 22 November. Thanking you.'

'Please send me a claim form as I have had a baby. I had one before, but it got dirty and I burned it.'

'Please correct this assessment. I have not worked for the past three months as I have broken my leg. Hoping you will do the same.'

'Re your request for P45 for new employee. You already have it and he isn't leaving here but coming, so we haven't got it.'

'I have not been living with my husband for several years, and have much pleasure in enclosing his last will and testament.'

'I cannot get sick pay. I have six children, can you tell me why?'

'I want money as quick as I can get it. I have been in bed with the doctor for two weeks and this doesn't seem to do me any good. If things don't improve I will be forced to send for another doctor.'

'My husband is in HM forces. I have no children. Trusting it will have your attention.'

'I am forwarding my marriage certificate and six children. I have seven but one died and was baptized on half sheet of paper.'

'I am writing to the Welfare Department to say that my baby was born two years old. When do I get my money?'

'Unless I get my money soon, I will be forced to lead an immortal life.'

'In accordance with your instructions, I have given birth to twins in the enclosed envelope.'

'Mrs Jones has not had any clothes for a year and has been visited regularly by the clergy.'

'I am very annoyed that you have branded my son illiterate, as this is a lie. I was married to his father a week before he was born.'

'I don't know why you should be interested in the length of my residence in Quebec, but I have nothing to hide. It is 31 feet 8 inches long and there's an attached garage.'

'Please send me an official letter advising that I can't claim the costs of taking my wife to conventions. I don't want her along but I need an excuse.'

'Thank you for explaining my income tax liability. You have done it so clearly that I almost understand it.'

THE BOOKER PRIZE

Two People Who Have Won The Booker Prize Twice: J.M. Coetzee for *Disgrace* in 1999, having won for *Life and Times of Michael K* in 1983, and Peter Carey for *True History of The Kelly Gang* in 2001, having won for *Oscar And Lucinda* in 1988.

Booker Prize Judge Who Became A Winner: A.S. Byatt is the only Booker Prize judge (1974) to subsequently become a winner (for *Possession* in 1990).

Judge Who Was On The Panel Which Shortlisted Her Husband: Elizabeth Jane Howard in 1974 (Kingsley Amis's *Ending Up* was shortlisted but didn't win).

Judges Who Resigned: Malcolm Muggeridge in 1971 (too much sex in the novels he had to read); Nicholas Mosley in 1991 (he couldn't get the book he wanted on to the shortlist).

First First Novel To Win: *The Bone People* (Keri Hulme).

Most Shortlisted Novelist: Dame Iris Murdoch (six times – winning once with *The Sea, The Sea* in 1978).

Novelists Who Have Been Shortlisted Without Ever Winning: Muriel Spark, Martin Amis, William Trevor, Doris Lessing, Beryl Bainbridge, Fay Weldon, Anthony Burgess.

When John Berger won (in 1972 for *G*), he attacked Booker McConnell, the sponsors, and declared that he was giving half the money to the Black Panthers.

In 1983, Selina Scott asked Fay Weldon, the chairman of the judges, on television whether she'd actually read all the books.

ALL THE WINNERS OF THE BOOKER PRIZE

2004 – Alan Hollinghurst, *The Line of Beauty*

2003 – D.B.C. Pierre, *Vernon God Little*

2002 – Yann Martel, *Life of Pi*

2001 – Peter Carey, *True History of The Kelly Gang*

2000 – Margaret Atwood, *The Blind Assassin*

1999 – J.M. Coetzee, *Disgrace*

1998 – Ian McEwan, *Amsterdam*

1997 – Arundhati Roy, *The God of Small Things*

1996 – Graham Swift, *Last Orders*

1995 – Pat Barker, *The Ghost Road*

1994 – James Kelman, *How Late It Was, How Late*

1993 – Roddy Doyle, *Paddy Clarke Ha Ha Ha*

1992 – Michael Ondaatje, *The English Patient* and Barry Unsworth, *Sacred Hunger*

1991 – Ben Okri, *The Famished Road*

1990 – A.S. Byatt, *Possession*

1989 – Kazuo Ishiguro, *The Remains of The Day*

1988 – Peter Carey, *Oscar And Lucinda*

1987 – Penelope Lively, *Moon Tiger*

1986 – Kingsley Amis, *The Old Devils*

1985 – Keri Hulme, *The Bone People*

1984 – Anita Brookner, *Hotel Du Lac*

1983 – J.M. Coetzee, *Life And Times of Michael K*

1982 – Thomas Keneally, *Schindler's Ark*

1981 – Salman Rushdie, *Midnight's Children*

1980 – William Golding, *Rites of Passage*

1979 – Penelope Fitzgerald, *Offshore*

1978 – Iris Murdoch, *The Sea, The Sea*

1977 – Paul Scott, *Staying On*

1976 – David Storey, *Saville*

1975 – Ruth Prawer Jhabvala, *Heat And Dust*

1974 – Nadine Gordimer, *The Conservationist*
and Stanley Middleton, *Holiday*

1973 – J.G. Farrell, *The Siege of Krishnapur*

1972 – John Berger, *G*

1971 – V.S. Naipaul, *In A Free State*

1970 – Bernice Rubens, *The Elected Member*

1969 – P.H. Newby, *Something To Answer For*

ELIGIBLE BOOKS THAT WEREN'T EVEN NOMINATED

Birdsong (Sebastian Faulks)

Captain Corelli's Mandolin (Louis de Bernières)

The Curious Incident of The Dog In The Night-time (Mark Haddon)

A Perfect Spy (John Le Carré)

Perfume (Patrick Süskind)

Trainspotting (Irvine Welsh)

White Teeth (Zadie Smith)

Monsignor Quixote (Graham Greene)

Girl With A Pearl Earring (Tracy Chevalier)

PEOPLE WHO HAVE SERVED AS BOOKER PRIZE JUDGES

Joanna Lumley

David Baddiel

Kenneth Baker

Mariella Frostrup

Gerald Kaufman

Nigella Lawson

Sir Trevor McDonald

WRITERS WHO HAD A MANUSCRIPT LOST OR STOLEN

Louis de Bernières (the first 50 pages of *A Partisan's Daughter*)

Ernest Hemingway

Malcolm Lowry

Thomas Wolfe (*Mannerhouse* – rewrote it entirely)

T.E. Lawrence (*Seven Pillars of Wisdom* – rewrote it in full after losing it while changing trains at Reading station in 1919)

John Steinbeck (*Of Mice And Men* – the first draft was eaten by his dog)

Jilly Cooper (*Riders*, her first big blockbuster book – she lost the first draft)

PEOPLE WHO WROTE JUST ONE NOVEL

Anna Sewell: *Black Beauty*

Margaret Mitchell: *Gone With The Wind*

Harper Lee: *To Kill A Mockingbird*

Emily Brontë: *Wuthering Heights*

Kenneth Grahame: *The Wind In The Willows*

PEOPLE (MORE FAMOUS FOR OTHER THINGS) WHO WROTE NOVELS

Robert Shaw (*The Sun Doctor*)

Anthony Sher (*Middlepost*)

Sarah Bernhardt (*In The Clouds*)

George Kennedy (*Murder On Location*)

Jean Harlow (*Today Is Tonight*)

Joan Collins (*Prime Time*)

Leslie Caron (*Vengeance*)

Mae West (*The Constant Sinner*)

Naomi Campbell (*Swan*)

Benito Mussolini (*The Cardinal's Mistress*)

Julie Andrews (*The Last of The Really Great Whangdoodles*)

Martina Navratilova (*Total Zone*)

Jilly Johnson (*Double Exposure*)

Sir Winston Churchill (*Savrola*)

Carly Simon (*Amy The Dancing Bear*)

Tony Curtis (*Kid Andrew Cody And Julie Sparrow*)

Whoopi Goldberg (*Alice*)

Jane Seymour (*This One And That One*)

Michael Palin (*Small Harry And The Toothache Pills*)

Ethan Hawke (*The Hottest State*)

Johnny Cash (*Man In White*)

SHAKESPEARE'S LONGEST ROLES

Falstaff (1,614 lines in *Henry IV, Parts 1 & 2* and *The Merry Wives of Windsor*)

Hamlet (1,422 lines in *Hamlet* – making Hamlet the longest role in any *single* Shakespeare play)

Richard III (1,124 lines in *Richard III*)

Iago (1,097 lines in *Othello*)

Henry V (1,025 lines in *Henry V*)

Othello (860 lines in *Othello*)

Vincentio (820 lines in *Measure For Measure*)

Coriolanus (809 lines in *Coriolanus*)

Timon (795 lines in *Timon of Athens*)

Marc Antony (766 lines in *Antony And Cleopatra*)

THINGS SAID ABOUT POETRY

'Poetry is the lava of the imagination whose eruption prevents an earthquake.' (Lord Byron)

'Poetry is what gets lost in translation.' (Robert Frost)

'Poetry is living proof that rhyme doesn't pay.' (Anon.)

'There's no money in poetry, but there's no poetry in money, either.' (Robert Graves)

'A poet in history is divine; but a poet in the next room is a joke.' (Max Eastman)

'Poetry is an evasion of the real job of writing prose.' (Sylvia Plath)

'Poetry often enters through the window of irrelevance.' (M.C. Richards)

'Genuine poetry can communicate before it is understood.' (T.S. Eliot)

'Most people ignore most poetry because most poetry ignores most people.' (Adrian Mitchell)

'Poetry is the language in which man explores his own amazement.' (Christopher Fry)

'Any healthy man can go without food for two days – but not without poetry.' (Charles Baudelaire)

'Poetry comes nearer to vital truth than history.' (Plato)

PEOPLE AND THE APPROXIMATE VALUE OF THEIR AUTOGRAPHS

Adolf Hitler: £6,000

Marilyn Monroe: £5,000

Sir Winston Churchill: £5,000

Harry Houdini: £4,000

Albert Einstein: £4,000

Horatio Nelson: £4,000

Bruce Lee: £4,000

John F. Kennedy: £3,500

Diana, Princess of Wales: £3,500

Oscar Wilde: £3,250

Napoleon: £3,000

John Lennon: £3,000

Charles Dickens: £3,000

Sir Alfred Hitchcock: £3,000

Pablo Picasso: £3,000

Elvis Presley: £2,500

Jimi Hendrix: £2,000

Cary Grant: £2,000

Judy Garland: £2,000

Bob Marley: £2,000

Yuri Gagarin: £1,500

Buddy Holly: £1,500

The Queen Mother: £1,250

Grace Kelly: £1,250
Andy Warhol: £1,000
Walt Disney: £1,000
Mother Teresa: £875
Errol Flynn: £775
River Phoenix: £775
Queen Victoria: £575
James Cagney: £575
Salvador Dalí: £475

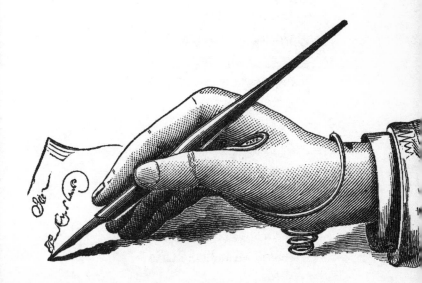

CHOCOLATE BARS, ETC, AND WHEN THEY MADE THEIR DEBUTS

Fry's Chocolate Cream – 1866

Hershey Bars – 1900

Toblerone – 1900

Cadbury's Dairy Milk – 1905

Cadbury's Bournville – 1910

Mars Bar – 1923

Crunchie – 1929

Terry's All Gold – 1932

Rowntree's Black Magic – 1933

Kit-Kat – 1935 (although for the first two years of its existence it was known as 'Chocolate Crisp')

Aero – 1935

Quality Street – 1936

Dairy Box – 1936

Rolo – 1937

Milky Bar – 1937

Smarties – 1937

Cadbury's Roses – 1938

Bounty – 1951

Galaxy – 1958

Picnic – 1958

After Eight – 1962

Toffee Crisp – 1963

Twix – 1967

Yorkie – 1976

CHOCOLATE BRANDS NO LONGER WITH US

Fry's Chocolate Cream

Fry's Five Boys

Nestle's Semi-sweet Smoker's Chocolate

Wispa

Fuse

Secret

Aztec

Amazin

Rumba

Caramac

WHAT CAR? CAR OF THE YEAR SINCE 1991

2004: VW Golf

2003: Seat Ibiza

2002: Toyota Corolla

2001: Ford Mondeo

2000: Skoda Fabia

1999: Rover 75

1998: Land Rover Freelander

1997: Renault Mégane Scenic

1996: Peugeot 406

1995: VW Polo

1994: Peugeot 306

1993: Ford Mondeo

1992: VW Golf

1991: Rover Metro

THINGS THAT BEGAN IN THE 1960s

Jiffy bags, aluminium kitchen foil, discotheques, flavoured potato crisps, plastic carrier-bags, trainers, hatchbacks, self-service petrol stations, tights (in the UK), fruit-flavoured yoghurts, football hooliganism, After Eight mints, pocket calculators, *Coronation Street*, fibre-tip pens, Weight Watchers, colour TV, MOT tests, longlife milk, *The Sun*, electric toothbrushes, the *QE2*, legal male homosexuality, the contraceptive pill, *Private Eye*, safety belts, abortion clinics, *Jackie* magazine, the Trimphone, Brut 33, Pedigree Chum, ASDA, Green Shield stamps, the mini skirt, James Bond films, pirate radio, the Booker Prize, Yellow Pages, Gold Blend coffee, Ibuprofen, Radio 1, *Top of the Pops*, the Homepride flour graders in their bowler hats, Peanuts, *Call My Bluff,* Shelter, *Songs of Praise*, BBC2, Mothercare, Habitat, Twister, Mr Kipling, Pringles, Fairy Liquid, clingfilm, the Jacuzzi, bar codes

THINGS THAT BEGAN IN THE 1970s

Bell bottoms, lava lamps, Argos catalogue, *The Antiques Road Show*, the CD, Grange Hill, *Scoobie Doo*, Mr Sheen, Pot Noodle, soft contact lenses, punk music, *Only Fools and Horses*, floppy disks, the VCR, Post-It Notes, liposuction, word processors, gay lib, North Sea oil, decimal currency, VAT, hotpants, (legal) commercial radio, three-day week, genetic engineering, cricket world cup, test-tube babies, palimony, *Fawlty Towers*, *Not The Nine O'Clock News*

THE WAY WE LIVE

The average person spends two weeks over their lifetime waiting for the traffic lights to change.

One in ten people live on an island.

Married men change their underwear twice as often as single men.

Every year one ton of cement is poured for every man, woman and child in the world.

If you are struck by lightning once, you are 100,000 times more likely to get struck another time than someone who has never been struck.

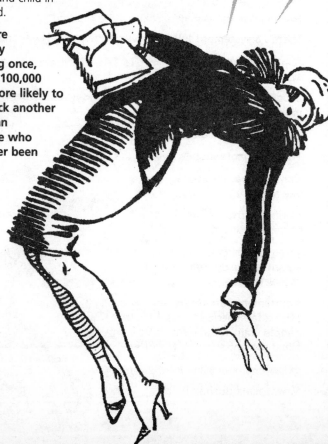

It is said that small particles of faecal matter can become airborne during toilet flushing, and dentists recommend keeping your toothbrush 2 metres away from the toilet to avoid contamination. If your bathroom isn't big enough, put the lid down before flushing.

62 per cent of email is spam.

After hours working at a computer display, look at a blank piece of white paper. It will probably appear pink.

There is no such thing as naturally blue food – even blueberries are purple.

Astronauts have to be under 6 feet in height.

There's a systematic lull in conversation every seven minutes.

Paranormal experts say we reach the peak of our ability to see ghosts at the age of seven.

Laughing lowers levels of stress hormones and strengthens the immune system.

Women burn fat more slowly than men.

There are more mobile phones than people in Britain.

Only a third of the people who can twitch their ears can twitch them one at a time.

During menstruation, the sensitivity of a woman's middle finger is reduced.

71 per cent of office workers stopped on the street for a survey agreed to give up their computer passwords in exchange for a chocolate bar.

Amusement park attendance goes up after a fatal accident. It seems that people want to take the same ride that killed someone.

64 per cent of people can roll their tongue.

Most toilets flush in E flat.

During a lifetime, the average person drinks 8,000 gallons of water and uses 68,250 gallons of water to brush their teeth.

Car drivers tend to go faster when other cars are around. It doesn't matter where the other cars are – whether in front, behind or alongside.

Most digital alarm clocks ring in the key of B flat.

In the average lifetime, a person will walk the equivalent of 5 times round the equator.

Newborn babies are given to the wrong mother 12 times a day in maternity wards across the world.

Wearing headphones for an hour increases the bacteria in your ear 700 times.

A computer user blinks on average seven times a minute.

If you gave each human on earth an equal portion of dry land, including the uninhabitable areas, everyone would get roughly 100 square feet (30.4 square metres).

The average person flexes the joints in their fingers 24 million times in a lifetime.

Fingerprints provide traction for the fingers.

We forget 80 per cent of what we learn every day.

50 per cent of lingerie purchases are returned to the shop.

The average smell weighs 760 nanograms.

At 200 miles (322 km) per hour, airbags explode.

There are 4.3 births and 1.7 deaths in the world every second.

If we had the same mortality rate now as in 1900, more than half the people in the world today would be dead.

If Britain's gas mains were laid end to end, they would go round the world a dozen times.

If all the carpets sold in a year in Britain were laid end to end, they would go all the way to the moon and halfway back again.

If all the credit cards used in Britain today were laid end to end, they would stretch from London to Istanbul.

If all the Easter eggs sold in Britain in one year were laid end to end, they'd go from London to Australia and halfway back again.

The QWERTY typewriter was designed so that the left hand typed the most common letters – it was a means of slowing down typists and keeping the typewriters from jamming.

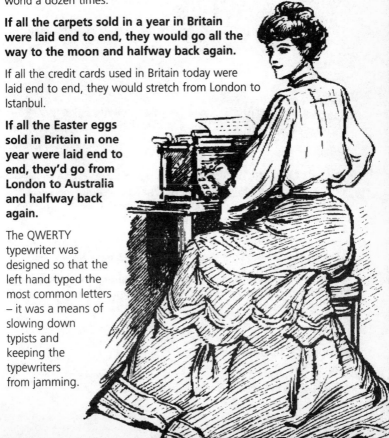

HONEY

The honeybee is the only insect that produces food eaten by humans.

Historically honey was used to treat cuts and burns.

The Romans used honey instead of gold to pay their taxes.

Honey was part of Cleopatra's daily beauty ritual.

Beehives were sometimes used in ancient warfare, lobbed at the enemy as a kind of bomb.

It takes the nectar from two million flowers to make one pound (450g) of honey. One bee would therefore have to fly around 90,000 miles – three times around the globe – to make a pound of honey.

A bee visits 50 to 100 flowers during a collection trip, and makes altogether about a twelfth of a teaspoon of honey during its life.

The buzz of a honeybee comes from its wings, which beat more than 11,000 times a minute.

Worker bees are all female.

An explorer who found a 2000-year-old jar of honey in an Egyptian tomb said it tasted delicious.

Bees use the shortest route possible to reach the flower of their choice, hence the expression 'making a beeline for …'.

POLITICANS WHO CHANGED PARTIES

Winston Churchill (Conservative-Liberal-Conservative)

Alan Howarth (Conservative-Labour)

Reg Prentice (Labour-Conservative)

Sir Oswald Mosley (Conservative-Labour-Fascist)

Dr David Owen (Labour-SDP)

Shirley Williams (Labour-SDP)

Roy Jenkins (Labour-SDP)

Bill Rodgers (Labour-SDP)

Christopher Mayhew (Labour-Liberal)

Emma Nicholson (Conservative-Liberal)

Sir Cyril Smith (Labour-Liberal)

Enoch Powell (Conservative-Ulster Unionist)

Robert Jackson (Conservative-Labour)

Shaun Woodward (Conservative-Labour)

Peter Hain (Liberal-Labour – although he never represented the Liberals in Parliament)

FORMER MPS

John Buchan, Hilaire Belloc, Andrew Marvell, Samuel Pepys, Daniel Defoe, Sir Thomas More, Richard Brinsley Sheridan, A.P. Herbert, Edward Gibbon, Jeffrey Archer

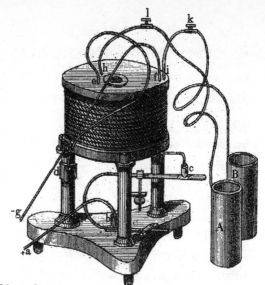

Science

Copper exposed to arsenic turns black.

The cracks in breaking glass move at speeds up to 3,000 miles (4,827 km) per hour.

A whip 'cracks' because its tip moves faster than the speed of sound.

Water freezes faster if it starts from a warm temperature than a cool one.

René Descartes came up with the theory of coordinate geometry by watching a fly walk across a ceiling.

Sound travels 15 times faster through steel than through air.

Methane gas can often be seen bubbling up in ponds. It is produced by decomposing plants and animals in the mud at the bottom.

An ounce of gold can be beaten into a thin film covering 100 square feet.

Lightning strikes our planet about 6,000 times a minute.

It is harder to reach the speed of sound at sea level than at altitude.

The silvery metal gallium is liquid at 29.8°C (85.6°F), which means it would melt in your hand. Cesium is another metal that would melt in your hand, but it would also react violently with your skin and possibly catch fire. The third metal that is liquid at more or less room temperature is mercury.

If you went unprotected into space, you would explode before you suffocated.

The holes in fly swatters are there to reduce air resistance. For the same reason, you should open your fingers when trying to kill mosquitoes by hand (it works).

Every megabyte sent over the internet needs two lumps of coal to power it.

A car travelling at 80 km/h needs half of its fuel just to overcome wind resistance.

A combustion engine wastes 75 per cent of the chemical energy contained in petrol.

The liquid inside young coconuts can be used as a substitute for blood plasma.

MUSIC

Johnny Depp played guitar on *Fade In-Out* by Oasis and appeared in the video for Tom Petty's *Into The Wide Great Open*.

John Cage composed 'Imaginary Landscape No.4', which was scored for twelve radios tuned at random.

Steve Davis once promoted a rock concert (for the French jazz-rock group Magma).

Matt Lucas appeared in the video for Blur's *Country House*.

Myleene Klass, the singer and pianist, insured her hands for £1 million.

Karen Carpenter's doorbell chimed the first six notes of *We've Only Just Begun*.

Rolf Harris played didgeridoo on *The Dreaming* by Kate Bush.

Actor Jon Voight's brother, Chip Taylor, wrote the song *Wild Thing*.

SONGS THAT DON'T FEATURE THEIR TITLES IN THE LYRICS

'Killer' (Adamski)

'Martha's Harbour' (All About Eve)

'Pure Shores' (All Saints)

'A Life Less Ordinary' (Ash)

'A Day In The Life' (The Beatles)

'Ballad of John And Yoko' (The Beatles)

'For You Blue' (The Beatles)

'Tomorrow Never Knows' (The Beatles)

'Ambulance' (Blur)

'Space Oddity' (David Bowie)

'For What It's Worth' (Buffalo Springfield)

'Superstar' (The Carpenters)

'Why I Can't Stand One-Night Stands' (Catatonia)

'Tubthumping' (Chumbawumba)

'Death of a Ladies' Man' (Leonard Cohen)

'The Scientist' (Coldplay)

'Badge' (Cream)

'Suite: Judy Blue Eyes' (Crosby, Stills and Nash)

'7 Days' (Craig David)

'Annie's Song' (John Denver)

'It Takes a Lot to Laugh, It Takes a Train to Cry' (Bob Dylan)

'Positively 4th Street' (Bob Dylan)

'Subterranean Homesick Blues' (Bob Dylan)

'The Circus' (Erasure)

'Guilty Conscience' (Eminem)

'Kinky Afro' (Happy Mondays)

'Earth Song' (Michael Jackson)

'Jilted John' (Jilted John)

'The Riddle' (Nik Kershaw)

'Black Dog' (Led Zeppelin)

'The Battle of Evermore' (Led Zeppelin)

'#9 Dream' (John Lennon)

'Act of Contrition' (Madonna)

'Creeque Alley' (The Mamas and The Papas)

'Porcelain' (Moby)

'Alternate Title' (The Monkees – the original title, which they were obliged to drop, was 'Randy Scouse Git', which also didn't feature in the lyrics)

'Suedehead' (Morrissey)

'Hate This and I'll Love You' (Muse)

'Blue Monday' (New Order)

'Smells Like Teen Spirit' (Nirvana)

'Complex' (Gary Numan)

'Shakermaker' (Oasis)

'The Riverboat Song' (Ocean Colour Scene)

'Brain Damage' (Pink Floyd)

'American Trilogy' (Elvis Presley)

'Disco 2000' (Pulp)

'Bohemian Rhapsody' (Queen – although it did contain the title of the song that knocked it off the top of the British charts – Abba's 'Mamma Mia')

'Talk Show Host' (Radiohead)

'Endless Cycle' (Lou Reed)

'The Sidewinder Sleeps Tonight' (R.E.M.)

'The Millennium Prayer' (Cliff Richard)

'Unchained Melody' (The Righteous Brothers)

'Sympathy for the Devil' (The Rolling Stones)

'Pyjamarama' (Roxy Music)

'The Immigrant Song' (Neil Sedaka)

'For Emily, Whenever I May Find Her' (Simon and Garfunkel)

'Pretzel Logic' (Steely Dan)

'The Caves of Altamira' (Steely Dan)

'Father and Son' (Cat Stevens)

'Richard III' (Supergrass)

'The Logical Song' (Supertramp)

'The Unforgettable Fire' (U2)

'Tom's Diner' (Suzanne Vega)

'Excerpt From A Teenage Opera' (Keith West)

'Ball Park Incident' (Wizzard)

'After The Gold Rush' (Neil Young)

PEOPLE WHO USED TO BE IN POP GROUPS

Fiona Bruce was the singer with Chez Nous.

Richard Hannon, the racehorse trainer, used to be a drummer with The Troggs.

Keith Chegwin was the lead singer in Kenny (which had a Number 3 hit in 1975 with 'The Bump').

Su Pollard was the singer with the pop group Midnight News.

Dani Behr started her career as one third of the group Faith, Hope and Charity.

Bruce Willis was in the band Loose Goose.

Martine McCutcheon was the lead singer of a three-girl group called Milan.

Emma Freud was a backing singer for Mike Oldfield.

Michael Howard played in a skiffle band.

Ken Stott sang with the group Keyhole.

Nigel Short, the chess champion and world title contender, played in a rock band called The Urge.

Asil Nadir played in a rock group called The Asils.

Neil Kinnock played guitar in a skiffle group called The Rebels.

Vince Earl (Ron Dixon in *Brookside*) played the tea-chest bass in a skiffle group called The Teenage Rebels.

Will Self was lead singer in a band called Will Self and the Abusers.

Woody Harrelson is lead singer in the band Manly Moondog and the Three Kool Hats.

Denise Van Outen was in a girl band called Those Two Girls.

River Phoenix was the vocalist in Aleka's Attic.

SONGS THAT PROVIDED NUMBER-ONE HITS FOR TWO (OR MORE) STARS

'I Believe': Frankie Laine (1953); Robson Green and Jerome Flynn (1995)

'This Ole House': Rosemary Clooney (1954); Shakin' Stevens (1981)

'Unchained Melody': Jimmy Young (1955); The Righteous Brothers (1990); Robson Green and Jerome Flynn (1995); Gareth Gates (2002)

'Young Love': Tab Hunter (1957); Donny Osmond (1973)

'Mary's Boy Child': Harry Belafonte (1957); Boney M (1978)

'Living Doll': Cliff Richard And The Drifters (1959); Cliff Richard And The Young Ones, Featuring Hank Marvin (1986)

'Can't Help Falling In Love': Elvis Presley (1962); UB40 (1993)

'You'll Never Walk Alone': Gerry And The Pacemakers (1963); The Crowd (1985)

'I Got You Babe': Sonny And Cher (1965); UB40 And Chrissie Hynde (1985)

'Somethin' Stupid': Nancy And Frank Sinatra (1967); Robbie Williams And Nicole Kidman (2001)

'Baby Come Back': The Equals (1968); Pato Banton (1994)

'With A Little Help From My Friends': Joe Cocker (1968); Wet Wet Wet (1988); Sam and Mark (2004)

'Dizzy': Tommy Roe (1969); Vic Reeves And The Wonder Stuff (1991)

'Spirit In The Sky': Norman Greenbaum (1970); Doctor And The Medics (1986); Gareth Gates Featuring The Kumars (2003)

'Without You': Nilsson (1972); Mariah Carey (1994)

'Seasons In The Sun': Terry Jacks (1974); Westlife (1999)

'Everything I Own': Ken Boothe (1974); Boy George (1987)

'Tragedy': The Bee Gees (1979); Steps (1999)

'The Tide Is High': Blondie (1980); Atomic Kitten (2002)

'Uptown Girl': Billy Joel (1983); Westlife (2001)

'Do They Know It's Christmas?': Band Aid (1984); Band Aid II (1989); Band Aid 20 (2004)

'When The Going Gets Tough, The Tough Get Going': Billy Ocean (1986); Boyzone (1999)

'Eternal Flame: The Bangles (1989); Atomic Kitten (2001)

'Lady Marmalade': All Saints (1998); Christina Aguilera, Lil' Kim, Mya And Pink (2001)

'Mambo No 5': Lou Bega (1999); Bob The Builder (2001)

Instruments and the People Who Play Them

Bass guitar (Gary Sinise)

Guitar (Paul Bettany)

Piano and cello (Rosamund Pike)

Violin (David James)

French horn and trumpet (Samuel L. Jackson)

Guitar (Minnie Driver)

Harmonica (Dan Aykroyd)

Banjo (Steve Martin)

Trombone (Fiona Phillips)

Bagpipes (Alastair Campbell)

Bagpipes (Ken Stott)

Tuba (Hannah Waterman)

Piano (Jeff Goldblum)

Guitar (Kate Hudson)

Bass Guitar (Vic Reeves)

Violin (Meryl Streep)

Guitar (Ricky Gervais)

BANDS WHO CAME UP WITH UNIMAGINATIVE SONG TITLES

Doop (Doop, 1994)

Immaculate Fools (Immaculate Fools, 1985)

Jilted John (Jilted John, 1978)

Living in a Box (Living in a Box, 1987)

Love and Money (Love and Money, 1987)

Natural Life (Natural Life, 1992)

The Singing Dogs (The Singing Dogs, 1955)

Small Ads (Small Ads, 1981)

Talk Talk (Talk Talk, 1982)

Tricky Disco (Tricky Disco, 1990)

THE BEATLES BY NUMBER

Note that some numbers appear in more than one song.

1/2 'Yesterday'

1 'Day Tripper'

2 'Two of Us'

3 'Come Together'

4 'You Never Give Me Your Money'

5 'She's Leaving Home'

6 'All Together Now'

7 'And Your Bird Can Sing'

8 'Eight Days A Week'

9 'Revolution 9'

10 'Being For The Benefit of Mr Kite'

12 'Cry Baby Cry'

15 'She Came In Through The Bathroom Window'

17 'I Saw Her Standing There'

19 'Taxman'

20 'Sergeant Pepper's Lonely Hearts Club Band'

31 'Maxwell's Silver Hammer'

50 'Maxwell's Silver Hammer'

64 'When I'm 64'

909 'One After 909'

1,000 'Paperback Writer' or 'The Fool On The Hill'

4,000 'A Day In The Life'

1,000,000 'Across The Universe'

1 2 3 4
can I have
a little more

AROUND THE WORLD IN BEATLES SONGS

Amsterdam 'The Ballad of John And Yoko'

Bishopsgate 'Being For The Benefit of Mr Kite'

Blackburn, Lancashire 'A Day In The Life'

California 'Get Back'

Dakota 'Rocky Raccoon'

France 'The Ballad of John And Yoko'

Georgia 'Back In The USSR'

Gibraltar 'The Ballad of John And Yoko'

Holland 'The Ballad of John And Yoko'

Isle of Wight 'When I'm 64'

Lime Street 'Maggie Mae'

Liverpool 'Maggie Mae'

London 'The Ballad of John And Yoko'

LA 'Los Angeles' 'Blue Jay Way'

Miami Beach 'Back In The USSR'

Moscow 'Back In The USSR'

Paris 'The Ballad of John And Yoko'

Penny Lane 'Penny Lane'

Southampton 'The Ballad of John And Yoko'

Spain 'The Ballad of John And Yoko'

Tucson, Arizona 'Get Back'

Ukraine 'Back In The USSR'

Vienna 'The Ballad of John And Yoko'

THE BEATLES IN NEWSPAPERS

Daily Mail 'Paperback Writer'

The News of The World
'Polythene Pam'

**The Sun 'Here Comes The Sun'
– with apologies**

JUST SOME OF THE BEATLES TRIBUTE BANDS

The Bootleg Beatles

Cavern

All You Need Is Love

Apple

The Backbeat Beatles

The Brazilian Beetles

Come Together

The Eggmen

The Fake Beatles

The Upbeat Beatles

The Fab Beatles

The Beatels

Revolver

Backbeat

Day Tripper

Day Trippers

The Fab Walrus

Help!

The Imagine

The Moptops

Rain

The Fab Four

The Beatleg

Apple Pies

Shout!

Strawberry Fields

Yesterday

ALL THE ACTS THAT HAD THREE – OR MORE – BRITISH NUMBER-ONE HITS IN THE SAME YEAR

Frankie Laine (1953: I Believe, Hey Joe!, Answer Me)

Elvis Presley (1961: Are You Lonesome Tonight?, Wooden Heart, Surrender, Little Sister/His Latest Flame)

Elvis Presley (1962: Rock-A-Hula Baby/Can't Help Falling In Love, Good Luck Charm, She's Not You, Return To Sender)

The Beatles (1963: From Me To You, She Loves You, I Want To Hold Your Hand)

Gerry and The Pacemakers (1963: How Do You Do It, I Like It, You'll Never Walk Alone)

The Beatles (1964: Can't Buy Me Love, A Hard Day's Night, I Feel Fine)

The Rolling Stones (1965: The Last Time, (I Can't Get No) Satisfaction, Get Off Of My Cloud)

The Beatles (1965: Ticket To Ride, Help!, Day Tripper/We Can Work It Out)

Slade (1973: Cum On Feel The Noize, Skweeze Me Pleeze Me, Merry Xmas Everybody)

Abba (1976: Mamma Mia, Fernando, Dancing Queen)

Blondie (1980: Atomic, Call Me, The Tide Is High)

Frankie Goes To Hollywood (1984: Relax, Two Tribes, The Power of Love)

Jason Donovan (1989: Especially For You, Too Many Broken Hearts, Sealed With A Kiss)

Take That (1993: Pray, Relight My Fire, Babe)

The Spice Girls (1996: Wannabe, Say You'll Be There, 2 Become 1)

The Spice Girls (1997: Mama/Who Do You Think You Are, Spice Up Your Life, Too Much)

All Saints (1998: Never Ever, Under The Bridge/Lady Marmalade, Bootie Call)

B*Witched (1998: C'Est La Vie, Rollercoaster, To You I Belong)

Westlife (1999: Swear It Again, If I Let You Go, Flying Without Wings, I Have A Dream/Seasons In The Sun)

Westlife (2000: Fool Again, Against All Odds, My Love)

Elvis Presley (2005: Jailhouse Rock, One Night, It's Now Or Never)

NB Will Young and Gareth Gates each had two solo number ones in 2002 and a joint number one – which means they don't qualify for this list

CLASSIC SINGLES THAT DIDN'T MAKE THE BRITISH TOP 20

'Someone Saved My Life Tonight' (Elton John)

'We've Only Just Begun' (The Carpenters)

'Stop Your Sobbing' (The Pretenders)

'Last Train To Clarksville' (The Monkees)

'I Don't Believe In Miracles' (Colin Blunstone)

'Wouldn't It Be Nice' (The Beach Boys)

'Rikki Don't Lose That Number' (Steely Dan)

'Angel of The Morning' (P.P. Arnold)

'Year of The Cat' (Al Stewart)

'What A Fool Believes' (The Doobie Brothers)

CELEBRITIES AND THE SINGLES THEY RELEASED

Patrick Swayze: 'Raisin' Heaven And Hell Tonight'

David Copperfield: 'Summer Days'

Farrah Fawcett: 'You'

Dame Elizabeth Taylor: 'Wings In The Sky'

Stefan Dennis: 'Don't It Make You Feel Good'

Tom Watt: 'Subterranean Homesick Blues'

Clint Eastwood: 'I Talk To The Trees'

Leonard Nimoy: 'Proud Mary'

Terry Wogan: 'Floral Dance'

Ingrid Bergman: 'This Old Man'

David McCallum: 'Louie Louie'

Lon Chaney Jnr: 'Monster Holiday'

Diego Maradona: 'La Mano De Dios' – 'The Hand of God'

Russell Crowe: 'I Want To Be Like Marlon Brando'

Billy Crystal: 'The Christmas Song'

Meryl Streep: 'Amazing Grace'

Peter Fonda: 'Catch The Wind'

Linda Evans: 'Don't You Need'

Britt Ekland: 'Do It To Me'

Sir Anthony Hopkins: 'A Distant Star'

Oliver Reed: 'Lonely For A Girl'

Rebecca De Mornay: 'Oh Jimmy'

Gene Wilder: 'Pure Imagination'

Raquel Welch: 'This Girl's Back In Town'

Burt Reynolds: 'I Like Having You Around'

Robert Mitchum: 'Ballad of Thunder Road'

Princess Stephanie of Monaco: 'Live Your Life'

Richard Chamberlain: 'Love Me Tender'

William Shatner: 'Mr Tambourine Man'

THE FIRST VIDEOS EVER SHOWN ON MTV (1981)

'Video Killed The Radio Star' (Buggles)

'You Better Run' (Pat Benatar)

'She Won't Dance With Me' (Rod Stewart)

'You Better You Bet' (The Who)

'Little Susie's On The Up' (PhD)

'We Don't Talk Anymore' (Cliff Richard)

'Brass In Pocket' (The Pretenders)

'Time Heals' (Todd Rundgren)

'Take It On The Run' (REO Speedwagon)

'Rockin' The Paradise' (Styx)

THE FIRST VIDEOS EVER SHOWN ON MTV EUROPE (1987)

'Money For Nothing' (Dire Straits)

'Fake' (Alexander O'Neal)

'U Got The Look' (Prince)

'It's A Sin' (The Pet Shop Boys)

'I Wanna Dance With Somebody (Who Loves Me)' (Whitney Houston)

'I Want Your Sex' (George Michael)

'Who's That Girl' (Madonna)

'I Really Didn't Mean It' (Luther Vandross)

'Misfit' (Curiosity Killed The Cat)

'Your Love Keeps Lifting Me Higher And Higher' (Jackie Wilson)

People who had songs written for them

Woody Harrelson – 'Woody' (Hootie and The Blowfish)

Gwyneth Paltrow – 'Moses' (Chris Martin)

Angie Bowie – 'Angie' (The Rolling Stones)

Nancy Sinatra – 'Nancy With The Laughing Face' (Frank Sinatra)

Carole King – 'Oh Carol' (Neil Sedaka)

Frances Tomelty – 'Every Breath You Take' (The Police)

Patti D'Arbanville – 'Lady D'Arbanville' (Cat Stevens)

Rosanna Arquette – 'Rosanna' (Toto)

Paula Yates – 'No-one Compares To You' (Michael Hutchence)

Paul McGrath – 'I Believe In God' (Nigel Kennedy)

Diana, Princess of Wales – 'Candle In The Wind 1997' (Elton John)

Magic Johnson – 'Positive' (Michael Franti)

David Geffen – 'A Free Man In Paris' (Joni Mitchell)

Eric Clapton – 'My Favourite Mistake' (Sheryl Crow)

Robert F. Kennedy – 'Long Time Gone' (David Crosby)

Syd Barrett – 'Shine On You Crazy Diamond' (Roger Waters)

Duke Ellington – 'Sir Duke' (Stevie Wonder)

Kari-Anne Jagger (wife of Chris Jagger) – 'Carrie Anne' (The Hollies)

ALL THE WINNERS OF THE AWARD FOR BEST BRITISH GROUP AT THE BRITS

2005: Franz Ferdinand

2004: The Darkness

2003: Coldplay

2002: Travis

2001: Coldplay

2000: Travis

1999: Manic Street Preachers

1998: The Verve

1997: Manic Street Preachers

1996: Oasis

1995: Blur

1994: Stereo MC's

1993: Simply Red

1992: The KLF/Simply Red (Joint Winners)

1991: The Cure

1990: Fine Young Cannibals

1989: Erasure

1988: Pet Shop Boys

1987: Five Star

1986: Dire Straits

1985: Wham!

1984: Culture Club

1983: Dire Straits

1982: The Police

SINGING DRUMMERS

Phil Collins, Kevin Godley, Don Henley, Dave Clark, Levon Helm, Ringo Starr, Stewart Copeland, Jim Capaldi, Karen Carpenter, Micky Dolenz

ALL THE DOUBLE-A SIDES THAT REACHED NUMBER ONE IN BRITAIN

Gamblin' Man/Putting On The Style (Lonnie Donegan 1957)

All I Have To Do Is Dream/Claudette (The Everly Brothers 1958)

Carolina Moon/Stupid Cupid (Connie Francis 1958)

One Night/I Got Stung (Elvis Presley 1959)

A Fool Such As I/I Need Your Love Tonight (Elvis Presley 1959)

Walk Right Back/Ebony Eyes (The Everly Brothers 1961)

Reach For The Stars/Climb Ev'ry Mountain (Shirley Bassey 1961)

Little Sister/His Latest Flame (Elvis Presley 1961)

Rock-A-Hula Baby/Can't Help Falling In Love (Elvis Presley 1961)

The Next Time/Bachelor Boy (Cliff Richard And The Shadows 1963)

Day Tripper/We Can Work It Out (The Beatles 1965)

Yellow Submarine/Eleanor Rigby (The Beatles 1966)

What A Wonderful World/Cabaret (Louis Armstrong 1968)

Daydreamer/The Puppy Song (David Cassidy 1973)

I Don't Want To Talk About It/First Cut Is The Deepest (Rod Stewart 1977)

Mull of Kintyre/Girls' School (Wings 1977)

Rivers of Babylon/Brown Girl In The Ring (Boney M 1978)

Going Underground/Dreams of Children (The Jam 1980)

Computer Love/The Model (Kraftwerk 1982)

A Town Called Malice/Precious (The Jam 1982)

Pump Up The Volume/Anitina (The First Time I See She Dance) (M/A/R/R/S 1987)

With A Little Help From My Friends/She's Leaving Home (Wet Wet Wet/Billy Bragg with Cara Tivey 1988)

Sacrifice/Healing Hands (Elton John 1990)

Bohemian Rhapsody/These Are The Days of Our Lives (Queen 1991)

Please Don't Go/Game Boy (KWS 1992)

Unchained Melody/(There'll Be Bluebirds Over) The White Cliffs of Dover (Robson Green and Jerome Flynn 1995)

I Believe/Up On The Roof (Robson Green and Jerome Flynn 1995)

Knockin' On Heaven's Door/Throw These Guns Away (Dunblane 1996)

Mama/Who Do You Think You Are (The Spice Girls 1997)

Candle In The Wind 1997/Something About The Way You Look Tonight (Elton John 1997)

Under The Bridge/Lady Marmalade (All Saints 1998)

Heartbeat/Tragedy (Steps 1999)

She's The One/It's Only Us (Robbie Williams 1999)

I Have A Dream/Seasons In The Sun (Westlife 1999)

Holler/Let Love Lead The Way (The Spice Girls 2000)

Eternity/Road To Mandalay (Robbie Williams 2001)

Evergreen/Anything Is Possible (Will Young 2002)

The Long And Winding Road/Suspicious Minds (Will Young/Gareth Gates 2002)

My Place/Flap Your Wings (Nelly 2004)

METEOROLOGY

It would take 7 billion particles of fog to fill a teaspoon. A cubic mile of fog is made up of less than a gallon of water.

No rain has ever been recorded in the Atacama desert in Chile.

The sunlight that strikes the earth at any given moment (in total) weighs as much as a large ocean liner.

500 million litres of rain can fall during a thunderstorm.

A snowflake can take up to an hour to land.

12 per cent of the earth's land surface is permanently covered by ice and snow.

The South Pole has no sun for 182 days each year.

On 17 July 1841, a shower of hail and rain in Derby was accompanied by a fall of hundreds of small fish and frogs – some of them still alive.

Small clouds that look like they have broken off from bigger clouds are called scuds.

A full moon always rises at sunset.

A full moon is nine times brighter than a half moon.

On 14 August 1979, a rainbow over North Wales lasted for three hours.

PEOPLE WHO GOT THEIR BREAK ON *NEW FACES*

Jim Davidson, Lenny Henry, Victoria Wood, Marti Caine, Michael Barrymore, Roger De Courcey, Patti Boulaye, Les Dennis, Malandra Burrows, Peter Andre

PEOPLE WHO GOT THEIR BREAK ON *OPPORTUNITY KNOCKS*

Les Dawson, Tom O'Connor, Mary Hopkin, Engelbert Humperdinck, Bobby Crush, Bonnie Langford, Freddie Starr

PEOPLE WHO APPEARED IN SOAP OPERAS

Derek Nimmo – *Neighbours*

Jenny Hanley – *Emmerdale*

Clive James – *Neighbours*

Peter Purves – *EastEnders*

Angela Thorne – *Emmerdale*

David Jason – *Crossroads*

Diane Keen – *Crossroads*

Cat Deeley – *Hollyoaks*

Christian Slater – *Ryan's Hope*

Ricky Martin – *General Hospital*; started as a singing bartender and then got a regular role

Russell Crowe – *Neighbours*

Val Kilmer – *Knot's Landing*

Brad Pitt – *Dallas*

Jude Law – *Families*

Holly Valance – *Neighbours*

Demi Moore – *General Hospital*

Kevin Kline – *Search For Tomorrow*

Alec Baldwin – *The Doctors*

Tommy Lee Jones – *One Life To Live*

Morgan Freeman – *Another World*

Kevin Bacon – *Guiding Light*

Meg Ryan – *As The World Turns*

Christopher Walken – *Guiding Light*

Marisa Tomei – *As The World Turns*

Sigourney Weaver – *Somerset*

Ray Liotta – *Another World*

Susan Sarandon – *Search For Tomorrow*

Paula Yates – *Brookside**

Lily Savage – *Brookside**

The Nolan Sisters – *Brookside**

Michael Parkinson – *Brookside**

Linda Lusardi – *Hollyoaks**

Ian Botham – *Emmerdale**

Eamonn Holmes – *Brookside**

Lorraine Kelly – *Brookside**

Sarah Greene – *Brookside**

*= appeared as themselves

People who appeared in *Coronation Street*

Richard Beckinsale (P.C. Willcocks)

Michael Ball (Malcolm Nuttall)

Prunella Scales (Eileen Hughes)

Davy Jones (Colin Lomax)

Martin Shaw (Robert Croft)

Dame Beryl Bainbridge (Ken Barlow's girlfriend)

Noddy Holder (Stan Potter)

Michael Elphick (Douglas Wormold)

Mel B. (Bettabuys worker)

Joanna Lumley (Elaine Perkins)

Peter Noone (Stanley Fairclough)

Gorden Kaye (Bernard Butler)

Sir Ben Kingsley (Ron Jenkins)

Max Wall (Harry Payne)

Bill Maynard (Mickey Malone)

Gilly Coman (Sugar La Marr)

Paul Shane (Frank Draper)

Kenneth Cope (Jed Stone)

Tony Anholt (David Law)

Kathy Staff (Vera Hopkins)

Leonard Sachs (Sir Julius Berlin)

Paula Wilcox (Janice Langton)

Mollie Sugden (Nellie Harvey)

Ian McKellen (Mel Hutchwright)

PEOPLE WHO APPEARED IN *GRANGE HILL*

Susan Tully (Suzanne Ross 1981–84)

Letitia Dean (Lucinda 1978)

Sean Maguire (Tegs Ratcliffe 1988–91)

Todd Carty (Peter 'Tucker' Jenkins 1978–82)

Alex Kingston (Jill Harcourt 1980)

Michelle Gayle (Fiona Wilson 1988–89)

Patsy Palmer (bit parts for three years)

John Alford (Robbie Wright 1985–90)

Naomi Campbell (Uncredited pupil 1978)

PEOPLE WHO MADE GUEST APPEARANCES IN *THE BILL*

Rik Mayall, Paul O'Grady, Brian Glover, Ray Winstone, Craig Charles, Leslie Phillips, Letitia Dean, Anita Dobson, Leslie Ash, Alex Kingston, Emma Bunton, Michelle Collins, Linda Robson, Robert Carlyle, Martin Kemp, Denise Van Outen, Leslie Grantham, Emmanuel Petit, Linda Lusardi, Tamzin Outhwaite

PEOPLE WHO MADE GUEST APPEARANCES IN *THE AVENGERS*

John Cleese, Donald Sutherland, Warren Mitchell, John Thaw, Charlotte Rampling, Ronnie Barker, Christopher Lee, Ron Moody, Joss Ackland, Peter Cushing, Arthur Lowe, Roy Kinnear, Gordon Jackson, Peter Wyngarde, Jon Pertwee, Yootha Joyce, Penelope Keith, Peter Bowles

PEOPLE WHO MADE GUEST APPEARANCES IN *CASUALTY*

Kate Winslet, Alfred Molina, Sadie Frost, Jonny Lee Miller, Julian Fellowes, Minnie Driver, Kathy Burke, Lionel Jeffries, Pete Postlethwaite, Amanda Redman, Christopher Eccleston, Sophie Okonedo, Nick Moran, Dorothy Tutin, Julia Sawalha

PEOPLE WHO MADE GUEST APPEARANCES IN *THE ADVENTURES OF ROBIN HOOD*

Peter Asher, Hubert Gregg, Richard O'Sullivan, Leo McKern, Leslie Phillips, Thora Hird, Nicholas Parsons, Jane Asher, Ian Bannen, John Schlesinger, Bernard Bresslaw, Patrick Troughton, Wilfrid Brambell, Harry H. Corbett, Nigel Davenport, Andrew Faulds, Lionel Jeffries, Geoffrey Bayldon, Ronald Allen, Billie Whitelaw, Gordon Jackson, Desmond Llewelyn, Michael Gough

PEOPLE WHO WERE ON *THIS IS YOUR LIFE* BEFORE THE AGE OF 30

Twiggy (aged 20)

Bonnie Langford (21)

Stephen Hendry (21)

Robin Cousins (22)

John Conteh (23)

George Best (25)

Ian Botham (25)

Kevin Keegan (27)

Elaine Paige (27)

Jim Davidson (29)

PEOPLE WHO WERE ON *THIS IS YOUR LIFE* TWICE

Lord Andrew Lloyd Webber, Frankie Vaughan, Richard Briers, Sir Jimmy Savile, Honor Blackman, Dame Shirley Bassey, Edward Woodward, Sir Harry Secombe, Dame Barbara Cartland, Dame Vera Lynn, Sir Peter Ustinov, George Best

PEOPLE WHO REFUSED TO GO ON *THIS IS YOUR LIFE*

Danny Blanchflower, Richard Gordon, Noel Gallagher

PEOPLE WHO WORKED ON
SPITTING IMAGE

Voices: Chris Barrie, Rory Bremner, Steve Coogan, Hugh Dennis, Adrian Edmondson, Harry Enfield, Alistair McGowan, Jan Ravens, John Sessions, Pamela Stephenson, John Thomson

Writers: Richard Curtis, Jack Docherty, Ben Elton, Ian Hislop, John O'Farrell, Steve Punt

PEOPLE WHO MADE GUEST APPEARANCES ON US TV SHOWS

Sir Richard Branson – *Baywatch*

Sir Paul McCartney – *Baywatch*

Leonard Cohen – *Miami Vice*

Ray Charles – *Moonlighting*

Norman Beaton – *The Cosby Show*

Peter Noone – *My Two Dads*

Phil Collins – *Miami Vice*

Frank Sinatra – *Magnum, P.I.*

Dionne Warwick – *The Rockford Files*

Carly Simon – *thirtysomething*

Boy George – *The A-Team*

Davy Jones – *My Two Dads*

Ewan McGregor – *ER*

TV SHOWS THAT STARTED AS RADIO SHOWS

Little Britain

What's My Line?

This Is Your Life

They Think It's All Over

Dragnet

Have I Got News For You

Hancock's Half-Hour

After Henry

Perry Mason

Gunsmoke

The Lone Ranger

FILMS THAT BECAME TV SERIES

Lock Stock And Two Smoking Barrels

Dixon of Dock Green

Doctor Kildare

Casablanca

In The Heat of The Night

The Third Man

The Saint

The Prime of Miss Jean Brodie

Quiller (from The Quiller Memorandum)

Man at the Top (from Room At The Top)

SITCOMS THAT WERE SPIN-OFFS FROM OTHER SITCOMS

George and Mildred (Man About The House)

Frasier (Cheers)

Going Straight (Porridge)

Empty Nest (The Golden Girls)

In Sickness And In Health (Till Death Us Do Part)

Laverne And Shirley (Happy Days)

Grace And Favour (Are You Being Served?)

Rhoda (The Mary Tyler Moore Show)

The Fenn Street Gang (Please Sir)

Tabitha (Bewitched)

Joey (Friends)

THE CONTESTANTS IN *CELEBRITY BIG BROTHER* AND HOW THEY FARED

SERIES 1 (2001)

Jack Dee – Winner
Claire Sweeney – Runner-up
Keith Duffy – 3rd
Anthea Turner – 4th
Vanessa Feltz – 5th
Chris Eubank – 6th

SERIES 2 (2002)

Mark Owen – Winner
Les Dennis – Runner-up
Melinda Messenger – 3rd
Sue Perkins – 4th
Anne Diamond – 5th
Goldie – 6th

SERIES 3 (2005)

Bez – Winner
Kenzie – Runner-up
Brigitte Nielsen – 3rd
Jeremy Edwards – 4th
Caprice – 5th
Lisa L'Anson – 6th
John McCririck – 7th
Jackie Stallone – 8th
Germaine Greer – walked out

GENUINE RESPONSES GIVEN BY CONTESTANTS ON *FAMILY FORTUNES*

Name something a blind person might use.
A sword.

Name an occupation where you need a torch.
A burglar.

Name a dangerous race.
The Arabs.

Name a bird with a long neck.
Naomi Campbell.

Name a famous royal.
Mail.

Name a number you have to memorize.
Seven.

Name something you might be allergic to.
Skiing.

Name a non-living object with legs.
A plant.

Name something a cat does.
Goes to the toilet.

Name something you do in the bathroom.
Decorate.

Name a domestic animal.
A leopard.

Name a part of the body beginning with 'N'.
Knee.

Name something associated with the police.
Pigs.

Dogs

There are some seven million dogs in the UK. The most popular breeds are Labradors, Alsatians, West Highland white terriers and Golden Retrievers.

The average lifespan of a dog is between 8 and 15 years, depending on the breed.

The largest amount of money left to a dog was £15 million – to a poodle in 1931 by one Ella Wendel of New York.

The most popular names for dogs in the UK are Sam, Trixie, Polly and Spot.

The Queen is the world's most famous owner of Corgis. The names she's given to her dogs include Fable, Myth, Shadow, Jolly and Chipper.

The breeds that bite the most are German Police Dogs, Chows and Poodles.

The breeds that bite the least are Golden Retrievers, Labradors and Old English Sheepdogs.

People who used to sleep with their dog in the bed next to them include the Duke of Windsor, General Custer and Elizabeth Barrett Browning.

The most intelligent dog breeds are (in order): Border Collie, Poodle, Alsatian and Golden Retriever.

Dogs on film: *Beethoven, The Fox And The Hound, 101 Dalmatians, K-9, Lady And The Tramp, Oliver & Company, Turner & Hooch* (but not *Reservoir Dogs*).

Dogs in Literature: Nana in *Peter Pan* by J.M. Barrie; Toto in *The Wizard of Oz* by Frank Baum; Timmy in *The Famous Five* books by Enid Blyton; Edison in *Chitty Chitty Bang Bang* by Ian Fleming; Montmorency in *Three Men In A Boat* by Jerome K. Jerome; Bullseye in *Oliver Twist* by Charles Dickens; Jip in *Dr Dolittle* by Hugh Lofting; Argos in *The Odyssey* by Homer.

'A dog teaches a boy fidelity, perseverance and to turn round three times before lying down.' (Robert Benchley)

'I loathe people who keep dogs. They are cowards who haven't got the guts to bite people themselves.' (August Strindberg)

'That indefatigable and unsavoury engine of pollution, the dog.' (John Sparrow)

'The censure of a dog is something no man can stand.' (Christopher Morley)

GANFYD

At the back of *This Book* and *That Book*, I asked readers to come up with ideas. One reader who did was Dr Peter Davies, who sent me some examples of extraordinary requests for doctors' notes – under the heading Get A Note From Your Doctor (GANFYD) – collected from the website www.doctors.net.uk.

LETTER REQUESTED ...

To confirm that 'I'm too breathless to cut the grass'.

To confirm that a patient has an artificial limb.

To confirm that a patient's daughter is female, because the passport office had issued a passport with no stated sex on it.

To confirm that a 16-year-old girl does not have chicken pox.

To state that the doctor knows of no reason why a student should not massage members of the public.

To give to a school so that the father isn't sent to jail for the child's non-attendance.

To 'say that my daughter can appear in the school play'.

To 'say that my old-fashioned mobile phone is causing me tension headaches'.

To 'say that chewing gum at the checkout helps me breathe'.

To confirm that a patient gets backache – so he can get a more comfortable BMW from his firm.

To confirm that a potential employee 'is fit to handle cheese'.

To confirm that a patient is fit to drive, even though she'd just received an 18-month driving ban.

To confirm that a patient has latex allergy – 'so I couldn't possibly be guilty of kerb crawling as with this I would not want to wear a condom'.

To say that a patient's acne is so bad she cannot go to the gym (and so can get a refund).

To say that a patient's new coat caused them a rash (so that the shop would give a refund).

IT'S NOT ONLY THE PATIENTS:

A holiday insurance company asked whether a GP would have said a patient was fit to travel had the GP seen him before he left.

A school required a doctor's note before allowing a child with a leg in plaster of Paris to be excused swimming lessons.

An American state asks doctors to certify condemned prisoners as fit to be executed.

At a hospital: 'That's a new problem so before we can do anything you'll need to get a note from your doctor.'

At a dentist's: 'Due to pressure on the system get a note from the doctor if you need to see the dentist.'

A local bank rang the doctor's surgery to ask for a note confirming that the customer 'is who she says she is'.

'Periodically it is necessary to obtain proof that pensioners are being paid correctly and we would be grateful if you could complete this form to confirm that [X] is still alive …'

PEOPLE WHO CHOSE 'MY WAY' ON *DESERT ISLAND DISCS*

Jimmy Tarbuck, Sir David Frost, Geoffrey Boycott, Russell Harty, Lord Norman Tebbit, David Broome, Jimmy Jewel, Gareth Edwards, Barry John, Johnny Speight, Alan Minter, Stewart Granger, Sir Stanley Kalms

PEOPLE WHO CHOSE PROUST'S *A LA RECHERCHE DU TEMPS PERDU* AS THEIR BOOK ON *DESERT ISLAND DISCS*

Tony Blair, Mary Archer, Sir Stephen Spender, Michael Portillo, Cyril Connolly, Michael White

PEOPLE WHO DECLINED TO GO ON *DESERT ISLAND DISCS*

Sir Laurence Olivier, George Bernard Shaw, Sir Albert Finney, Prince Charles, Leo Sayer (after the BBC couldn't find his favourite records)

EXTRAORDINARY LUXURIES CHOSEN ON *DESERT ISLAND DISCS*

Haemorrhoid cream – Jimmy McGovern

New York's Chrysler building – Terry Pratchett

Model of the Tower of London – Denis Norden

A suicide pill – Stephen Fry

The *Mona Lisa* – Arthur Scargill

Silk underwear – Dame Helen Mirren

A stick of marijuana – Norman Mailer

A car to clean – Rowan Atkinson

A replica of Broadcasting House – Sir Harry Secombe

Madge Allsop – Dame Edna Everage (the only time a 'person' has been allowed as a luxury on the show)

Electrical device to heat shaving foam – Billy Connolly

Big bag of plaster to make heads of friends – Virginia Ironside

A Barclaycard – Spike Milligan

The laws of the land (so he could break them) – Benjamin Zephaniah

A hot bath with extra tap for cold champagne – Jane Asher

The front seat of a Porsche – Iain Banks

Notting Hill Pizza Express – Richard Curtis

Space invaders – Clive James

A car to listen to music in – Sir Michael Gambon

A life-sized papier maché model of Margaret Thatcher and a baseball bat – John Cleese

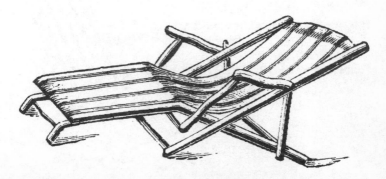

Having *The Sporting Life* delivered daily – Des O'Connor

An inflatable rubber woman – Oliver Reed

An inflatable woman and a puncture repair kit – Michael Crawford

A deckchair – Eric Morecambe

A deckchair ticket-machine – Ernie Wise

Nelson's Column – Lionel Bart

Nothing (he's had enough luxury to last a lifetime) – Colin Montgomerie

PEOPLE WHO CHOSE THEIR OWN SONGS ON *DESERT ISLAND DISCS*

Cilla Black ('Anyone Who Had A Heart')

Hylda Baker ('Give Us A Kiss')

Tony Bennett ('Smile')

Gary Glitter ('Rock And Roll I Gave You The Best Years Of My Life')

Dame Edna Everage ('My Bridesmaid And I')

Alan Price ('House of The Rising Sun')

Mel Brooks ('Springtime For Hitler')

Clive Dunn ('Grandad')

Dudley Moore ('Little Miss Britten')

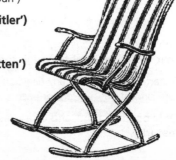

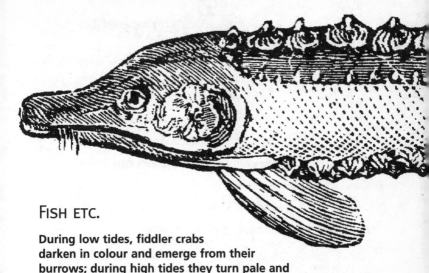

Fish etc.

**During low tides, fiddler crabs
darken in colour and emerge from their
burrows; during high tides they turn pale and
retreat. Kept in a laboratory far away from the ocean, they still
keep time with the tide, changing colour as it ebbs and flows.**

Dolphins don't breathe autonomically; breathing for them is a
conscious act.

Jellyfish sometimes evaporate.

The Weddell seal can travel underwater for seven miles without
surfacing for air.

A male sea lion can go for three months without eating.

In the Caribbean there are oysters that can climb trees.

**The lantern fish has a glowing spot on its head
that would be bright enough to read by.**

A starfish can move in any direction without having to
turn since it has no front or back.

**Only one in a thousand creatures born in the sea reaches
maturity.**

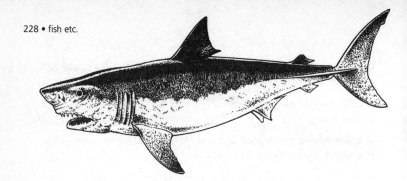

Next to man, the porpoise is the most intelligent creature on earth.

Shrimps swim backwards.

A barnacle has the largest penis of any creature relative to its size.

The embryos of tiger sharks fight each other in the womb and only survivors get born.

Octopuses have gardens (as Ringo knew).

An octopus's eye has a rectangular pupil.

Tuna swim at a steady rate of 9 miles (14 km) per hour until they die – they never stop moving.

The mudskipper is a fish that can walk on land.

A blue whale's heart beats nine times a minute.

The blue whale, the largest creature on earth, weighs approximately as much as 224,000 copies of *Moby Dick*.

A lobster can lay 150,000 eggs at one time.

Texas horned toads can fire blood out of the corners of their eyes.

A sea squirt found in the seas near Japan has occasion at a certain point in its life to digest its own brain. When it reaches maturity, it attaches itself to a rock, and with no further need to move, dispenses with its brain by consuming it.

If you are served a crayfish with a straight tail, you shouldn't eat it. It was dead before it was cooked.

A baby grey whale drinks enough milk to fill more than 2,000 baby bottles a day.

A killer whale torpedoes a shark from underneath, bursting the shark by entering its stomach.

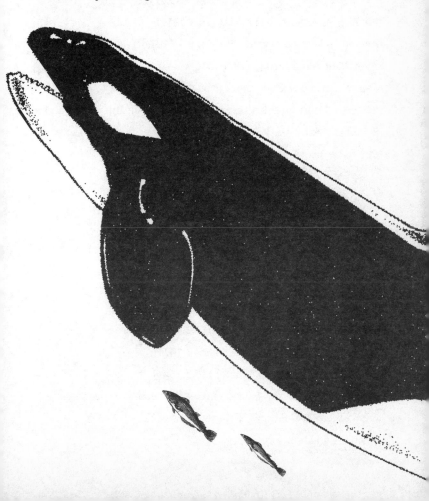

PAIRS OF PEOPLE BORN ON THE SAME DAY

Joan Baez & Susannah York (9.1.1941)

Robert Palmer & Dennis Taylor (19.1.1949)

Federico Fellini & DeForest Kelley (20.1.1920)

Heather Small & Sophie, Countess of Wessex (20.1.1965)

Vic Reeves & Nastassja Kinski (24.1.1959)

Andrew Ridgeley & Jose Mourinho (26.1.1963)

Alan Alda & Bill Jordan (28.1.1936)

Carol Channing & Mario Lanza (31.1.1921)

Stephen McGann & Eva Cassidy (2.2.1963)

Roberta Flack & Peter Purves (10.2.1939)

Christina Ricci & Sarah Lancaster (12.2.1980)

Clare Short & Marisa Berenson (15.2.1946)

Gene Pitney & Julia McKenzie (17.2.1941)

Robin Cook & Syreeta (28.2.1946)

Andrew Strauss & Chris Martin (2.3.1977)

Eddy Grant & Elaine Paige (5.3.1948)

Rachel Weisz & Matthew Vaughn (7.3.1971)

Terry Holmes & Osama Bin Laden (10.3.1957)

Joe Bugner & William H. Macy (13.3.1950)

Gail Porter & Natascha McElhone (23.3.1971)

Eric Clapton & Johnnie Walker (30.3.1945)

Celine Dion & Donna D'Errico (30.3.1968)

Camille Paglia & Emmylou Harris (2.4.1947)

David Letterman & Tom Clancy (12.4.1947)

Sarah Michelle Gellar & Freddie Ljungberg (14.4.1977)

Claire Sweeney & Jennifer Garner (17.4.1972)

Penelope Cruz & Vernon Kay (28.4.1974)

Benjamin Spock & Bing Crosby (2.5.1903)

Sonny Liston & Phyllida Law (8.5.1932)

Olga Korbut & Debra Winger & Hazel O'Connor (16.5.1955)

Caroline Charles & Nobby Stiles (18.5.1942)

Malcolm X & Pol Pot (19.5.1925)

Busta Rhymes & Tina Hobley (20.5.1972)

Leo Sayer & Ian McEwan (21.5.1948)

Herge & Sir Laurence Olivier (22.5.1907)

Joseph Fiennes & Robert Di Matteo (27.5.1970)

Lisa 'Left Eye' Lopes & Paul Bettany (27.5.1971)

Gladys Knight & Faith Brown (28.5.1944)

Heidi Klum & Saffron Burrows (1.6.1973)

Sir Wilfred Thesiger & Paulette Goddard (3.6.1910)

Michael J. Fox & Aaron Sorkin (9.6.1961)

Newt Gingrich & Barry Manilow (17.6.1943)

Barry Hearn & Nick Drake (19.6.1948)

John Goodman & Vikram Seth (20.6.1952)

Jane Russell & Judy Holliday & Jean Kent (21.6.1921)

Patrick Kluivert & Ruud Van Nistelrooy (1.7.1976)

Beck & Todd Martin (8.7.1970)

Marc Almond & Tom Hanks (9.7.1956)

Gough Whitlam & Reg Varney (11.7.1916)

Blake Edwards & Jason Robards (26.7.1922)

Jason Robinson & Hilary Swank (30.7.1974)

Alexander Fleming & Louella Parsons (6.8.1881)

Gillian Anderson & Eric Bana (9.8.1968)

Adrian Lester & Darren Clarke (14.8.1968)

Robert Redford & William Rushton (18.8.1937)

Martin Freeman & David Arquette (8.9.1971)

David Copperfield & Mickey Rourke (16.9.1956)

Lance Armstrong & Jada Pinkett Smith (18.9.1971)

Bruce Springsteen & Floella Benjamin (23.9.1949)

Mika Hakkinen & Naomi Watts (28.9.1968)

Rula Lenska & Marc Bolan (30.9.1947)

John Entwistle & Peter Tosh (9.10.1944)

Nicholas Parsons & Murray Walker (10.10.1923)

Ann Jones & Evel Knievel (17.10.1938)

Susan Tully & Monica Ali (20.10.1967)

Larry Mullen Jr & Peter Jackson (31.10.1961)

Griff Rhys Jones & Tony Parsons (6.11.1953)

Dame Elizabeth Frink & Big Daddy (14.11.1930)

Lucy Liu & David Batty (2.12.1968)

Jeff Bridges & Pamela Stephenson (4.12.1949)

Janet Street-Porter & Polly Toynbee (27.12.1946)

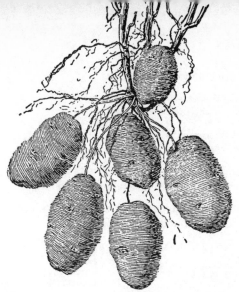

POTATOES

Potatoes were first eaten more than six thousand years ago by natives (later Incas) living in the Andes mountains of Peru.

The Incas measured time by how long it took for potatoes to cook.

Their descendants, the Quechua Indians, have more than a thousand different names for potatoes.

Sir Walter Raleigh introduced potatoes to Europe in the late 16th century and grew them at his Irish estate near Cork.

Religious leaders denounced the potato because it wasn't mentioned in the Bible.

Potatoes are the world's fourth food staple – after wheat, corn and rice.

Every year enough potatoes are grown worldwide to cover a four-lane motorway circling the world six times.

Potatoes are grown worldwide in over 125 countries (even in space – in 1995).

China is the world's largest producer.

King Louis XVI of France wore potato blossoms in his buttonhole while Marie Antoinette wore them in her hair.

The word 'spud' comes from the name for a narrow flat spade that was used for digging potatoes.

We each eat an average of 110 kilograms (240 pounds) of potatoes every year – not quite as much as the Germans consume.

The potato is about 80 per cent water and 20 per cent solids and is related to the tomato and tobacco.

Mr Potato Head was the first toy to be advertised on American television.

Some superstitious people say you should carry a potato in your pocket to ease toothache.

The botanical name for the common potato is *Solanum tuberosum*.

If you unscrew a light bulb and the bulb breaks, cut a potato in half and push the potato in the socket and turn. It should remove the remainder of the bulb.

Storing potatoes with apples stops them from sprouting.

In 1778 Prussia and Austria fought the Potato War in which each side tried to starve the other by consuming their potato crop.

Until the late 18th century, the French believed that potatoes caused leprosy.

During the Alaskan Klondike gold rush of the 1890s, potatoes were so valued for their vitamin C content that miners traded gold for them.

BODIES

Patrick Swayze has broken his left knee five times.

Will Carling can't cross his legs because they're too muscular.

Ashton Kutcher has two webbed toes on his left foot.

Shania Twain has used cow-udder balm as a moisturizer.

Joe Pesci, Christopher Walken, Kiefer Sutherland, Barbara Kellerman, Dan Aykroyd and Kate Bosworth each have eyes of different colours.

Julian Clary, Denise Van Outen and Princess Michael of Kent have all had Botox treatment.

PEOPLE AND WHAT THEY ARE ALLERGIC TO

Warren Beatty – oysters

Lindsay Lohan – blueberries

David Duchovny – metal (on his body)

Carol Channing – bleach

Rosie O'Donnell – cats and horses

Ian Kelsey – wood

Simon Mayo – sunlight

Gary Webster – animals

Philippa Forrester – bread

Drew Barrymore – bee stings and perfume

Charles Kennedy – dogs, grass and make-up

Ross Kemp – wasps

Darius Danesh – mushrooms

Kathy Burke – white wine

Anne Diamond – wine and beer

Tricia Penrose – dust

David Cassidy – garlic

Lleyton Hewitt – grass, horses and cats

Gail Porter – oil

Cleo Rocos – shellfish

Kyle MacLachlan – wool

Ioan Gruffudd – cats

Chris Bisson – sawdust

Nadia Sawalha – yeast

Alice Beer – wheat

Julia Sawalha – caffeine

Belinda Carlisle – wheat

Rene Russo – sesame

Gareth Gates – oranges, coffee and cheese

Gillian Anderson – cat hair

Alistair McGowan – wig glue

Brad Pitt – dogs

HAY FEVER SUFFERERS

Philippa Forrester, Tyra Banks, Jeremy Clarkson, Tiger Woods, Michelle Wie, Michael Fish, Simon Mayo, Chris Evans, Suzanne Charlton, John Major, Steffi Graf, Nigel Mansell, Bruce Oldfield, Paul Young, Sergio Garcia, Jesper Parnevik, Jimmy Hill

PEOPLE WHO SURVIVED TUBERCULOSIS

Nelson Mandela, Paul Eddington, Saffron Burrows, Stewart Granger, Sir Leonard Cheshire, Bill McLaren, Engelbert Humperdinck, Richard Harris, Alan Sillitoe, Sir Gordon Richards, Ray Galton, Alan Simpson (indeed, it was while convalescing from TB that Galton and Simpson met – and then went on to write *Hancock* **and** *Steptoe and Son***), Tom Jones, Archbishop Desmond Tutu**

INSOMNIACS

Mia Farrow, Sir Magdi Yacoub, Una Stubbs, Damon Albarn, Dame Eileen Atkins, Dulcie Gray, Sarah Kennedy, Sir Winston Churchill, Jeremy Clarkson, Derek Jameson, Michael Aspel, Phil Edmonds, Alexander Dumas, Alexander Pope, Sebastian Faulks, Jenni Falconer, J 5ive, Colin Farrell, Justin Timberlake, Richard Burton, Ernest Hemingway, Groucho Marx, Audie Murphy

SLEEPWALKERS

Ann Widdecombe (during her late teens at school)

Antony Worrall Thompson (along Brighton seafront as a boy)

GOUT SUFFERERS

Greg Dyke, Jonathan King, Ronnie Biggs, Terry Wogan, Fran Cotton, Tony Robinson, Sam Torrance, Antonio Carluccio, Sam Mendes, Carl Wilson, Nicholas Coleridge, Joseph Conrad, Julius Caesar, John Milton, Dr Samuel Johnson

PEOPLE WHO SUFFERED FROM GALLSTONES

Dawn French, Aristotle Onassis, Alexandra Bastedo, Larry Hagman, Linda Robson, Rosemary Conley, Pam Ferris, Benazir Bhutto, Claire Rayner, Pope John Paul II, Harold Macmillan, Yasser Arafat

PEOPLE WHO HAVE HAD A HEART MURMUR

Tony Blair, Barbara Windsor, Keith Duffy, Sir Alex Ferguson, Judy Finnigan, Arnold Schwarzenegger, Bridget Fonda, Gareth Hale, Retief Goosen, Rachel Hunter, Evander Holyfield, Dame Elizabeth Taylor

PEOPLE WHO SUFFERED FROM OBSESSIVE COMPULSIVE DISORDER

Emily Lloyd, Michelle Pfeiffer, Billy Bob Thornton, Winona Ryder, David Beckham, Woody Allen, Jane Horrocks, Harrison Ford, Paul Gascoigne, Charles Dickens, Leonardo DiCaprio

NB Art Carney's father suffered from OCD

PEOPLE WHO HAD BAD ADOLESCENT ACNE

Sienna Guillory, Vanessa Redgrave, Rob Brydon ('Professional acne'), Charlotte Salt, Trinny Woodall, Sir Derek Jacobi, Elvis Presley, Ricky Martin, Tim Vincent

PEOPLE WHO HAVE SUFFERED FROM ECZEMA

Liz Earle, Liam Gallagher, Trudie Goodwin, Brett Anderson, Michaela Strachan, Neil Hamilton, Claire Sweeney

PEOPLE WITH BEAUTY SPOTS

Madonna, Robert De Niro, Cheryl Ladd, Sir Roger Moore, Cindy Crawford, Lisa Stansfield, Sherilyn Fenn, Lynsey De Paul, Chesney Hawkes, Marilyn Monroe

PEOPLE WHO HAVE USED HYPNOSIS

Lisa Kudrow (for stopping smoking)

Melanie Griffith (for stopping smoking)

Britney Spears (for stopping biting her nails)

Jennifer Aniston (for stopping smoking)

Pat Benatar (for relaxing her vocal cords)

Courteney Cox (for stopping smoking)

Tori Spelling (for her fear of flying)

Christy Turlington (for stopping smoking)

Salma Hayek (for fear of snakes)

Catherine Deneuve (for stopping smoking)

PEOPLE WHO ARE COLOUR-BLIND

William Hague, Paul Newman, Rod Stewart, Jack Nicklaus, Nicky Piper, Peter Bowles, Peter Ebdon, Sir Donald Sinden, Mark Williams, Bill Beaumont, George Michael

PEOPLE WHO HAVE SUFFERED FROM SERIOUS DEPRESSION

Billy Joel, Jill Gascoine, Charlotte Rampling, Judy Finnigan, Sir Elton John, Claire Rayner, Axl Rose, Paul Gascoigne, Sheryl Crow, Kenneth Branagh, Patsy Kensit, Sarah Lancashire, Bill Paxton, Marie Osmond, Kerry Katona, Lenny Henry, Trisha Goddard, Frances Barber, Paul O'Grady, Monty Don

PEOPLE WHO USED TO CUT THEMSELVES

Johnny Depp used to cut himself (the small knife-marks on his arms marked certain rites of passage)

Christina Ricci used to stub out burning cigarettes on her body and gouge herself with bottle tops. Interestingly, Ricci and Depp co-starred in *Sleepy Hollow*

Princess Diana used to cut herself with a penknife

Shirley Manson, as a teenager, used to slash her legs with a razor

PEOPLE WHO WORE BRACES ON THEIR TEETH AS ADULTS

Jill St John, Jack Klugman, Diana Ross, Carol Burnett, Cher, Tom Cruise

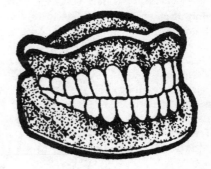

PEOPLE WHO SAY THEY HATE THEIR FEET

Britney Spears, Naomi Campbell, Claudia Schiffer, Will Young, Angela Griffin, Badly Drawn Boy (Damon Gough), Freya Copeland, Kevin McNally, Amanda Holden, Dani Behr, Ruth Madoc, Anna Walker, Gwyneth Strong, Kate Hardie, Gina Bellman

PEOPLE WHO HAD THEIR SPLEENS REMOVED

Keanu Reeves, Bob Hawke, Burt Reynolds, Geoffrey Boycott

PEOPLE WHO HAD A LUNG REMOVED

Tupac Shakur, Malcolm Allison, Auberon Waugh, Hughie Green, Vaclav Havel, Doug Mountjoy, Link Wray, Stewart Granger, King George VI, Robert Maxwell, Viscount Bernard Montgomery

INSECTS ETC.

Anteaters would rather eat termites.

The world's smallest winged insect is the Tanzanian parasitic wasp, which is smaller than a housefly's eye.

A large swarm of locusts can eat 80,000 tons of corn in a day.

A spider dismantling its web is a sure sign of a storm on the way.

It is said that 80 per cent of the creatures on earth have six legs.

The cockroach is the fastest thing on six legs: it can cover a metre a second.

Blood-sucking hookworms inhabit 700 million people worldwide.

Crickets 'hear' through their knees.

Maggots were once used to treat a bone infection called osteomyelitis.

There are 1 million ants for every person in the world.

The Madagascan hissing cockroach gives birth to live young (rather than laying eggs) – it is one of very few insects to do this.

The Venus flytrap takes less than half a second to slam shut on an insect.

Tarantulas extend and withdraw their legs by controlling the amount of blood pumped into them.

If you put a drop of alcohol on a scorpion, it will go mad and sting itself to death.

Dragonflies can fly at 30 miles per hour, but live for only 24 hours.

A species of earthworm in Australia can grow to 3 metres (about 10 feet) long.

Many hairy caterpillars carry a toxin that can be painful to humans if touched.

On waking, ants stretch and appear to yawn in a very human manner.

From hatching to pupation, a caterpillar increases its body size 30,000 times.

Only full-grown male crickets can chirp.

The largest insect on earth is the South American acteon beetle (*Megasoma acteon*), which measures 9cm by 5cm, and is 4cm thick.

The largest insects that ever lived were giant dragonflies with wingspans of 91cm.

The heaviest insect is the goliath beetle, weighing in at 100 grams.

The neck of the male long-necked weevil is twice as long as its body.

The colour of a head louse can depend on the colour of its human host's hair.

The sound made by bees, mosquitoes and other buzzing insects comes from their rapidly moving wings.

Monarch butterflies regularly migrate beween southern Canada and central Mexico, a distance of 2,500 miles. They weigh 0.5 gram, travel at 20 miles per hour and reach altitudes of 3,000 metres.

A scorpion could withstand 200 times more nuclear radiation than a human could.

Cockroaches like to eat the glue on the back of stamps.

The fastest Lepidoptera are the sphinx moths. They have been recorded at speeds of 60 kilometres (37 miles) per hour.

Mosquito repellents don't repel mosquitoes but rather prevent the mosquitoes from knowing you are there by blocking their sensors.

 Termites will eat your house twice as fast if you play them loud music.

The silkworm, *Bombix mori*, is the only truly domesticated insect. The adult moths are so tame they can barely fly and must be fed by hand. About 10 pounds of mulberry leaves are needed for silkworms to manufacture 1 pound of cocoons, from which can be spun 100 miles of silk thread.

The millipede has approximately 750 legs.

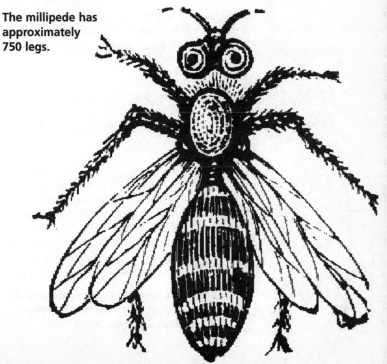

KEEN PAINTERS

Michelle Pfeiffer, Josh Hartnett, Heath Ledger, Marilyn Manson, Pierce Brosnan, Christopher Walken, Arnold Schwarzenegger, Donna Summer, Sir Sean Connery, Dame Beryl Bainbridge, Prince Charles, David Bowie, Eric Cantona, David Bailey, Robbie Coltrane, Will Carling, Cherie Lunghi, Björk, Holly Johnson, Lauren Hill, Sting, Sir Elton John, Peter Gabriel, Sir Cliff Richard, Brian May, Debbie Harry, Jarvis Cocker, Bob Dylan, Graham Coxon, Lulu, Bob Geldof, John Lithgow, Jane Seymour, Jeff Bridges, Viggo Mortensen, Dennis Hopper

GOOD AT DIY

Bill Wyman, Craig Phillips, Daniel Day-Lewis, Dennis Waterman, Nick Knowles, Sandra Bullock, Tim Allen, Adrian Mills

KEEN POKER PLAYERS

Tobey Maguire, Jennifer Aniston, James Woods, Leonardo DiCaprio, Mark Williams, Eric Bristow, Phil Taylor, Stephen Fry, Ricky Gervais, Joan Collins, Guy Ritchie, Vinnie Jones, Salman Rushdie, Michael Owen, Caprice, Claire Goose, Jason Flemyng, Mike Tindall, Samuel West, Zara Phillips

RAILWAY ENTHUSIASTS

Peter Snow, Chris Donald, Jim Bowen, Keith Floyd, Timothy West, Phil Collins, Michael Palin, Pete Waterman, Jools Holland, Rod Stewart (collects Hornby train sets), Patrick Stewart

KEEN SCRABBLE PLAYERS

Jo Brand, Norman Cook (Fatboy Slim), Delia Smith, Jeremy Clarkson, Jonathan Ross, Nicky Haslam, Eno, Ginger Baker, Laura Davies, Guy Ritchie, Ant, Dec, Damon Albarn, Chris Martin, Alistair McGowan, Sean Hughes, Moby

KEEN PHOTOGRAPHERS

Lord Denis Healey, John Suchet, David Suchet, Steven Berkoff, Viggo Mortensen, Michael Bond, Prince Harry, Prince Andrew, Sir Ranulph Fiennes, Karl Lagerfeld, Helena Christensen, Morten Harket, Ben Kay, Bryan Adams, Jamie Theakston, Jeff Bridges, Mary-Kate Olsen, Michael Ancram, Penny Lancaster

Keen ornithologists

Bill Oddie, Norman Lamont, Prince Andrew, Judith Chalmers, Jack Cunningham, Nigel Planer, Magnus Magnusson, Daryl Hall, Bernard Cribbins, Neil Buchanan, Robin Oakley, Kenneth Clarke, Jarvis Cocker, Vic Reeves, Keith Flint

Keen gardeners

Penelope Keith, Sir Michael Caine, Anna Ford, Prunella Scales, Jimmy Greaves, Siân Phillips, Ken Livingstone, Roger Lloyd Pack, Elizabeth Hurley, Lord Michael Heseltine, Edward Fox, Nigel Havers, Sam Neill, Robert Kilroy-Silk, Richard Briers, Trevor Phillips, Hannah Gordon, Susannah York, Lynn Redgrave, Matthew Modine, Jenny Seagrove, Liza Tarbuck

Keen bridge players

Omar Sharif, Alan Coren, Raymond Illingworth, David Nobbs, Maeve Binchy, Joel Cadbury, Nick Ross, Gordon Honeycombe, James Mates, Bruce Critchley, Arnold Palmer, Ian Hislop, Sue Lawley, Angus Deayton, Clive Anderson, Damon Albarn, Honor Fraser, Martina Navratilova, Mike Gatting, Stephen Fry, Sting

Hobbies include sleeping

Terry Jones, Jon Bon Jovi, Jeremy Paxman, Phil Tufnell, Dame Beryl Bainbridge, Jane Corbin, Roy Hudd, Lord St John of Fawsley, Sir Jonathan Miller, Mel Giedroyc, Tim Vincent

Keen cyclists

Madonna, Jon Snow, Brad Pitt, Alexei Sayle, Jeremy Paxman, Boris Johnson, Eva Mendes, Jason Lewis, Matthew Marsden, Mena Suvari, Olivia Williams, Paul Usher, Robin Williams, Woody Harrelson

Keen divers

Anthony Head, Brian May, Brooke Shields, David Hasselhoff, Duncan James, Elijah Wood, Goran Visnjic, Heidi Klum, John Hannah, Josh Brolin, Julianna Margulies, Juliette Binoche, Martin Clunes, Michael Palin, Sir Mick Jagger, Natalie Imbruglia, Natasha Bedingfield, Neil Morrissey, Nick Carter, Pierce Brosnan, Prince Harry, Prince William, Ron Howard, Salma Hayek, Sandra Bullock, Tom Hanks, Val Kilmer

Bungee jumpers

Orlando Bloom, Dominic Monaghan, Jodie Marsh, Prince William, Richard Dunwoody, Robbie Williams

AROUND THE WORLD

In Italy, the entire town of Capena, just north of Rome, lights up cigarettes each year at the Festival of St Anthony. This tradition is centuries old, and even young children take part (though there are now moves to stop the smoking or at least revert to smoking rosemary, the traditional substance).

A difference of almost three inches in height separates the average North Korean seven-year-old from the average South Korean seven-year-old – the South Korean child is the taller.

It is the custom in Morocco for a bride to keep her eyes closed throughout the marriage ceremony.

The province of Alberta in Canada has been completely free of rats since 1905.

The letter 'O' in Irish surnames means 'grandson of'.

There are more Barbie dolls in Italy than Canadians in Canada.

There are more than 15,000 different varieties of rice.

The Amayra guides of Bolivia are said to be able to keep pace with a trotting horse for a distance of 100 kilometres.

In China, the entire population of over a billion shares only about 200 family names.

The Philippine flag is displayed with its blue field at the top in times of peace and the red field at the top in times of war.

The largest employer in the world is the Indian railway system, which employs over a million people.

Where the stones are of equal size, a flawless emerald is worth more than a flawless diamond.

In the Hebrides, what defines an island is the ability of the land to support at least one sheep.

At any one time, 0.7 per cent of the world's population is estimated to be drunk.

In Lima, Peru, there is a large brass statue of Winnie the Pooh – even though it's Paddington Bear who came from Peru.

Aircraft are not allowed to fly over the Taj Mahal.

The harmonica is the world's most popular musical instrument.

It used to be against the law in Swiss cities to slam the car door.

About 5,000 languages are spoken on earth.

After oil, coffee is the most traded commodity in the world.

More than a hundred cars can drive side by side on the Monumental Axis in Brazil, the world's widest road.

Panama hats come from Ecuador.

Soldiers from every country salute with their right hand.

Bulgarians eat more yogurt than anyone else.

The Tibetan mountain people use yak's milk as a form of currency.

Churches in Malta show two different (wrong) times in order to confuse the devil.

ECCENTRIC EVENTS FROM AROUND THE WORLD

The World Wife Carrying Championships (Finland)

World Screaming Championships (Poland)

World Mosquito Killing Championship (Finland)

Stilton Cheese Rolling Competition (Stilton, Cambridgeshire)

World Nettle Eating Championships (Marshwood, Dorset)

Air Guitar World Championships (Finland)

World Walking The Plank Championships (Isle of Sheppey, Kent)

World Bog Snorkelling Championships (Llanwrtyd Wells, Wales)

World Gurning Championships (Egremont, Cumbria)

The Munich Festival Beer Drinking Challenge (Germany)

Polar Bear Jump Off (Alaska, USA)

World Pea Throwing Competition (Lewes, East Sussex)

Trie-sur-Baïse Pig Screaming Championship (France)

Odalengo Truffle Hunting Competition (Italy)

Biggest Liar In The World Competition (Santon Bridge, Cumbria)

Kiruna Snowball Throwing Contest (Sweden)

Burning Tar Barrels (Ottery St Mary, Devon)

Australia Day Cockroach Races (Australia)

Annual Roadkill Cook-off (West Virginia, USA)

Tuna Throwing (Australia)

Goat Racing (Pennsylvania, USA)

World Worm Charming Championships (Nantwich, Cheshire)

World Shovel Race Championships (New Mexico, USA)

Penny Farthing World Championships (Tasmania)

The Great Mushroom Hunt Championships (Illinois, USA)

Annual Bat Flight Breakfast (New Mexico, USA)

Bognor Birdman Competition (Bognor Regis, West Sussex)

The Great Tomato Fight (Spain)

Summer Redneck Games (Georgia, USA – includes spitball bug zapping, hubcap hurling, watermelonseed spitting, bobbing for pigs' feet and the mud pit bellyflop)

World's Championship Duck Calling Contest and Wings Over The Prairie Festival (Arkansas, USA)

Annual World Elephant Polo Association Championships (Kathmandu, Nepal)

Scarecrow Festival (Wray, Lancashire)

THE WIT OF OSCAR WILDE

'The only thing to do with good advice is pass it on. It is never any use to oneself.'

'Experience is the name everyone gives to their mistakes.'

'Illness of any kind is hardly a thing to be encouraged in others. Health is the primary duty of life.'

'Fashion is a form of ugliness so intolerable that we have to alter it every six months.'

'I am not young enough to know everything.'

'I think that God in creating Man somewhat overestimated his ability.'

'Seriousness is the only refuge of the shallow.'

'It is better to have a permanent income than to be fascinating.'

'Whenever people agree with me I always feel I must be wrong.'

'A little sincerity is a dangerous thing, and a great deal of it is absolutely fatal.'

'To disagree with three-fourths of the British public is one of the first requisites of sanity.'

'Only dull people are brilliant at breakfast.'

'It is absurd to divide people into good and bad. People are either charming or tedious.'

'One should always play fairly when one has the winning cards.'

'Anybody can sympathize with the sufferings of a friend, but it requires a very fine nature to sympathize with a friend's success.'

'We're all in the gutter, but some of us are looking at the stars.'

GEOGRAPHY

The surface of the Dead Sea is 400 metres below the surface of the Mediterranean Sea.

Every gallon of seawater holds more than 100 grams (about 4oz) of salt.

20 per cent of the land's surface is desert.

As a result of precipitation, for a few weeks every year K2 is bigger than Everest.

Finland has more islands than any other country: 179,584.

Five hundred million years ago, Antarctica was on the equator.

More than 75 per cent of the countries in the world are north of the equator.

Two minor earthquakes occur every minute.

Sahara means 'desert' in Arabic.

The largest iceberg ever recorded was larger than Belgium. It was 200 miles long and 60 miles wide.

Five countries in Europe touch only one other: Portugal, Denmark, San Marino, Vatican City and Monaco.

The US national anthem doesn't mention the name of the country; neither does the Dutch one. (In fact, you have to find an ancient and no longer sung verse of God Save The Queen to find any mention of Britain.)

The Swiss flag is square.

Less than 2 per cent of the water on earth is fresh.

Canada derives its name from an Indian word meaning 'big village'.

The oldest exposed surface on earth is New Zealand's South Island.

England is smaller than New England.

The Eiffel Tower has 2.5 million rivets, 1,792 steps and can vary in height (according to the temperature) by as much as 15cm (6 inches).

If the earth were smooth, the ocean would cover the entire surface to a depth of 3,700 metres (12,000 feet).

The earth's surface area is 197,000,000 square miles.

2,000 pounds of space dust and other debris lands on earth every day.

The forests on Kauai in Hawaii are fertilized by dust from the deserts of China, 9,660 miles away.

It would take about 3,085,209,600,000 rolls of wallpaper to cover the Sahara.

The African baobab tree is pollinated by bats and its blossom opens only to moonlight.

The name of Spain comes from

DEBERNY

A sizeable oak tree gives off 28,000 gallons of moisture during the growing season.

The national anthem of the Netherlands, the 'Wilhelmus', takes the form of an acrostic. The first letters of each of the fifteen verses represent the name 'Willem Van Nassov', or William of Orange. It is also the oldest anthem in the world.

Olympus Mons on Mars is the largest volcano in our solar system.

In May 1948, Mount Ruapehu and Mount Ngauruhoe, both in New Zealand, erupted simultaneously.

The Indonesian island of Sumatra has the world's largest flower: the *Rafflesia arnoldi*, which can grow to the size of an umbrella.

South Africa produces two-thirds of the world's gold.

The Angel falls in Venezuela are nearly 20 times taller than Niagara falls.

'the land of rabbits'.

ALL THE UK OVERSEAS TERRITORIES

Anguilla

Bermuda

British Antarctic Territory (BAT)

British Indian Ocean Territory (BIOT)

British Virgin Islands (BVI)

Cayman Islands

Falkland Islands

Gibraltar

Montserrat

Pitcairn Islands

St Helena and its Dependencies (Ascension Island and Tristan da Cunha)

South Georgia and the South Sandwich Islands

The Sovereign Base Areas of Akrotiri and Dhekelia in Cyprus

The Turks and Caicos Islands (TCI)

TODAY THERE ARE ABOUT 6,486,000,000 PEOPLE ON OUR PLANET ...

Here are the best projections for the future:

2006: 6,581,000,000

2007: 6,676,000,000

2008: 6,773,000,000

2009: 6,872,000,000

2010: 6,972,000,000

2015: 7,494,000,000

2020: 8,056,000,000

2025: 8,660,000,000

2030: 9,308,000,000

2035: 10,006,000,000

WORDS

The word 'had' can be used eleven times in a row in the following sentence about two boys, John and Steve, who had written similar sentences in their essays: John, where Steve had had 'had', had had 'had had'; 'had had' had had the higher mark.

The word 'and' can be used five times in a row in the following sentence about a sign being painted above a shop called Jones And Son: Mr Jones looks at the sign and says to the painter, 'I would like bigger gaps between Jones and and, and and and Son.'

The words loosen and unloosen mean the same thing.

'Hippopotomonstrosesquippedaliophobia' is the fear of long words.

 We get the expression 'nosy parker' from Matthew Parker who was Archbishop of Canterbury in the 16th century. He had a very long nose and was extremely inquisitive – hence Nosy Parker.

The first letters of the months July to November spell the name JASON.

The word 'samba' means 'to rub navels together'.

Cerumen is the technical term for earwax.

The oldest word in the English language is 'town'.

The word 'coffee' came from Arabic and meant 'excitement'.

The word 'voodoo' comes from a West African word that means 'spirit' or 'deity' and has no negative connotations.

'Crack' gets its name from the crackling sound it makes when smoked.

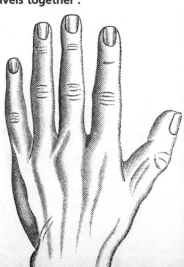

'Alma mater' means 'bountiful mother'.

The youngest letters in the English language are 'j', 'v' and 'w'.

The word 'diastema' describes a gap between the front teeth.

The stars and colours you see when you rub your eyes are called phosphenes.

No word in the English language rhymes with pint, diamond or purple.

The magic word 'abracadabra' was originally intended for the specific purpose of curing hay fever.

John Milton used 8,000 different words in *Paradise Lost*.

The word 'monosyllable' has five syllables.

The names for the numbers 'eleven' and 'twelve' in English come from the Anglo-Saxon for 'one left' (*aend-lefene*) and 'two left' (*twa-lefene*). They represented going back to your left hand and starting again after reaching ten counting on your fingers.

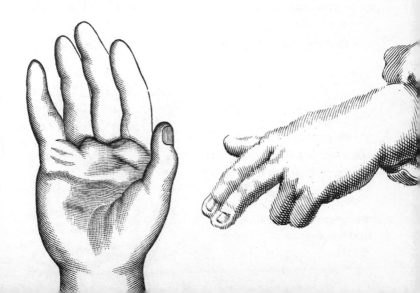

The phrase 'sleep tight' originated when ropes round a wooden frame were used to support a mattress. Sagging ropes could be tightened with a bed key.

Ten human body parts are only three letters long: eye, hip, arm, leg, ear, toe, jaw, rib, lip, gum.

The word 'lethologica' describes the state of forgetting the word you want.

The word 'mafia' was created as an acronym for *Morte alla francia italia adela*, meaning 'Death to the French is Italy's cry'.

The suffix 'ology' means the study of something. The shortest 'ology' is 'oology' – the study of eggs.

The word 'starboard' is derived from the Old English word for the paddle that Vikings used on the right side of their ships to steer: *steorbord*.

PEOPLE WHO HAVE SUFFERED FROM DYSLEXIA

Salma Hayek, Keira Knightley, Ozzy Osbourne, Jamie Oliver, Ruth Madoc, Lord Michael Heseltine, Duncan Goodhew, General George Patton, James Hewitt, Brian Conley, Sid Owen, Sir Steve Redgrave, Sonique, Richie Neville, Princess Beatrice

THE MOST BEAUTIFUL WORDS IN THE ENGLISH LANGUAGE?

In 2004, to mark its 70th anniversary, the British Council polled seven thousand people in 46 countries to ask them what they considered to be the most beautiful words in the English language. There was also an online poll that attracted over 35,000 votes. Here are the results:

1 mother	13 sunshine
2 passion	**14 sweetheart**
3 smile	15 gorgeous
4 love	**16 cherish**
5 eternity	17 enthusiasm
6 fantastic	**18 hope**
7 destiny	19 grace
8 freedom	**20 rainbow**
9 liberty	21 blue
10 tranquillity	**22 sunflower**
11 peace	23 twinkle
12 blossom	**24 serendipity**

25 bliss

26 lullaby

27 sophisticated

28 renaissance

29 cute

30 cosy

31 butterfly

32 galaxy

33 hilarious

34 moment

35 extravaganza

36 aqua

37 sentiment

38 cosmopolitan

39 bubble

40 pumpkin

41 banana

42 lollipop

43 if

44 bumblebee

45 giggle

46 paradox

47 delicacy

48 peek-a-boo

49 umbrella

50 kangaroo

51 flabbergasted

52 hippopotamus

53 gothic

54 coconut

55 smashing

56 whoops

57 tickle

58 loquacious

59 flip-flop

60 smithereens

61 oi

62 gazebo

63 hiccup

64 hodgepodge

65 shipshape

66 explosion

67 fuselage

68 zing

69 gum

70 hen-night

NAA

LOST IN TRANSLATION

According to a poll of a thousand translators, the most untranslatable word in the world is ILUNGA, from the Bantu language of Tshiluba, and means a person ready to forgive an abuse the first time, tolerate it the second time, but neither the third time. The runners-up were:

SHLIMAZL Yiddish for a chronically unlucky person

RADIOUKACZ Polish for a person who worked as a telegrapher for the resistance movements on the Soviet side of the Iron Curtain

NAA Japanese word used only in Kansai area of Japan for emphasis or to agree with someone

ALTAHMAM Arabic for a kind of deep sadness

GEZELLIG Dutch for cosy

SAUDADE Portuguese for a certain type of longing

SELATHIRUPAVAR Tamil for a certain type of truancy

POCHEMUCHKA Russian for a person who asks a lot of questions

KLLOSHAR loser in Albanian

PANGRAMS

The quick brown fox jumps over a lazy dog

Xylophone wizard begets quick jive form

Wet squid's inky haze veils sex of jumping crab

Jackdaws love my big sphinx of quartz

Pack my box with five dozen liquor jugs

The five boxing wizards jump quickly

Quick wafting zephyrs vex bold Jim

Mr Jock, TV quiz PhD, bags few lynx

Six plump boys guzzling cheap raw vodka quite joyfully

XV quick nymphs beg fjord waltz

PALINDROMES

Some men interpret nine memos

Star comedy by Democrats

We panic in a pew

Won't lovers revolt now?

Step on no pets

No, it is opposition

Live not on evil

Was it a car or a cat I saw?

Never odd or even

Sex at noon taxes

Able was I ere I saw Elba

Nurse, I spy gypsies – run!

Pull up if I pull up

Madam, I'm Adam

A nut for a jar of tuna

A Santa lived as a devil at NASA

A Toyota

Race fast, safe car

A slut nixes sex in Tulsa

Desserts, I stressed

Doom an evil deed, liven a mood

Not New York, Roy went on

Rot can rob a born actor

**Sit on a
potato pan,
Otis**

People who've been 'inside'

James Brown (carrying a gun and assault in 1988 – served 2 years; he had also served 3 years for theft when he was a teenager)

Ozzy Osbourne (burglary – 2 months in 1966)

Glen Campbell (sentenced to 10 days for drink-driving in 2004)

Don King (manslaughter in 1966 – served 3 years 11 months)

Zsa Zsa Gabor (slapping a cop – 3 days in 1989)

Kelsey Grammer (drugs – 2 weeks in jail for not doing the community service imposed for his offence in 1988)

George Best (drink-driving – 12 weeks in 1984)

Sean Penn (assault and violation of a probation order for an earlier assault – 32 days in 1987)

Chuck Berry (violating the Mann Act by taking a girl across state borders for 'immoral purposes' – 2 years in 1962)

Ryan O'Neal (brawling – served 51 days in 1960)

Stephen Fry (stealing credit cards – spent 3 months in a young offenders' institution in 1975)

Sir Paul McCartney (drugs – 9 days in Japan in 1980)

Evel Knievel (assault in 1977 – served 6 months)

Christian Slater (attacking policemen under the influence of cocaine – 3 months in 1997)

Oliver Stone (drugs – 2 weeks in 1969 while waiting to be tried for possession of marijuana)

Taki (drugs – served 3 months in 1984/5)

Robert Downey Jnr (drugs – sentenced to 6 months in 1997)

Nick Nolte (reckless driving – 30 nights in jail while at college, though he was released during the day to practise his football)

Stacy Keach (drugs – sentenced to 6 months in 1984)

Gregg Allman (drink-driving – served 3 days in 1986)

Jimmy Nail (GBH – 6 months in 1977)

Hugh Cornwell (drugs – 5 weeks in 1980)

Wilson Pickett (drink-driving and causing injury – served a year in 1992)

Mark Morrison (threatening a policeman – served 3 months in 1997, and sentenced to a year in 1998 for getting an impostor to do his community service)

David Crosby (drugs and possession of an illegal weapon – sentenced in 1983 to 5 years but served about a year and a half)

Johnny Vaughan (drugs – 4 years in 1988)

Anthony Newley (served a month in jail for driving while disqualified)

Muhammad Ali (one week in jail in 1968 for driving without a licence. He was sentenced in 1967 to 5 years in jail for refusing to serve in the army, but he challenged the verdict, it was overturned and he didn't spend any time in jail for it)

Ricky Tomlinson (served 2 years for conspiracy to intimidate other builders during picket-line violence in 1972)

Tim Allen (served 28 months in jail in 1978 for attempting to sell cocaine)

Mark Wahlberg (convicted at the age of 16 for his part in a robbery in which 2 Vietnamese were beaten – he served 45 days in jail)

Barry White (at the age of 16, for stealing tyres)

David Dickinson (at the age of 19, for mail-order fraud)

Jeffrey Archer (sentenced to 4 years in 2001 for perjury and perverting the course of justice)

Isaac Hayes (in 1989 for failing to pay alimony and child support)

CELEBRITIES WHO SHOPLIFTED

Michael Winner ('I stole from shops and from pupils at school')

Nick Ross (admitted shoplifting at his local Woolworth in Wallington, Surrey)

Farrah Fawcett (was twice arrested for shoplifting in LA before she was famous and was fined £280 – although she claimed that she was acting in revenge because the stores in question refused to take back defective goods)

Liam Gallagher (spent a volatile childhood shoplifting – as disclosed on a TV documentary)

Noel Gallagher (in the same documentary, Noel pointed out where he got nicked for shoplifting)

Tracy Shaw (stole from stores in Belper without realizing what she was doing. Was caught three times – including once with 99p-worth of strawberries – but was let off with warnings. 'Shoplifting is associated with anorexia')

Quentin Tarantino (as a teenager, stole an Elmore Leonard novel from a local store)

Roseanne

Julie Burchill

Jeremy Beadle

Groucho Marx

Alan Davies (as a kid)

Hedy Lamarr

Steve Strange (caught stealing a £10.99 Teletubbies doll)

Bruce Oldfield (sweets in Woolworth)

Mark Lamarr (shoplifted in his hometown of Swindon. 'One of the older punks would say he needed a new T-shirt so I'd just walk into a shop and nick one')

Béatrice Dalle (in 1992, she was given a six-month suspended sentence for shoplifting £3,000-worth of jewellery in Paris)

Rufus Sewell (stole records in Woolworth and, as a starving drama student, was caught stealing food)

John Lennon (shoplifted the harmonica he used on *Love Me Do* in Holland)

Jill Clayburgh (caught stealing at Bloomingdale's)

Courtney Love (in her early teens, she stole a Kiss T-shirt from a department store and was sent to a juvenile detention centre)

Jennifer Capriati

Winona Ryder (she claimed she was trying out a role. So how does she explain the stories going around LA that she has been caught several times before – only by shops who were less keen to press charges against someone so famous?)

Patsy Palmer (she was once caught stealing toys from Hamleys. 'We was nicking all these toys and they caught us. They gave us a warning. I don't know how we got away with it.')

Fiona Phillips (given a police caution for stealing cosmetics from Boots when she was a schoolgirl)

Goldie (Burton's)

Tom Jones (he and his friends would nick singles from record shops: 'In those days, all the records used to be on display and, as a gang, we would buy one and come out with six or seven')

Zoë Ball ('I used to shoplift quite a lot – just chocolate and stuff like that. I still feel bad about nicking a Marathon bar from a baker's shop when I was eight or nine. A woman caught me, but my parents never found about it')

Jade Goody

Chris Eubank ('from the age of 14 to 16, I was one of the best shoplifters in London')

Claire Sweeney (a chocolate bar from a shop when she was eight)

PEOPLE JAILED FOR TAX EVASION

Lester Piggott (1 year in 1987)

Al Capone (11 years in 1931)

Sophia Loren (17 days in 1982)

Chuck Berry (4 months in 1979)

Leona Helmsley (hotelier; 4 years in 1990)

Allen Klein (former Beatles manager; 2 months in 1979)

Marvin Mitchelson (American divorce lawyer; 2 years, 6 months in 1993)

Rev. Sun Myung Moon (14 months in 1984)

Aldo Gucci (fashion boss; 1 year in 1986)

Peter Max (artist; 2 months in 1998)

Maria O'Sullivan (Ronnie's mother; 7 months in 1995)

PEOPLE WHO HAD THEIR ROLEX WATCHES STOLEN

Britt Ekland, Alexandra Heseltine, Michael Green, Bernie Ecclestone, Jilly Johnson, Caprice, Steve Norris, Gary Mabbutt, Gwen Humble, Lesley Clarke (Mrs Nicky Clarke), Julian Clary, Ian Wright

PEOPLE WHO WERE ARRESTED

Hugh Grant (for performing a 'lewd act' with Divine Brown in 1995 – he was fined and given two years' probation)

Brigitte Bardot (for castrating a donkey that was trying to mount her donkey – later she was not only discharged but was also awarded costs against the plaintiff)

Johnny Depp (for trashing a hotel suite in 1994 – he agreed to pay for the damage)

Billy Preston (for drink-driving and cocaine possession – given a suspended jail sentence and probation in 1992)

Johnny Cash (for being drunk and disorderly many times in the early 1960s)

Jodie Foster (for possession of cocaine – given a year's probation in 1983)

Harry Connick Jr (for having a gun in his luggage at New York's JFK airport)

Brian de Palma (for stealing a motorcycle and for resisting arrest – he was given a suspended sentence in 1963)

Carlos Santana (for marijuana possession – community service in 1991)

Paul Reubens (aka Pee-Wee Herman; for 'indecent exposure' in a cinema – he was fined and ordered to do community service)

Sean P. Diddy Combs (for possession of a firearm after a shooting incident in a bar in 1999) and Jennifer Lopez (arrested in the same incident and held in jail for 16 hours before being released without charge)

Chrissie Hynde (for demonstrating for animal rights in 2000. She used a knife to tear into leather and suede clothes in a Gap shop window in New York)

Jason Priestley (for drink-driving)

Vanilla Ice (after being accused of attacking his wife during a row in a car in 2001; he spent a night in jail in Florida)

Jennifer Capriati (for possession of marijuana in 1994; she was arrested in a hotel room and spent 23 days in a rehabilitation clinic)

PEOPLE WITH FATHERS WHO HAVE BEEN IN JAIL

Matt Lucas (John Lucas – fraud)

Ronnie O'Sullivan (Ronnie O'Sullivan Sr – murder)

Keanu Reeves (Samuel Reeves – drugs)

Heather Mills (John Mills – fraud)

Woody Harrelson (Charles Harrelson – murder)

Steffi Graf (Peter Graf – tax evasion)

Tatum O'Neal (Ryan O'Neal – brawling)

Lorraine Chase (Charlie 'Scarface' Parsons – robbery)

Patsy Kensit (Jimmy 'The Dip' Kensit – pickpocketing)

Stella McCartney (Sir Paul McCartney – drugs)

Brittany Murphy (Angelo Bertolotti – a convicted mobster. After three jail sentences he's alleged to have said: 'I got friends who make Tony Soprano look like an altar boy')

Jade Goody (Andrew Goody – robbery)

PEOPLE WHO HAD COMPUTER VIRUSES NAMED AFTER THEM

Osama bin Laden, Avril Lavigne, Michelangelo, Leela Zahir, Tonya Harding

THE BIBLE

The word 'and' appears in the Bible 46,277 times.

The longest name in the Old Testament is Mahershalalhashbaz.

The book of Esther in the Bible is the only book that doesn't mention the name of God.

The chapters in the New Testament weren't there originally. When medieval monks translated the Bible from the Greek, they divided it into chapters.

Scholars believe that what we now read as 'forty', in Aramaic meant 'many'. So that 'forty days', for example, simply meant many days.

THE HUMAN CONDITION

Your feet are bigger in the afternoon than at any other time of day.

The average talker sprays 300 microscopic saliva droplets per minute, about 2.5 droplets per word.

A foetus acquires fingerprints at the age of 3 months.

The Neanderthal's brain was bigger than yours is.

The human body has 600 muscles, which make up 40 per cent of the body's weight. We use 300 of these muscles to stand still. We need 72 muscles to speak. If all 600 muscles in your body pulled in one direction, you could lift 25 tons.

A nail grows from base to tip in about 6 months.

Every human spent about half an hour as a single cell.

Beards have the fastest-growing hair on the human body. If a man never trimmed his beard, it could grow to over 9 metres (30 feet) in his lifetime.

One human hair can support 3 kilograms (over 6 1/2 pounds).

The average man's speed of sperm emission is 11 miles (18 kilometres) per hour.

Every square inch of the human body has an average of 32 million bacteria on it.

Six-year-olds laugh about 300 times a day. Adults laugh about 15 times a day.

The attachment of the skin to muscles is what causes dimples.

Kidneys filter about 500 gallons of blood each day.

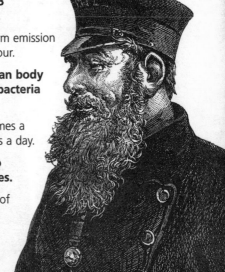

One in every 2,000 babies is born with a tooth.

The largest cell in a woman is the ovum. The smallest cell in a man is the sperm.

The most common blood type in the world is type O. The rarest, A-H, has been found in fewer than a dozen people since the type was discovered.

The tendency towards ingrown toenails is hereditary.

The most sensitive finger is the forefinger.

Weight for weight, men are stronger than horses.

The digestive tract is more than 9 metres (about 30 feet) long.

The ashes of the average cremated person weigh 4 kilograms (9 pounds).

Blood makes up about 8 per cent of the body's weight.

Due to gravitational effects, you weigh slightly less when the moon is directly overhead.

Every year about 98 per cent of the atoms in your body are replaced.

The entire length of all the eyelashes shed in a lifetime is about 30 metres (100 feet).

Your skull is made up of 29 different bones.

Hair is made from the same substance as fingernails.

Each square inch (2.5cm) of human skin contains 20 feet (6 metres) of blood vessels.

During a 24-hour period, the average human breathes 23,040 times.

The sound you hear when you put a shell to your ear is not the sea but blood flowing through your head.

Jaw muscles can provide about 200 pounds of force for chewing.

The human brain has about 100 billion nerve cells. Nerve impulses travel to and from the brain as fast as 170 miles (274 kilometres) per hour.

If you unfolded your brain, it would cover an ironing board. The more wrinkles your brain has, the more intelligent you are.

Alcohol does not kill brain cells, but detaches them. Reattachment would require new nervous tissue, which cannot be produced after about the age of five.

Your skin weighs twice as much as your brain.

There are 450 hairs in an average eyebrow.

The human brain stops growing at about the age of 18.

Your foot is the same length as the distance between your wrist and your elbow.

The chemicals in a human body are estimated to have a combined worth of 6.25 euro.

It's physically impossible to lick your elbow.

A cough comes out of your mouth at about 60 miles (96.5 kilometres) per hour.

STARS AND THEIR FIRST FILMS

Dame Julie Andrews – *Mary Poppins* (1964)

Dan Aykroyd – *1941* (1979)

Lauren Bacall – *To Have And Have Not* (1943)

Drew Barrymore – *Altered States* (1980)

Ned Beatty – *Deliverance* (1972)

Warren Beatty – *Splendor In The Grass* (1961)

Hywel Bennett – *The Family Way* (1966)

Orlando Bloom – *Wilde* (1997)

Helena Bonham Carter – *Lady Jane* (1984)

Marlon Brando – *The Men* (1950)

James Caan – *Irma La Douce* (1963)

Nicolas Cage – *Fast Times At Ridgemont High* (1982)

Sir Sean Connery – *No Road Back* (1955)

Tom Cruise – *Endless Love* (1981)

Willem Dafoe – *Heaven's Gate* (1980)

Robert De Niro – *The Wedding Party* (1963)

Johnny Depp – *A Nightmare On Elm Street* (1984)

Danny DeVito – *Dreams of Glass* (1968)

Clint Eastwood – *Revenge of The Creature* (1955)

Jane Fonda – *Tall Story* (1960)

Richard Gere – *Report To The Commissioner* (1975)

Whoopi Goldberg – *The Color Purple* (1985)

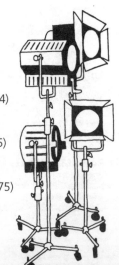

Jeff Goldblum – *Death Wish* (1974)

Hugh Grant – *Privileged* (1982 – credited as 'Hughie Grant')

Melanie Griffith – *The Harrad Experiment* (1973)

Gene Hackman – *Mad Dog Coll* (1961)

Goldie Hawn – *The One And Only Genuine Original Family Band* (1968)

Dustin Hoffman – *The Tiger Makes Out* (1967)

Sir Anthony Hopkins – *The Lion In Winter* (1968)

Holly Hunter – *The Burning* (1981)

William Hurt – *Altered States* (1980)

Anjelica Huston – *Sinful Davey* (1968)

Jeremy Irons – *Nijinsky* (1980)

Scarlett Johansson – *North* (1994)

Michael Keaton – *Night Shift* (1982)

Kevin Kline – *Sophie's Choice* (1982)

Keira Knightley – *A Village Affair* (1994)

Lindsay Lohan – *The Parent Trap* (1998)

Jennifer Lopez – *My Little Girl* (1986)

Rob Lowe – *The Outsiders* (1983)

Shirley Maclaine – *The Trouble With Harry* (1955)

Tobey Maguire – *The Wizard* (1989)

Steve Martin – *Sgt Pepper's Lonely Hearts Club Band* (1978)

Bette Midler – *Hawaii* (1965)

Sarah Miles – *Term of Trial* (1962)

Liza Minnelli – *Charlie Bubbles* (1968)

Eddie Murphy – *48 Hours* (1982)

Paul Newman – *The Silver Chalice* (1954)

Al Pacino – *Me, Natalie* (1969)

Sean Penn – *Taps* (1981)

Robert Redford – *War Hunt* (1961)

Keanu Reeves – *Youngblood* (1986)

Dame Diana Rigg – *The Assassination Bureau* (1968)

Julia Roberts – *Blood Red* (1986)

Cybill Shepherd – *The Last Picture Show* (1971)

Sylvester Stallone – *A Party At Kitty And Stud's* (1970)

Terence Stamp – *Billy Budd* (1962)

Sharon Stone – *Stardust Memories* (1980)

Barbra Streisand – *Funny Girl* (1968)

Meryl Streep – *Julia* (1977)

Donald Sutherland – *The World Ten Times Over* (1963)

Lily Tomlin – *Nashville* (1975)

John Travolta – *The Devil's Rain* (1975)

Kathleen Turner – *Body Heat* (1981)

Jon Voight – *The Hour of The Gun* (1967)

Orson Welles – *Citizen Kane* (1941)

Robin Williams – *Popeye* (1980)

Bruce Willis – *Blind Date* (1987)

Sir Norman Wisdom – *Trouble In Store* (1953)

Susannah York – *Tunes of Glory* (1960)

ACTORS WITHOUT A SINGLE OSCAR BETWEEN THEM*

Gene Kelly, Steve McQueen, Cary Grant, Glenn Ford, James Mason, Stewart Granger, Charles Boyer, Anthony Quayle, Montgomery Clift, Kirk Douglas, Greta Garbo, Agnes Moorehead, Carole Lombard, Barbara Stanwyck, Lana Turner, Judy Garland, Lee Remick, Natalie Wood, Rita Hayworth, Gloria Swanson

*Apart from honorary Oscars

ACTORS WITHOUT EVEN A SINGLE OSCAR NOMINATION BETWEEN THEM

Al Jolson, Tallulah Bankhead, Audie Murphy, Yvonne De Carlo, Errol Flynn, Hedy Lamarr, Sir Dirk Bogarde, Raquel Welsh, Boris Karloff, Veronica Lake, Olivia Hussey, Glenn Ford, Jacqueline Bisset, Martin Sheen, Dorothy Lamour, Peter Cushing, Brigitte Bardot, Roger Moore, Jane Russell, Harry Belafonte

ALL THE YEARS WHEN ENGLISH LANGUAGE FILMS WON THE PALME D'OR AT THE CANNES FILM FESTIVAL

2004 *Fahrenheit 9/11*

2003 *Elephant*

2002 *The Pianist*

1996 *Secrets and Lies*

1994 *Pulp Fiction*

1993 *The Piano*

1991 *Barton Fink*

1990 *Wild at Heart*

1989 *Sex, Lies and Videotape*

1986 *The Mission*

1984 *Paris, Texas*

1982 *Missing*

1980 *All That Jazz*

1979 *Apocalypse Now*

1976 *Taxi Driver*

1974 *The Conversation*

1973 *Scarecrow and The Hireling*

1971 *The Go-Between*

1970 *M*A*S*H*

1969 *If...*

1967 *Blow-Up*

1965 *The Knack … And How to Get It*

1957 *Friendly Persuasion*

1955 *Marty*

1949 *The Third Man*

PEOPLE WHOSE NAMES APPEARED IN FILM TITLES

John Malkovich – *Being John Malkovich* (2000)

Greta Garbo – *Garbo Talks* (1984)

Brigitte Bardot – *Dear Brigitte* (1965)

Bela Lugosi – *Bela Lugosi Meets A Brooklyn Gorilla* (1952)

Douglas Fairbanks – *F As In Fairbanks* (1975)

Fred Astaire – *The Curse of Fred Astaire* (1984)

Ginger Rogers – *Ginger And Fred* (1986)

James Dean – *Come Back To The Five And Dime, Jimmy Dean, Jimmy Dean* (1982)

Humphrey Bogart – *The Man With Bogart's Face* (1980)

Clark Gable – *The Woman Who Married Clark Gable* (1985)

Errol Flynn – *In Like Flynn* (1985)

David Beckham – *Bend It Like Beckham* (2002)

Pete Tong – *It's All Gone Pete Tong* (2004)

UNCREDITED MOVIE APPEARANCES

Paula Abdul (in *Can't Buy Me Love* – as a cheerleader)

Steve Buscemi (in *Pulp Fiction* – as a waiter)

Cyd Charisse (in *Ziegfeld Follies* – as a dancer)

Don Cheadle (in *Rush Hour 2* and *Ocean's Eleven* – both times as a criminal)

Phil Daniels (in *Bugsy Malone* – as a waiter)

Richard Dreyfuss (in *The Graduate* – as a student)

Kirsten Dunst (in *The Day After Tomorrow* – as a student)

Leif Garrett (in *Bob and Carol and Ted and Alice* – as the son of Dyan Cannon and Elliott Gould)

Charlton Heston (in the 2001 remake of *Planet of The Apes*)

Jason Isaacs (in *Resident Evil* as Dr Birkin)

Steve McQueen (in *Dixie Dynamite* as a motorcyclist)

Christian Slater (in *Austin Powers: International Man of Mystery* as a security guard)

Jaclyn Smith (in *Charlie's Angels: Full Throttle* as Kelly Garrett, her character in the original TV series)

ACTRESSES WHO SHAVED THEIR HEADS FOR ROLES

Persis Khambatta (*Star Trek: The Motion Picture* 1979)

Emma Thompson (*Wit* 2001)

Vanessa Redgrave (*Playing For Time* 1980)

Demi Moore (*G.I. Jane* 1997)

Sigourney Weaver (*Alien III* 1992)

Dervla Kirwan (*The Dark Room* 1998)

Alison Lohman (*Dragonfly* 2002 – though her scenes were cut)

Natalie Portman (*V For Vendetta* 2005)

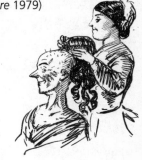

ALL THE WINNERS OF THE AMERICAN FILM INSTITUTE'S LIFETIME ACHIEVEMENT AWARD

Meryl Streep 2004

Robert De Niro 2003

Tom Hanks 2002

Barbra Streisand 2001

Harrison Ford 2000

Dustin Hoffman 1999

Robert Wise 1998

Martin Scorsese 1997

Clint Eastwood 1996

Steven Spielberg 1995

Jack Nicholson 1994

Elizabeth Taylor 1993

Sidney Poitier 1992

Kirk Douglas 1991

David Lean 1990

Gregory Peck 1989

Jack Lemmon 1988

Barbara Stanwyck 1987

Billy Wilder 1986

Gene Kelly 1985

Lillian Gish 1984

John Huston 1983

Frank Capra 1982

Fred Astaire 1981

James Stewart 1980

Alfred Hitchcock 1979

Henry Fonda 1978

Bette Davis 1977

William Wyler 1976

Orson Welles 1975

James Cagney 1974

John Ford 1973

PEOPLE WHO WROTE/CO-WROTE SCREENPLAYS

Jack Nicholson (*Head*)

Melvyn Bragg (*Isadora*)

Martin Amis (*Saturn 3*)

Erich Segal (*Yellow Submarine*)

John Wells (*Princess Caraboo*)

George MacDonald Fraser (*Octopussy*)

Roald Dahl (*You Only Live Twice*)

Christopher Logue (*Savage Messiah*)

Denis Norden (*Buona Sera, Mrs Campbell*)

Mike Sarne (*The Lightship*)

Paul Theroux (*Saint Jack*)

Clare Boothe Luce (*Come To The Stable*)

ACTRESSES WHO TESTED FOR THE ROLE OF SCARLETT O'HARA IN *GONE WITH THE WIND*

Lana Turner	**Claudette Colbert**
Bette Davis	Katharine Hepburn
Norma Shearer	**Loretta Young**
Miriam Hopkins	Jean Harlow
Tallulah Bankhead	**Carole Lombard**

PEOPLE WHO HAVE PLAYED GOD IN FILMS OR ON TV

Morgan Freeman (*Bruce Almighty* 2003)

James Garner (*God, The Devil And Bob* 2000)

Alanis Morissette (*Dogma* 1999)

Robbie Fowler (*Soccer AM* 1994)

Marianne Faithfull (*Absolutely Fabulous* 1992)

Robert Morley (*Second Time Lucky* 1984)

George Burns (*Oh, God!* 1977)

Groucho Marx (*Skidoo* 1968)

Valentine Dyall (*Bedazzled* 1967)

Martin Sheen (*Insight* 1960)

POP/ROCK GROUPS THAT APPEARED IN FILMS

All Saints – *Honest* (2000)

The Spice Girls – *Spiceworld The Movie* (1997)

Madness – *Take It Or Leave It* (1981)

The Sex Pistols – *The Great Rock 'N' Roll Swindle* (1980)

The Who – *The Kids Are Alright* (1979)

Led Zeppelin – *The Song Remains The Same* (1976)

Slade – *Flame* (1975)

T-Rex – *Born To Boogie* (1972)

The Monkees – *Head* (1968)

Gerry and The Pacemakers – *Ferry Cross The Mersey* (1965)

The Beatles – *Hard Day's Night* (1964) etc

Bill Haley and His Comets – *Rock Around The Clock* (1956)

THE *SIGHT AND SOUND* POLLS

Every ten years since 1952, the British Film Institute's magazine *Sight and Sound* has asked distinguished movie critics to vote for the greatest film of all time. Here are the results of those polls.

1952

1. *Bicycle Thieves* (De Sica)

2= *City Lights* (Chaplin)

2= *The Gold Rush* (Chaplin)

4. *Battleship Potemkin* (Eisenstein)

5= *Intolerance* (Griffith)

5= *Louisiana Story* (Flaherty)

7= *Greed* (von Stroheim)

7= *Le Jour Se Lève* (Carné)

7= *The Passion of Joan of Arc* (Dreyer)

10= *Brief Encounter* (Lean)

10= *Le Million* (Clair)

10= *La Règle du Jeu* (Renoir)

1962

1. *Citizen Kane* (Welles)

2. *L'Avventura* (Antonioni)

3. *La Règle du Jeu* (Renoir)

4= *Greed* (von Stroheim)

4= *Ugetsu Monogatari* (Mizoguchi)

6. *Battleship Potemkin* (Eisenstein)

7= *Bicycle Thieves* (De Sica)

7= *Ivan the Terrible* (Eisenstein)

9. *La terra trema* (Visconti)

10. *L'Atalante* (Vigo)

1972

1. *Citizen Kane* (Welles)

2. *La Règle du Jeu* (Renoir)

3. *Battleship Potemkin* (Eisenstein)

4. *8 ¹/₂* (Fellini)

5= *L'avventura* (Antonioni)

5= *Persona* (Bergman)

7. *The Passion of Joan of Arc* (Dreyer)

8= *The General* (Keaton)

8= *The Magnificent Ambersons* (Welles)

10= *Ugetsu Monogatari* (Mizoguchi)

10= *Wild Strawberries* (Bergman)

1982

1. *Citizen Kane* (Welles)

2. *La Règle du Jeu* (Renoir)

3= *Seven Samurai* (Kurosawa)

3= *Singin' in the Rain* (Kelly, Donen)

5. *8 1/2* (Fellini)

6. *Battleship Potemkin* (Eisenstein)

7= *L'Avventura* (Antonioni)

7= *The Magnificent Ambersons* (Welles)

7= *Vertigo* (Hitchcock)

10= *The General* (Keaton)

10= *The Searchers* (Ford)

1992

1. *Citizen Kane* (Welles)

2. *La Règle du Jeu* (Renoir)

3. *Tokyo Story* (Ozu)

4. *Vertigo* (Hitchcock)

5. *The Searchers* (Ford)

6= *L'Atalante* (Vigo)

6= *Battleship Potemkin* (Eisenstein)

6= *The Passion of Joan of Arc* (Dreyer)

6= *Pather Panchali* (S. Ray)

10. *2001: A Space Odyssey* (Kubrick)

2002

1. *Citizen Kane* (Welles)

2. *Vertigo* (Hitchcock)

3. *La Règle du Jeu* (Renoir)

4. *The Godfather and The Godfather Part II* (Coppola)

5. *Tokyo Story* (Ozu)

6. *2001: A Space Odyssey* (Kubrick)

7= *Battleship Potemkin* (Eisenstein)

7= *Sunrise* (Murnau)

9. *8 ½* (Fellini)

10. *Singin' in the Rain* (Kelly, Donen)

THINGS SAID ABOUT TAX

'Income tax returns are the most imaginative fiction being written today.' (Herman Wouk)

'I have always paid income tax. I object only when it reaches a stage when I am threatened with having nothing left for my old age – which is due to start next Tuesday or Wednesday.' (Noel Coward)

'Next to being shot at and missed, nothing is really quite as satisfying as an income tax refund.' (F. J. Raymond)

'There's no such thing as a good tax.' (Sir Winston Churchill)

'In this world nothing can be said to be certain, except death and taxes.' (Benjamin Franklin)

'When they fire a rocket at Cape Canaveral, I feel as if I own it.' (William Holden)

'There should be no taxation without comprehension.' (John Gummer)

'The income tax has made more liars out of the American people than golf has.' (Will Rogers)

'The avoidance of taxes is the only intellectual pursuit that carries any reward.' (John Maynard Keynes)

'There's always somebody who is paid too much, and taxed too little – and it's always somebody else.' (Cullen Hightower)

'The wages of sin are death, but by the time taxes are taken out, it's just sort of a tired feeling.' (Paula Poundstone)

'Tax reform means "Don't tax you, don't tax me, tax that fellow behind the tree."' (Russell Long)

'Man is not like other animals in the ways that are really significant: Animals have instincts, we have taxes.' (Erving Goffman)

'Noah must have taken into the Ark two taxes, one male and one female. And did they multiply bountifully!' (Will Rogers)

THE LONGEST-SERVING BRITISH MONARCHS SINCE 1066

Queen Victoria (64 years: 1837–1901)

King George III (60 years: 1760–1820)

King Henry III (56 years: 1216–1272)

Queen Elizabeth II (53 years: 1952–)

King Edward III (50 years: 1327–1377)

Queen Elizabeth I (45 years: 1558–1603)

King Henry VI (39 years: 1422–1461)

King Henry VIII (38 years: 1509–1547)

King Henry I (35 years: 1100–1135)

King Henry II (35 years: 1154–1189)

King Edward I (35 years: 1272–1307)

ANAGRAMS

LESS IN HARMONY – Shirley Manson

TRASH IN AIMING – Martina Hingis

BELT MERITED – Bette Midler

CAMEL NOISES – Monica Seles

VERY COOL TUNE – Courtney Love

BOIL JELLY – Billy Joel

CHIEF CROWD ALARM – Michael Crawford

NEAT APPELLATION – Natalie Appleton

I'M LONE SNOB – Simon Le Bon

GOAL ANGER HELL – Noel Gallagher

ARTICLES TARNISH – Christian Slater

LOW BORE – Rob Lowe

EMERGE ANGRIER – Germaine Greer

HELL IS HER HAUNT – Ruthie Henshall

INHALE? CHEERS! – Charlie Sheen

WE'LL SEND ANYONE – Lesley Anne Down

CREEP DID WARN – Prince Edward

SUIT U WHOLE HEAP – Paul Whitehouse

EDIT WASN'T COOL – Clint Eastwood

I'M SENILE, SORRY – Neil Morrissey

RANDOM CAR LOVER – Carol Vorderman

MEANT TO CRUNCH MICE – Martine McCutcheon

NOW EVEN WIVES DO IT – Vivienne Westwood

AUTUMN HARM – Uma Thurman

DREARY MILD ACHE – Richard Madeley

BETRAY IN PRESS – Britney Spears

SEND MY OLD MAN – Desmond Lynam

NO! DO CENSOR! – Des O'Connor

DARN SAD MALE – Adam Sandler

MERRY WARDROBE – Drew Barrymore

GERMANY – Meg Ryan

A PRETENDER – Peter Andre

LIKES EASY MEN – Melanie Sykes

RAMPANT TOENAIL – Natalie Portman

LOWERS ULCERS – Russell Crowe

ME THIN MAN – Tim Henman

FINE TICKLE LADY – Felicity Kendal

A NIGHTMARE SELL – Leslie Grantham

VAST EGO ONCE – Steve Coogan

RANK LIES? CHAMPION! – Michael Parkinson

CAR EPIC – Caprice

SO ANGRY OR MAD – Gordon Ramsay

IMAGINED UNION – Dannii Minogue

A ZIP SHALL RIP – Zara Phillips

SURE AM VAIN – Mena Suvari

I BULL, I SCREW – Bruce Willis

THAT SNAIL CHARM – Alan Titchmarsh

AN ACUTE GIRLISH AIR – Christina Aguilera

BUT MEN MOAN – Emma Bunton

HER MEN COLLAPSE – Elle MacPherson

VERY LESS TALL ON SET – Sylvester Stallone

I AM A PLONKER, NOT SMART – Tara Palmer-
Tomkinson

SEMI-BARKING – Kim Basinger

VOICE SELLS LOT – Elvis Costello

**EXPOSE THIS ILL BORE – Sophie Ellis-
Bextor**

TALL, NOT DIM – Matt Dillon

ORNATE PLUM – Paul Merton

TAKE JOINT SHAME – Jamie Theakston

IMAGINABLE RITUAL – Natalie Imbruglia

A COMIC MILK HERD – Charlie Dimmock

INTENSE HARM – Martin Sheen

AID THE SLIM – Delia Smith

TRY OLDER RAGE – Roger Daltrey

SMOKES? TA! – Kate Moss

NO SNOB INANER – Anne Robinson

SMALL EASIER WIN – Serena Williams

AND A FILM ROLE – Alfred Molina

SHE'LL CHARGE MALE LIAR – Sarah Michelle Gellar

NIGHTLY INSTRUCTOR – Christy Turlington

I WIN SMALL BIRO – Robin Williams

OUR WAY IS REVENGE – Sigourney Weaver

PUT ON A RAVIOLI ACT – Luciano Pavarotti

DRY AND OKAY – Dan Aykroyd

O FAT MALE – Meatloaf

UNSTABLE JERK? I'M IT! – Justin Timberlake

HAILED POSH – Sophie Dahl

WOW! LENGTHY PART – Gwyneth Paltrow

WORK? DIAL US! – Lisa Kudrow

I AM A SCOWLING RAT – Alistair McGowan

I'M A KIND CLONE – Nicole Kidman

I'M SOLE CLOWN – Simon Cowell

OK, MAN, CROON – Norman Cook (Fatboy Slim)

CASH IN NAME – Ian McShane

MAJOR LASS IN HEAT – Melissa Joan Hart

NOT INSANE ABROAD – Antonio Banderas

LET'S WIPE THE TEAPOT – Pete Postlethwaite

WARM TRIPE? CHEERIO! – Marco Pierre White

RAVAGE SAD NERVES – Vanessa Redgrave

WARM AND INTENSE – Dennis Waterman

RENT RISES? WHOOPEE! – Reese Witherspoon

ONE'S NOT RASH – Sharon Stone

REVENUE SAKE – Keanu Reeves

TART JEERS TO REPENT – Janet Street-Porter

IS LASS INFLATED? – Lisa Stansfield

SARDONIC WHIRL – Richard Wilson

DOCILE FARTS – Fidel Castro

I DRAG ODD TRASH – Trisha Goddard

GOSH DREARY! – Gary Rhodes

INTO NEW LAD – Dale Winton

RESPECT MEANT – Terence Stamp

GIRLS' HEAVEN – Nigel Havers

THE THREE WISE MONKEYS

Mizaru (See no evil)

Mikazaru (Hear no evil)

Mazaru (Say no evil)

Dealing with cold calls

Ask them if they're real or just one of the voices in your head.

Ask them to spell their name. Then ask them to spell the name of their company. Then ask them where the company is located. Then ask them to spell the company's location.

Tell them to talk very VERY S-L-O-W-L-Y, because you want to write down every single word.

If they're phoning from a kitchen company, tell them you live in a squat.

If they say they're not selling anything, tell them that that's a pity because you're in the mood for buying.

If they give you their name – 'Hi, I'm Sharon' – say, 'oh, Sharon, how ARE you?' as though they are a long-lost friend.

Tell them you're busy at the moment and could you have their home phone number to call them back later.

ADOLF HITLER (WITH EVERYTHING YOU ALREADY KNEW ABOUT HIM TAKEN OUT)

As a child, he was once beaten into a two-day coma by his father, Alois.

From 1925 to 1945, Hitler held the official title of SS Member #1. The man who was Member #2 wasn't Heinrich Himmler but Emil Maurice, Hitler's personal bodyguard/chauffeur and the man who is credited with founding the SS. Maurice, incredibly, was half-Jewish and, when this came to light in 1935, he was thrown out of the SS. However, he was allowed to retain all his privileges.

Hitler's suicide in 1945 was not his first attempt. In 1923, after the failure of his putsch, he was hiding out in the attic of his follower, Ernst 'Putzi' Hanfstangl. When the police arrived, Hitler tried to shoot himself, but a policeman managed to stop him before he could pull the trigger.

Hitler had Chaplin's _The Great Dictator_ banned but he was curious to see the film himself and so he had a print of the film smuggled into Germany from Portugal, and watched it not once, but twice.

He collected pornography and used to draw it.

He had an affair with his half-sister's daughter who eventually killed herself.

Each of his two Mercedes Benz cars had a false floor fitted to make him look taller when he stood up.

Car manufacturer Henry Ford was the only American to get a favourable mention in Hitler's autobiography, _Mein Kampf_.

Myrna Loy, Bertolt Brecht and cartoonist David Low were all on Hitler's personal blacklist.

Hitler was awarded the Iron Cross after being recommended for one by a Jewish officer.

Hitler esteemed Clark Gable above all other actors, and during the war offered a sizeable reward to anyone who could capture and return Gable unscathed to him.

He was taking 92 different drugs towards the end of his life.

Four male descendants through his father's line were born between 1949 and 1965 in New York State. None of them had any children.

THE USA

About a third of Americans flush the lavatory while they are still sitting on it.

In Kentucky, 50 per cent of people getting married for the first time are teenagers.

The dollar symbol ($) is a U combined with an S.

Tennessee has more neighbours than any other state in the US. It is bordered by eight states: Kentucky, Missouri, Arkansas, Mississippi, Alabama, Georgia, North Carolina and Virginia.

Many businesses in Nebraska have the word 'Aksarben' in their names: such as 'Aksarben Five and Dime Store' or 'Aksarben Transmission Service.' Aksarben is Nebraska spelt backwards.

Deafness was once so common on Martha's Vineyard that all the people who lived there, both the hearing and the deaf, were fluent in their own dialect of sign language. No distinction was made in working or social life between those who could hear and those who could not. The gene for deafness was brought over in the 17th century by settlers from the Weald in Kent, and by the 19th century the rate of hereditary deafness on the island was 37 times the American average. Marriage to off-islanders eventually saw deafness disappear from the population; the last deaf islander died in 1952 (though deafness was still so unremarkable that her brief obituary in the *Vineyard Gazette* saw no reason to mention it).

In Alaska, it is an offence to push a living moose out of a moving aeroplane.

During the time the atomic bomb was being hatched by the United States at Alamogordo, New Mexico, applicants for routine jobs were disqualified if they could read. Illiteracy was a job requirement. The reason: the authorities did not want their papers being read.

The name 'California' was taken from a 16th-century Spanish novel, *The Exploits of Esplaidian*, by Garcia Ordonez de Montalvo. In the novel it was the name of an imaginary island, described as an Amazon kingdom ruled by black women.

The three US presidents who have faced real or impending impeachment – Andrew Johnson, Richard Nixon and Bill Clinton – also have in common that their names are euphemisms for the penis: johnson, dick and willie.

Every rise in the US divorce rate is matched by a rise in toy sales.

There are more plastic flamingos in the US than real ones.

The average American chews 190 pieces of gum each year.

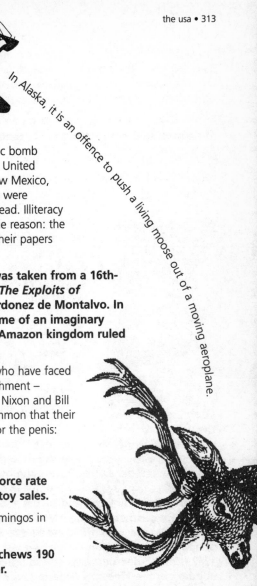

Point Roberts in Washington State is cut off from the rest of the state by British Columbia, Canada. In order to get to Point Roberts from any other part of the state, you have to go through Canadian and US customs.

In the 1940s, the name of the Bich pen was changed to Bic out of concern that Americans would pronounce it 'Bitch'.

In Los Angeles, there are more cars than people.

Americans drink an average of 25 gallons of milk a year.

New Yorker magazine has more subscribers in California than in New York.

The main library at Indiana University sinks by several centimetres a year. When it was built, no one took into account the weight of all the books it would hold.

Ted Turner owns 5 per cent of New Mexico.

In 1976, a Los Angeles secretary 'married' her 50-pound pet rock.

In 1980, a Las Vegas hospital suspended workers for running a book on when patients would die.

Since 1 January 2004, the population of the United States has been increasing by one person every 12 seconds. Every 13 seconds someone dies, every 8 seconds someone is born and every 25 seconds an immigrant arrives.

In Vermont, there are 10 cows for every person.

72 per cent of Americans sign their pets' names on the greeting cards they send.

The United States consumes 25 per cent of the world's energy.

On a clear day, you can see five states from the top of the Empire State Building: New York, New Jersey, Connecticut, Massachusetts and Pennsylvania.

The largest living thing on earth (by volume) is the General Sherman Tree in Sequoia National Park. It is 275 feet tall (84m) and its trunk is 37 feet (11m) in diameter at the widest point.

Second Street is the first choice of street name in the US.

The US government keeps its supply of silver at the military academy in West Point.

The murder capital of the US is Gary, Indiana.

A party boat filled with 60 men and women capsized in Texas after it passed a nudist beach and all its passengers rushed to one side.

More than 8,100 US troops are still listed as missing in action from the Korean War.

All the earthworms in America weigh 55 times what all the people weigh.

The slogan on New Hampshire number plates is 'Live Free or Die'. The plates are made by inmates in the state prison.

There's enough concrete in the Hoover Dam to make a 4-foot/1.2-m wide belt around the equator.

In American there's a lawsuit every 30 seconds.

The average American walks four miles a year making the bed.

Every day, 7 per cent of the US eats at McDonald's.

Names

Kiefer Sutherland's full name is Kiefer William Frederick Dempsey George Rufus Sutherland

People known by their initials

W.H. (Wystan Hugh) Auden

A.J. (Alfred Jules) Ayer

J.G. (James Graham) Ballard

P.T. (Phineas Taylor) Barnum

J.M. (James Mathew) Barrie

H.E. (Herbert Ernest) Bates

A.S. (Antonia Susan) Byatt

J.J. (John Junior) Cale

G.K. (Gilbert Keith) Chesterton

J.M. (John Maxwell) Coetzee

e.e. (Edward Estlin) Cummings

F.W. (Frederik Willem) de Klerk

E.L. (Edgar Lawrence) Doctorow

T.S. (Thomas Stearns) Eliot

W.C. (William Claude) Fields

E.M. (Edward Morgan) Forster

W.S. (William Schwenck) Gilbert

A.A. (Adrian Anthony) Gill

W.G. (William Gilbert) Grace

D.W. (David Wark) Griffith

W.C. (William Christopher) Handy

L.P. (Leslie Poles) Hartley

P.J. (Polly Jean) Harvey

A.E. (Alfred Edward) Housman

P.D. (Phyllis Dorothy) James

C.E.M. (Cyril Edwin Mitchinson) Joad

k.d. (Kathryn Dawn) lang

R.D. (Ronald David) Laing

D.H. (David Herbert) Lawrence

T.E. (Thomas Edward) Lawrence

C.S. (Clive Staples) Lewis

A.A. (Alan Alexander) Milne

V.S. (Vidiadhar Surajprasad) Naipaul

P.J. (Patrick Jake) O'Rourke

J.C. (James Cash) Penney

J.B. (John Boynton) Priestley

J.K. (Joanne Kathleen) Rowling

A.L. (Alfred Leslie) Rowse

J.D. (Jerome David) Salinger

R.C. (Robert Cedric) Sherriff

O.J. (Orenthal James) Simpson

F.E. (Frederick Edwin) Smith

W.H. (William Henry) Smith

C.P. (Charles Percy) Snow

A.J.P. (Alan John Percivale) Taylor

B.J. (Billy Joe) Thomas

E.P. (Edward Palmer) Thompson

J.R.R. (John Ronald Reuel) Tolkien

P.L. (Pamela Lyndon) Travers

J.M.W. (Joseph Mallord William) Turner

H.G. (Herbert George) Wells

J.P.R. (John Peter Rhys) Williams

P.G. (Pelham Grenville) Wodehouse

W.B. (William Butler) Yeats

PEOPLE WHO DON'T APPEAR TO HAVE MIDDLE NAMES

John Major, Michael Howard, Lorraine Chase, Geoffrey Boycott, Lynn Redgrave, Jonathan Dimbleby, John Fashanu, David Hamilton, John Francome, Glenn Hoddle, Wendy Richard, Nerys Hughes, David Suchet, Keith Michell, Gerry Cottle, Ron Moody, Gary Barlow, Nasser Hussain, Elaine Paige, Annabel Croft, Mo Mowlam

UNUSUAL NAMES GIVEN BY CELEBRITIES TO THEIR CHILDREN

Dixie Dot – Anna Ryder Richardson

Pilot Inspektor Riesgraf Lee – Jason Lee

Seven & Puma – Erykah Badu

Tu – Rob Morrow (i.e. Tu Morrow)

Salvador – Ed O'Brien

Raven – Gary Numan

Ace Howlett – Natalie Appleton and Liam Howlett

Geronimo – Alex James

Deacon – Reese Witherspoon

Apple – Gwyneth Paltrow and Chris Martin

MaKena Lei – Helen Hunt (after a Hawaiian island)

Salome – Alex Kingston

William True – Kirstie Alley

Camera – Arthur Ashe

Jack Daniel – Ellen Barkin and Gabriel Byrne

J.C. – Jackie Chan

Erika, Erinn, Ensa, Evin and Ennis – Bill Cosby

Lolita & Piper – Brian De Palma

Brandi & Buck – Roseanne

Cruz – David and Victoria Beckham

Ross & Chudney – Diana Ross

Gib & Prima – Connie Sellecca

Jesse Mojo – Sam Shepard

China – Grace Slick

Weston – Nicolas Cage

Paris & Brielle – Blair Underwood

Rio – Sean Young

Lourdes – Madonna

Cuathemoc – Louis Malle

Shelby – Reba McEntire

Imani – Jasmine Guy

Atherton – Don Johnson

Paris – Michael Jackson

Paris – Pierce Brosnan

Libbi-Jack (daughter) – Gaby Roslin

Eja (boy) – Shania Twain

**Vanessa Feltz, Tony Curtis,
John Huston, John Leguizamo,
Lord Byron and Donatella Versace
all named a daughter Allegra**

Good boy Eja.

PEOPLE WHO FOUND FAME WITH JUST A FIRST NAME

Jamelia (Davis)

Beck (Hansen)

Prince (Rogers Nelson)

Sinitta (Malone)

Madonna (Ciccone)

Dion (Dimucci)

Sade (Adu)

Caprice (Bourret)

Ann-Margret (Olsson)

Toyah (Willcox)

Cher (La Piere)

Yanni (Chrysomallis)

RuPaul (Charles)

Donovan (Leitch)

Melanie (Safka)

Nicole (Hohloch)

Björk (Gudmundsdottir)

Seal (Seal is short for Sealhenry and his surname is Samuel)

Taki (Theodoracopulos)

Arletty (Arletty was short for Arlette-Leonie and her surname was Bathiat)

Eusebio (da Silva Ferreira)

Heinz (Burt)

Charlene (Duncan)

Regine (Regine was a variation on Regina and her surname was Zylberberg)

Des'ree (Des'ree is a variation on Desiree and her surname is Weekes)

Fabian (Fabian is short for Fabiano and his surname is Forte)

Louise (Nurding/Redknapp)

Tiffany (Darwish)

Wynonna (Judd)

Dido (Dido Florian Cloud de Bounevialle Armstrong)

Aaliyah (Dana Haughton)

Brandy (Norwood)

Iman (Abdulmajid)

Jewel (Kilcher)

Kelis (Rogers)

Roseanne (Arnold/Barr)

Vendela (Thomessen)

PEOPLE WHO FOUND FAME WITH JUST A SURNAME

(Annunzio Paolo) Mantovani

(Stephen) Morrissey

(Chaim) Topol

(Harry) Nilsson

(Wladziu Valentino) Liberace

(Michael) D'Angelo

(Josip Broz) Tito

PEOPLE WHO FOUND FAME WITH JUST A NICKNAME/SOBRIQUET

Marilyn (Peter Robinson)

Capucine (Germaine Lefebvre)

Whigfield (Sannia Carlson)

Dana (Rosemary Brown)

Sting (Gordon Sumner)

Hammer (Stanley Burrell)

Pele (Edson Arantes do Nascimento)

Twiggy (Lesley Hornby)

Enya (Eithne Ni Bhraonain)

Suggs (Graham McPherson)

Martika (Marta Marrera)

Fish (Derek Dick)

Lulu (Marie Lawrie)

Yazz (Yasmin Evans)

2Pac (Tupac Shakur)

Twinkle (Lynn Ripley)

Fernandel (Fernand Contandin)

Aneka (Mary Sandeman)

Limahl (Chris Hamill – Limahl is an anagram of Hamill)

Falco (Johann Holzel)

Sabrina (Norma Ann Sykes)

Vangelis (Evangelos Papathanassiou)

Cantinflas (Mario Moreno Reyes)

Sonique (Sonia Clarke)

Bez (Mark Berry)

Coolio (Artis Ivey Jr)

Divine (Harris Glen Milstead)

Eminem (Marshall Mathers)

Flea (Michael Balzary)

Hergé (Georges Remi)

Saki (Hector Munro)

Molière (Jean-Baptiste Poquelin)

Sapper (Cyril McNeile)

Voltaire (François Marie Arouet)

Jordan (Katie Price)

Kool (Robert Bell)

Lemmy (Ian Fraser Kilminster)

Moby (Richard Hall)

Nena (Gabriele Kerner)

Nico (Christa Paffgen)

Pink (Alecia Moore)

Bono (Paul Hewson)

MEN WITH WOMEN'S NAMES

Dana Andrews

Gay Byrne

Kerry Packer

Val Kilmer

Marilyn Manson

Shirley Crabtree (original name of the wrestler Big Daddy)

Mandy Patinkin

Gert Frobe

Kay Kyser

Marion Morrison (original name of the actor John Wayne)

Lilian Thuram

By George

WOMEN WITH MEN'S NAMES

Leslie Ash

Sean Young

Michael Learned

Billie Piper

George Eliot

Cameron Diaz

Glenn Close

Jerry Hall

Charlie Dimmock

Daryl Hannah

George Sand

Teddy Beverley

Bye Mandy

PEOPLE WHO NAMED THEIR CHILDREN AFTER OTHER FAMOUS PEOPLE

Neneh Cherry: named daughter Tyson, after Mike Tyson

Dave Stewart and Siobhan Fahey: named son Django, after Django Reinhardt

Gyles Brandreth: named daughter Aphra, after the writer Aphra Behn

Woody Allen: named his son Satchel, after the baseball player Satchel Paige

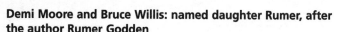

Paul Young: named daughter Levi, after Levi Stubbs of The Four Tops

Demi Moore and Bruce Willis: named daughter Rumer, after the author Rumer Godden

Ricky Schroder: named son Holden, after William Holden

Nicky Henson: named son Keaton, after Buster Keaton

Mickey Stewart: named his son Alec, after Alec Bedser

Bryan Ferry: named son Otis, after Otis Redding

Will Self: named son Luther, after Luther Vandross

PEOPLE WHO WERE NAMED AFTER SOMEONE/SOMETHING FAMOUS

Nasser Hussain (after Colonel Nasser)

Penelope Cruz (after the song 'Penélope' by Joan Manuel Serrat)

Sadie Frost (after the song 'Sexy Sadie' by The Beatles)

Celine Dion (after the song 'Celine' by Hugues Aufray)

Paul Gascoigne (after Paul McCartney)

Jude Law (after the song 'Hey Jude' by The Beatles)

PEOPLE WHO CHOSE TO USE THEIR MIDDLE NAME AS A FIRST NAME

Christopher Ashton Kutcher

George Roger Waters

Patrick Ryan O'Neal

Lee Alexander McQueen

Robert Oliver Reed

Alexander Boris Johnson

John Anthony Quayle

Johan Jordi Cruyff

James Harold Wilson

Marie Dionne Warwick

Michael Vincent O'Brien

Henry Antony Worrall Thompson

Richard Geoffrey Howe

Ernestine Jane Russell

John Enoch Powell

Ruth Bette Davis

Alfred Alistair Cooke

Norvell Oliver Hardy

Isaac Vivian Richards

Sir Peter Norman Fowler

Georgina Davinia Murphy

Leonard James Callaghan

Robert Edward (i.e. Ted) Turner

Eldred Gregory Peck

Alexander James Naughtie

Mary Sean Young

Daniel Patrick Macnee

George Anthony Newley

Sir Edwin Hardy Amies

Arthur Nigel Davenport

Mark Trevor Phillips

Alastair Brian Walden

Thomas Richard Dunwoody

David Paul Scofield

Christopher Nicholas Parsons

James Paul McCartney

Michael Jeremy Bates

Mary Farrah Fawcett

Lord Michael Colin Cowdrey

William Clark Gable

Nigel Keith Vaz

Christopher Rob Andrew

Ernest Ingmar Bergman

George Richard Chamberlain

Terrence Stephen (Steve) McQueen

Sir Arthur John Gielgud

John Michael Crichton

George Orson Welles

Howard Andrew (Andy) Williams

Troyal Garth Brooks

Audrey Faith Hill

Nelust Wyclef Jean

Carole Penny Marshall

Margaret Jane Pauley

Isaac Donald Everly

Ellen Tyne Daly

Holly Michelle Phillips

Peter Marc Almond

Winnifred Jacqueline Bisset

Henry Ken(neth) Russell

NICKNAMES

Natalie Imbruglia – Jagger Lips and Frog Eyes

Benjamin Bratt – Scarecrow (because he was so thin)

Donna Air – Lego Legs

Macy Gray – Bum Jiggy

Lucy Liu – Curious George (her friends' nickname for her)

Nicole Appleton – Fonzie

Madonna – Nonni (family nickname)

Josie Lawrence – Big Bird ('I'm five foot ten inches tall')

Johnny Depp – Mr Stench

Kathy Bates – Bobo

Helen Mirren – Popper

Rachel Stevens – Ratz

J.C. Chasez – Mr Sleepy

PEOPLE WITH UNUSUAL MIDDLE NAMES

Robbie MAXIMILIAN Williams

Anthea MILLICENT Turner

Richard TIFFANY Gere

Noah STRAUSSER SPEER Wyle

Courteney BASS Cox

Dom ROMULUS Joly

Hugh MARSTON Hefner

Bob XENON Geldof

FAMOUS SIBLINGS WITH DIFFERENT SURNAMES

Joan Fontaine & Olivia de Havilland

A.S. Byatt & Margaret Drabble

Emilio Estevez & Charlie Sheen

Warren Beatty & Shirley Maclaine

Keith Chegwin & Janice Long

Sheila Mercier & Lord Brian Rix

Lord Lew Grade & Lord Bernard Delfont

George Sanders & Tom Conway

Talia Shire & Francis Coppola

Peter Graves & James Arness

Gypsy Rose Lee & June Havoc

Ashley Judd & Wynonna

Beauty Culture

GENUINE NAMES FOR LIPSTICKS

Amour, Firecracker, Censored, Strawberry Fair, Corsaire, Nutmeg, Moon Beam, Neon Nude, Cool Candy, Passionate Pink, Mad Mauve, Risky Ruby, Portobello Plum, True Terracotta, Hot Honey, Barely Blush, Crazy Caramel, Too Truffle, Rolling Stone, Warm Platinum, Golden Spice, Chocoholic, Whisper, Fig, Parma Argent, Buttermilk, Sherbet Twist, Wine & Dine, Just Peachy, Hearts A Fire, So Cinnamon, In The Nude, Summer Daze, Let's Go Crazy

COUNTRIES THAT CHANGED THEIR NAMES

Rhodesia (to Zimbabwe)

Upper Volta (to Burkina Faso)

Aden (to Yemen)

Abyssinia (to Ethiopia)

Belgian Congo (to Zaire and back to Congo)

Dahomey (to Benin)

Siam (to Thailand)

Persia (to Iran)

Basutoland (to Lesotho)

British Honduras (to Belize)

Gold Coast (to Ghana)

Dutch Guiana (Suriname)

Nyasaland (Malawi)

The Afars and The Issas (Djibouti)

Portuguese Guinea (Guinea-Bissau)

Dutch East Indies (Indonesia)

New Hebrides (Vanuatu)

Bechuanaland (Botswana)

FICTITIOUS PLACES

Nutwood (Rupert Bear)

Walmington-On-Sea (*Dad's Army*)

Holby (*Casualty*)

Fulchester (*Viz*)

Llareggub (*Under Milk Wood*)

Erinsborough (*Neighbours*)

Gotham City (*Batman*)

Newtown (*Z Cars*)

Melchester (*Roy of The Rovers*)

St Mary Mead (*The Murder At The Vicarage* and all the Agatha Christie films and novels featuring Jane Marple)

WITCHES

In 2000, students at St Andrew's University tried to recruit 400 witches for a pagan coven.

Some years ago, Italian soccer was hit by a witchcraft scandal when it was revealed that the manager of the first division club, Pescara, had consulted a witch named Miriam Lebel. Apparently, this was just the tip of the iceberg and witchcraft is rife in the Italian game.

In New York, witches organized themselves into an 'Anti-Discrimination Lobby' in order to fight discrimination and to get a paid day off on Halloween.

In Gloucester in 1992, a new minister demanded his church be exorcised after he discovered that the organist, Shaun Pickering-Merrett, had been a practising witch for six years.

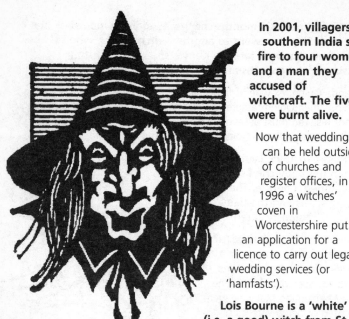

In 2001, villagers in southern India set fire to four women and a man they accused of witchcraft. The five were burnt alive.

Now that weddings can be held outside of churches and register offices, in 1996 a witches' coven in Worcestershire put in an application for a licence to carry out legal wedding services (or 'hamfasts').

Lois Bourne is a 'white' (i.e. a good) witch from St Albans. When a friend complained that they hadn't been able to sell their house for four years, she cast a spell and the next day the house went under offer. Mrs Bourne modestly admitted that it could be a coincidence but anyway later said, 'Selling houses is very boring magic and I refuse to do it.'

In 1995, Susan Leybourne, 29, a witch who had been ordained a pagan priestess at the Circle University in Louisiana, became the first witch to become a chaplain at a British university after her (unpaid) appointment was requested by 40 members of Leeds University's Occult Society.

In 1978, the British writer Nesta Wynn Ellis visited a witch doctor in Zimbabwe who told her that in six months she would marry a man she hadn't yet met. She then went to another witch doctor, who told her the same. A month later, in Kenya, she met her future husband. Five months after that, they were married.

Iolanda Quinn, ex-wife of film star Anthony Quinn, is a self-confessed witch. When Quinn fathered a 'love-child', Mrs Quinn said, 'This baby is not his. You must believe me, I am a witch and I know.' Unfortunately for her, Quinn admitted being the father.

In Russia in 1995, Lyuba Lagutina, a publisher, went to a witch when her baby cried so much that he developed a hernia. The witch said a few spells and the baby was miraculously cured.

In South Africa, two so-called witches were recently burned to death after a bus crash killed 14 children. Speelman Matsipane and Mamiagabo Makwele were accused of being witches on account of their advanced age. They were dragged from their homes and murdered. This is not the only case of witches (or women who are accused of being witches) being blamed for accidents that had nothing to do with them. Whenever someone is struck by lightning in parts of South Africa, it is said to be the work of witches, and old ladies suspected of being witches are driven out of their homes.

In 1989, Leicester Polytechnic had to cancel an 'exhibition on folk history' when 3,000 witches decided to descend on the college.

WISE WORDS FROM ALBERT EINSTEIN

'Only two things are infinite, the universe and human stupidity, and I'm not sure about the former.'

'I never think of the future. It comes soon enough.'

'The hardest thing in the world to understand is income tax.'

'An empty stomach is not a good political adviser.'

'Nationalism is an infantile disease.
It is the measles of mankind.'

**'I can't believe that God
plays dice with the
universe.'**

PEOPLE WHO WOULD HAVE TURNED 100 IN 2006

Carol Reed, British film director

Oscar Levant, American musician

Lew Grade, British film producer

Leonid Brezhnev, Russian politician

Laurens Van Der Post, British mystic and writer

Otto Preminger, American film director

Hermione Baddeley, British actress

Louise Brooks, American actress

Sir Alec Issigonis, British car designer

Luchino Visconti, Italian film director

Sir Fred Pontin, British holiday camp boss

Bob Danvers-Walker, British broadcaster

Primo Carnera, American boxer

Janet Gaynor, American actress

Dmitri Shostakovich, Russian composer

Aristotle Onassis, Greek shipping billionaire

John Betjeman, British poet

Joan Blondell, American actress

Bunny Austin, British tennis player

Elizabeth, Countess of Longford, British writer

Joan Hickson, British actress

John Huston, American film director

Clifford Odets, American playwright

George Sanders, British actor

Catherine Cookson, British writer

Billy Wilder, American film director

Roger Livesey, British actor

Josephine Baker, American singer

Libby Holman, American singer

Mary Astor, American actress

Roberto Rossellini, Italian film director

William Joyce (aka Lord Haw-Haw), Nazi propagandist

Samuel Beckett, Irish playwright

Hugh Gaitskell, British politician

A.J.P. Taylor, British historian

Henny Youngman, American comedian

Lou Costello, American comedian

Bugsy Siegel, American gangster

Madeleine Carroll, British actress

John Carradine, American actor

Dietrich Bonhoeffer, German clergyman

Lon Chaney Jnr, American actor

PEOPLE WHO TURN 90 IN 2006

Olivia de Havilland, American actress

Kirk Douglas, American actor

June Havoc, Canadian actress

Van Johnson, American actor

Walter Cronkite, American TV presenter

Gough Whitlam, Australian politician

Robert McNamara, American politician

Glenn Ford, American actor

Lord Robert Carr, British politician

Dom Mintoff, Maltese politician

Reg Varney, British actor

Alfred Shaughnessy, British writer

P.W. Botha, South African politician

Richard Fleischer, American film director

PEOPLE WHO WOULD HAVE TURNED 90 IN 2006

Sir Edward Heath, British politician

Max Faulkner, British golfer

Johnny Morris, British zoologist

Bill Waddington, British actor

Sirimavo Bandaranaike, Sri Lankan politician

Morris West, British writer

Peter Brough, British actor

Hans Eysenck, German psychologist

Irwin Allen, American writer/producer

Sterling Hayden, American actor

Robert Hanbury Brown, British astronomer

Mercedes McCambridge, American actress

Brian Inglis, British writer

Maxene Andrews, American singer

Harry James, American musician

Jackie Gleason, American actor

Irene Worth, American actress

(Carl) Giles, British cartoonist

Sir Leonard Hutton, British cricketer

Bernard Braden, Canadian broadcaster

Noel Annan, British writer and academic

Ray Conniff, American musician

Peggy Mount, British actress

Harold Robbins, American writer

Betty Grable, American actress

Yehudi Menuhin, British musician

Gregory Peck, American actor

Irving Wallace, American writer

Francis Crick, British scientist

Sir Harold Wilson, British politician

Roald Dahl, British writer

François Mitterrand, French politician

Peter Finch, British actor

Margaret Lockwood, British actress

Keenan Wynn, American actor

James Herriot, British writer

Rossano Brazzi, Italian actor

Dick Haymes, Argentinian singer and actor

Raf Vallone, American actor

Dinah Shore, American TV presenter

PEOPLE WHO TURN 80 IN 2006

Frank Finlay, British actor

Tony Bennett, American singer

Queen Elizabeth II

Sir George Martin, British music producer

William Franklyn, British actor and TV presenter

Lionel Jeffries, British actor

Jan Morris, British writer

Lord Geoffrey Howe, British politician

Alan Greenspan, American economist

Norman Jewison, Canadian film director

Bryan Forbes, British writer, actor and director

Sir David Attenborough, British natural historian

Don Rickles, American comedian

David Coleman, British sports commentator

Katie Boyle, British TV presenter

David Jacobs, British broadcaster

Valéry Giscard d'Estaing, French politician

Leslie Nielsen, Canadian actor

Bill Pertwee, British actor

Bernard Kops, British writer

Beryl Cook, British artist

Ian Paisley, British politician

Warren Mitchell, British actor

Sir Jimmy Savile, British broadcaster

Hugh Hefner, American publisher

Chuck Berry, American singer/songwriter

Mel Brooks, American actor, writer and director

George Melly, British singer and broadcaster

Sir Alan Walters, British economist

Frank Carson, British comedian

Moira Shearer, British ballerina

Stanley Baxter, British comedian

Sir Jack Brabham, Australian racing driver

June Haver, American actress

J.P. Donleavy, Irish writer

Shelley Berman, American comedian

Stuart Whitman, American actor

Clive Donner, British film director

Andy Griffith, American actor

Maria Schell, Austrian actress

Peter Shaffer, British playwright

Harper Lee, American writer

Peter Graves, American actor

Dr Garret Fitzgerald, Irish politician

Andrzej Wajda, Polish film director

Buddy Greco, American singer

Jeane Kirkpatrick, American diplomat

Dame Joan Sutherland, Australian singer

Harry Dean Stanton, American actor

Soupy Sales, American TV personality

Irene Papas, Greek actress

Bud Yorkin, American film director

Donald Carr, British cricketer and administrator

Harry Fowler, British actor

Milo O'Shea, Irish actor

Christopher Logue, British poet

Lord Peter Archer, British politician

Richard Pasco, British actor

Lord Ian Gilmour, British politician

Jackie Pallo, British wrestler

Lord Patrick Jenkin, British politician

Jean Alexander, British actress

Lord Gerry Fitt, Irish politician

Gillian Lynne, British choreographer

John Berger, British writer

Glyn Houston, British actor

H.R.F. Keating, British writer

Michael Bond, British writer

Sir Clyde Walcott, West Indian cricketer

Cloris Leachman, American actress

PEOPLE WHO WOULD HAVE TURNED 80 IN 2006

Evan Hunter, American writer

Anthony Sampson, British writer

Patricia Neal, American actress

Steve Reeves, American actor

Clive Jenkins, British trade unionist

Karel Reisz, British film director

Fred Winter, British racehorse trainer

Neal Cassady, American beat generation icon

Richard Crenna, American actor

Virgil 'Gus' Grissom, American astronaut

Jeffrey Hunter, American actor

H.R. Haldeman, American political aide

Leonard Rossiter, British actor

Anthony Shaffer, British playwright

Klaus Kinski, German actor

Fred Gwynne, American actor

Eric Morecambe, British comedian

John Aspinall, British zoo keeper and casino owner

John Derek, American actor

Marilyn Monroe, American actress

John Schlesinger, British film director

John Coltrane, American musician

Kenneth Williams, British actor

Pat Coombs, British comedienne

Allen Ginsberg, American poet

Victor Kiam, American businessman

Ted Moult, British TV presenter

Miles Davis, American musician

PEOPLE WHO TURN 70 IN 2006

Alan Alda, American actor

Lord Bill Jordan, British trade unionist

Sir Ivan Lawrence, British politician

Princess Alexandra, British royal

The Aga Khan

David Carradine, American actor

John Bird, British comedian and actor

Gary Hart, American politician

Tommy Steele, British entertainer

James Burke, British TV presenter

Louis Gossett Jr, American actor

Roy Hudd, British comedian and actor

Ralph Steadman, British cartoonist

Dennis Hopper, American actor

Ian Kennedy Martin, British writer

Bobby Simpson, Australian cricketer

Elizabeth Dole, American politician

Richard Wilson, British actor

Yves Saint-Laurent, French fashion designer

Mary Tyler Moore, American actress

Laurie Taylor, British academic and broadcaster

Keith Barron, British actor

Trevor Bannister, British actor

Seamus Mallon, British politician

Peter Bowles, British actor

John Blashford-Snell, British explorer

Bill Wyman, British musician

Sir Martin Gilbert, British historian

Carl Davis, British composer and conductor

Roy Emerson, Australian tennis player

Burt Reynolds, American actor

Jess Conrad, British singer and actor

Sir John Tusa, British broadcaster

Robin Hanbury-Tenison, British explorer

Tony O'Reilly, Irish businessman

Zubin Mehta, Indian orchestral conductor

Engelbert Humperdinck, British singer

Terry Downes, British boxer

Albert Finney, British actor

Glenda Jackson, British actress and politician

Gerald Scarfe, British cartoonist

Andrew Davies, British dramatist

A.S. Byatt, British writer

Hugh Hudson, British film director

Toby Balding, British horseracing trainer

Colin Meads, New Zealand rugby union legend

Bruce Dern, American actor

Levi Stubbs, American singer

Richard Rodney Bennett, British composer

F.W. de Klerk, South African politician

Ursula Andress, Swiss actress

Roger Whittaker, Kenyan singer

Glen Campbell, American singer

Dean Stockwell, American actor

Jean Boht, British actress

Joe Don Baker, American actor

Stella Stevens, American actress

Gordon Honeycombe, British TV newsreader and writer

Winnie Mandela, South African politician

Vaclav Havel, Czech playwright and politician

Judith Chalmers, British TV presenter

Don Black, British lyricist

Hugh Whitemore, British playwright

Kris Kristofferson, American actor and singer/songwriter

Ken Loach, British film director

David Vine, British TV sports commentator

John Gorman, British singer

El Cordobes, Spanish bullfighter

Arthur Scargill, British trade unionist

Keir Dullea, American actor

PEOPLE WHO WOULD HAVE TURNED 70 IN 2006

Ismail Merchant, Indian film producer

Michael Landon, American actor

Troy Donahue, American actor

Jill Ireland, British actress

Dave Allen, Irish comedian

Roger Miller, American singer

Jim Clark, British racing driver

Juliet Prowse, American actress and dancer

Nyree Dawn Porter, New Zealand actress

Peter Tinniswood, British writer

John Wells, British actor and writer

Roy Orbison, American singer

Frank Serpico, American policeman

Buddy Holly, American singer/songwriter

Wilt Chamberlain, American basketball player

Robert Sangster, British racehorse owner

Bobby Darin, American actor and singer

Jim Henson, American puppeteer

Duncan Edwards, British footballer

People who turn 60 in 2006

Rosie Barnes, British politician

Robert Fripp, British musician

George Best, British footballer

Simon Hoggart, British journalist

David Gilmour, British musician

Sue Townsend, British writer

Tim Curry, British actor

King Carl Gustaf of Sweden

Joanna Lumley, British actress

John Woo, Chinese film director

David Suchet, British actor

John Watson, British motor racing driver

Candice Bergen, American actress

Donovan, British singer/songwriter

Graham Gouldman, British musician

Maureen Lipman, British actress

Dave Mason, British musician

Tim Pigott-Smith, British actor

Talia Shire, American actress

Srinivas Venkataraghavan, Indian cricketer

John Waters, American film director

Lord George Robertson, British politician

Alan Knott, British cricketer

Nicholas Ball, British actor

Bob Harris, British DJ

Clare Francis, British yachtswoman and author

Nicole Farhi, French fashion designer

Barry Richards, South African cricketer

Paul Schrader, American film director

Al Green, American singer

Danny Glover, American actor

Ilie Nastase, Romanian tennis player

Diane Keen, British actress

Bill Forsyth, British film director

Jack Straw, British politician

Susan Saint James, American actress

Tony Robinson, British actor

William Waldegrave, British politician

Jimmy Webb, American songwriter

Lesley Ann Warren, American actress

Bill Clinton, American politician

Henry Kelly, Irish broadcaster

Hayley Mills, British actress

John Virgo, British snooker player

Jane Asher, British actress

John Paul Jones, British rock musician

Alan Rickman, British actor

Elkie Brooks, British singer

Tyne Daly, American actress

Robin Cook, British politician

Malcolm McLaren, British rock group manager

Lynda La Plante, British writer

Susan Sarandon, American actress

Charles Dance, British actor

Chris Tarrant, British DJ and TV presenter

Sir Willard White, Jamaican opera singer

Edwina Currie, British politician and writer

Justin Hayward, British singer/songwriter

Richard Carpenter, American musician

Sir Cameron Mackintosh, British theatrical impresario

Liza Minnelli, American actress and singer

Sylvester Stallone, American actor

George W. Bush, American politician

Sue Lyon, American actress

Derek Griffiths, British actor

Linda Ronstadt, American singer

The Sultan of Brunei

Timothy Dalton, British actor

Alan Bleasdale, British playwright

Catherine Walker, British fashion designer

Mike Procter, South African cricketer

Oliver Stone, American film director

Tommy Lee Jones, American actor

Billy Bonds, British footballer

Bishen Bedi, Indian cricketer

Felicity Kendal, British actress

Helen Shapiro, British singer

Patricia Hodge, British actress

Michael Buerk, British TV newsreader

Clare Short, British politician

Jenny Pitman, British horse racing trainer

Donald Trump, American businessman

Noddy Holder, British singer

Simon Williams, British actor

Duchess of Gloucester, British royal

Kate Hoey, British politician

Sir Malcolm Rifkind, British politician

Lord Maurice Saatchi, British advertising executive

Marisa Berenson, American actress

Penelope Wilton, British actress

Roy Wood, British singer/songwriter

Sally Field, American actress

Marianne Faithfull, British singer

Patti Smith, American singer/songwriter

Edgar Winter, American musician

Chip Hawkes, British singer

Cher, American actress and singer

Debbie Moore, British businesswoman

Brian Cox, British actor

Lasse Hallström, Swedish film director

Brenda Blethyn, British actress

Alison Steadman, British actress

Bob Beamon, American athlete

Barry Gibb, British-born singer/songwriter

Billy Preston, American musician

Buddy Miles, American musician

Loudon Wainwright III, American singer/songwriter

Christopher Hampton, British playwright

Victoria Principal, American actress

Stephen Rea, Irish actor

Kelvin Mackenzie, British journalist

José Carreras, Spanish singer

Diana Quick, British actress

Emerson Fittipaldi, Brazilian motor racing driver

Stan Smith, American tennis player

Benny Andersson, Swedish musician

Steven Spielberg, American film director

Rosemary Conley, British diet expert

Uri Geller, Israeli spoon-bender

Lesley Judd, British TV presenter

Janet Street-Porter, British TV presenter and executive

Gilbert O'Sullivan, Irish singer

Ivan Reitman, American film director

Peter Green, British musician

Ian McGeechan, British rugby union player and coach

Alan Jones, Australian racing driver

Diane Keaton, American actress

Syd Barrett, British rock musician

Julian Barnes, British writer

Dolly Parton, American singer

Lesley Joseph, British actress

David Lynch, American film director

PEOPLE WHO WOULD HAVE TURNED 60 IN 2006

Ronnie Lane, British musician

Robert Urich, American actor

Mick Ronson, British musician

Roger Tonge, British actor

Michael Elphick, British actor

Gilda Radner, American actress

Gram Parsons, American singer/songwriter

Andrea Dworkin, American academic and writer

Ric Grech, British musician

Keith Moon, British musician

Gene Siskel, American film critic

Sanjay Gandhi, Indian politician

Gianni Versace, Italian fashion designer

Duane Allman, American musician

Freddie Mercury, British singer

Les Gray, British singer

Ted Bundy, American serial killer

Robin Nedwell, British actor

Gregory Hines, American actor and dancer

Carl Wilson, American musician

Arthur Conley, American singer

Syreeta, American singer

PEOPLE WHO TURN 50 IN 2006

Sugar Ray Leonard, American boxer

Richard Madeley, British TV presenter

Oliver Letwin, British politician

LaToya Jackson, American singer

Björn Borg, Swedish tennis player

Rory McGrath, British comedian

Ingemar Stenmark, Swedish skier

Joan Allen, American actress

Kim Cattrall, American actress

Glen Matlock, British musician

Paul Allott, British cricketer and commentator

Ray Wilkins, British footballer

David Copperfield, American magician

Jono Coleman, Australian DJ

Mark Todd, New Zealand equestrian

Mel Gibson, Australian actor

David Caruso, American actor

Angus Deayton, British actor and TV presenter

Paul King, British rock musician

Phyllis Logan, British actress

Paul Young, British singer

Wayne Daniel, West Indian cricketer

Mimi Rogers, American actress

Geena Davis, American actress

Johnny Rotten/Lydon, British singer

Nathan Lane, American actor

Sue Barker, British tennis player and TV presenter

Andy Garcia, American actor

Koo Stark, British actress

Nicholas Hytner, British theatre and film director

Liam Brady, Irish footballer

David Willetts, British politician

Tessa Sanderson, British athlete

Tom Watt, British actor

Desmond Haynes, West Indian cricketer

Chris Isaak, American singer

Patricia Cornwell, American writer

Joe Montana, American footballer

Anthony Bourdain, American chef

Jerry Hall, American model

Viv Anderson, British footballer

Danny Boyle, British film director

Juliet Stevenson, British actress

Richard Curtis, British writer and film director

Nigel Kennedy, British musician

Keith Vaz, British politician

Bo Derek, American actress

John McCarthy, British journalist

Fiona Armstrong, British TV newsreader

Andrew Lansley, British politician

Michele Alboreto, Italian racing driver

Mickey Rourke, American actor

Rita Rudner, American comedienne

Tim McInnerny, British actor

Marc Almond, British singer/songwriter

Tom Hanks, American actor

Frank Stapleton, Irish footballer

Carrie Fisher, American actress and writer

Martina Navratilova, Czech-born tennis player

Sebastian Coe, British athlete

Theresa May, British politician

Amanda Burton, British actress

Fiona Fullerton, British actress

PEOPLE WHO TURN 40 IN 2006

Jason Flemyng, British actor

George Weah, Liberian footballer

Tony Adams, British footballer

John Regis, British athlete

Shaun Edwards, British rugby league player

Sinitta, British singer

Michaela Strachan, British TV presenter

Teddy Sheringham, British footballer

Samantha Robson, British actress

Roger Black, British athlete

Chris Evans, British broadcaster

Cynthia Nixon, American actress

Romario, Brazilian footballer

Wendy James, British singer

Stefan Edberg, Swedish tennis player

José Maria Olazabal, Spanish golfer

Rick Astley, British singer

Alan Davies, British comic

Wasim Akram, Pakistani cricketer

Jonathan Edwards, British athlete

Darius Rucker, American singer/songwriter

Greg Wise, British actor

Janet Jackson, American singer

Graeme Hick, British cricketer

Eric Cantona, French footballer

Helena Bonham Carter, British actress

Zola Budd, South African athlete

Chris Eubank, British boxer

Charlie Dimmock, British gardener and TV presenter

Halle Berry, American actress

Lisa Stansfield, British singer

Sinéad O'Connor, Irish singer

Carl Fogarty, British motorcycle racer

Kiefer Sutherland, American actor

Stephen Twigg, British politician

Martin Offiah, British rugby player

Shirley Manson, British singer and guitarist

Peter Cunnah, British singer

Salma Hayek, Mexican actress

Adam Sandler, American actor

John Cusack, American actor

Fay Ripley, British actress

Mike Tyson, American boxer

Annabel Croft, British tennis player

Dennis Wise, British footballer

Samantha Beckinsale, British actress

Martin Keown, British footballer

Sally Gunnell, British athlete

Kerry Fox, New Zealand actress

Dean Cain, American actor

Marina Ogilvy, British royal

Gianfranco Zola, Italian footballer

Gina Bellman, British actress

Julianna Margulies, American actress

David Platt, British footballer

Diane Modahl, British athlete

Jason Patric, American actor

Jennifer Grant, American actress

Johnny Vaughan, British TV presenter

Samantha Fox, British model and singer

Allan Donald, South African cricketer

David Schwimmer, American actor

Gordon Ramsay, British chef

Phil Tufnell, British cricketer

Cindy Crawford, American model

Billy Zane, American actor

Tea Leoni, American actress

John Daly, American golfer

PEOPLE WHO TURN 30 IN 2006

Dame Ellen Macarthur, British sailor

Isla Fisher, Australian actress

Kirsty Gallacher, British TV presenter

Paulo Wanchope, Costa Rican footballer

Lisa Scott-Lee, British singer (Steps)

Mark Philippoussis, Australian tennis player

Lady Victoria Hervey, British socialite

Tina Barrett, British singer (S Club 7)

Ronaldo, Brazilian footballer

Melissa George, Australian actress

J.C. Chasez, American singer ('N Sync)

Stephen Gately, Irish singer (Boyzone)

Freddie Prinze Jr, American actor

Reese Witherspoon, American actress

Keri Russell, American actress

H (Ian Watkins of Steps)

Martine McCutcheon, British actress and singer

Will Mellor, British actor

Colin Farrell, Irish actor

Lisa Riley, British actress

Jason Brown (aka J), British singer (5ive)

Kym Marsh, British singer (Hear'Say)

Camilla Power, British actress

Virginie Ledoyen, French actress

Jennifer Capriati, American tennis player

Emma Bunton, British singer

Melissa Joan Hart, American actor

Sean Maguire, British actor and singer

Candace Cameron Bure, American actress

Patrick Vieira, French footballer

Shane Lynch, Irish singer (Boyzone)

Anna Friel, British actress

50 Cent, American rapper

Cat Deeley, British TV presenter

Angela Griffin, British actress

PEOPLE WHO TURN 25 IN 2006

Elijah Wood, American actor

Justin Timberlake, American singer

Graeme Smith, South African cricketer

Ralf Little, British actor

Paris Hilton, American socialite

Julia Stiles, American actress

Lleyton Hewitt, Australian tennis player

Hannah Spearritt, British singer (S Club 7)

Liz McLarnon, British singer (Atomic Kitten)

Lady Gabriella Windsor, British royal

Jessica Alba, American actress

Emma Pierson, British actress

Craig David, British singer

Zara Phillips, British royal

Sean Conlon, British singer (5ive)

Anna Kournikova, Russian tennis player

Beyoncé Knowles, American singer (Destiny's Child)

Jonathan Taylor Thomas, American actor

Jack Ryder, British actor (EastEnders)

Natalie Portman, American actress and model

Bradley Mcintosh, British singer (S Club 7)

Serena Williams, American tennis player

Suzanne Shaw, British singer (Hear'Say)

Ben Adams (aka Soul a1), British singer

Britney Spears, American singer

Joe Cole, British footballer

Bryce Dallas Howard, American actress

Roger Federer, Swiss tennis player

Jamelia, British singer

Shaun Wright-Phillips, British footballer

Natasha Bedingfield, British singer/songwriter

Sienna Miller, British actress

PEOPLE WHO TURN 21 IN 2006

Wayne Rooney, British footballer

Jack Osbourne, Ozzy's son

Keira Knightley, British actress

Michelle Trachtenberg, American actress

Sammy Winwood, British actress

PEOPLE WHO TURN 20 IN 2006

Charlotte Church, British singer

Jamie Bell, British actor

Mary-Kate & Ashley Olsen, American actresses

Lindsay Lohan, American actress

Coleen McLoughlin, Wayne Rooney's girlfriend

Amir Khan, British boxer

WHAT PEOPLE DID IN WORLD WAR TWO

Jimmy Young served in the RAF as a physical training instructor with the rank of sergeant.

Baroness Barbara Castle was an administration officer in the Ministry of Food and served as an air-raid warden.

Sam Kydd was a private in the army but was captured and sent to a German POW camp. His book about his time there – *For You, The War is Over* – illustrated just how different POW camps were for officers compared to non-officers. He was also the POW adviser on the movie *The Captive Heart*.

Billy Wright was a corporal in the Shropshire Light Infantry and also made his debut for Wolves (as a winger) and for England (at right-half) in an 'unofficial' wartime international.

Lord Robert Runcie served with the Scots Guards and was a tank officer seeing action in Normandy and being awarded the Military Cross.

Lord Brian Rix served in the RAF and also down the mines as a Bevin Boy. (NB One in ten conscripts in the latter stages of the war were sent down the mines as Bevin Boys, named after the cabinet minister Ernest Bevin.)

Jack Palance was a pilot and was shot down – sustaining severe facial burns resulting in major plastic surgery. He was awarded the Purple Heart.

Ray Lindwall served with the Australian army in New Guinea and in the Solomon Islands.

Eli Wallach served in the US Army Medical Corps and helped battle casualties in Europe.

Peter Sellers was in the Entertainments Division of the RAF and was attached to the Ralph Reader Gang Show.

Dame Vera Lynn raised morale for Britons everywhere with concerts and radio performances at home and abroad in Egypt, India and Burma.

Leslie Nielsen joined the Royal Canadian Air Force and trained as an air gunner but the war ended before he could see combat.

Michael Bentine served in the RAF as an intelligence officer.

Brian Johnston was a Grenadier Guards officer who was awarded the Military Cross for, among other reasons, his 'cheerfulness under fire' in Normandy.

Donald Swann was a Quaker and so registered as a conscientious objector but he still joined the Friends Ambulance Unit working with refugees in Greece and the Middle East.

Dora Bryan served with the army entertainment organization ENSA at home and abroad (Italy).

David Tomlinson served as a flight lieutenant in the RAF.

Aaron Spelling served in the US Army Air Force and was awarded the Bronze Star and Purple Heart with Oak Leaf Cluster.

Lord Home was an MP throughout the war but also saw active service as a major in the Lanarkshire Yeomanry before being invalided out with tuberculosis of the spine.

Arthur English served in the Army for six years, ending the war as a sergeant.

Lord Bernard Weatherill served in the 4/7 Royal Dragoon Guards & Indian Army and the 19th KGVO Lancers.

Sir Edward Heath served in the Royal Artillery, rising to the rank of major and getting a mention in despatches as well as being awarded a military MBE.

Bill Travers was dispatched to India's North-West Frontier to join a Gurkha regiment that was operating behind enemy lines alongside General Wingate's Chindits. He parachuted into the Malayan jungle in command of a small group of men to harass the Japanese.

Ian Carmichael served as a major in the 22 Dragoons in north-west Europe, gaining a mention in despatches.

Telly Savalas served with the US Army towards the end of the war and was injured in action.

Rossano Brazzi joined the Italian Resistance after his parents were murdered by the Fascists. He also continued to make films during the war.

Lord Roy Jenkins served in the Royal Artillery and then in special intelligence, where he reached the rank of captain.

George Cole served in the RAF but spent most of his time making films.

Dinah Shore travelled more miles than any other American entertainer to entertain the troops.

Robert Kee spent much of the war in a German POW camp. His book on his experiences – *A Crowd Is Not Company* – was described by *The Times* as 'arguably the best POW book ever written'.

Viscount Whitelaw served as a major in the Scots Guards, winning the Military Cross.

Leo Abse served in the RAF but was arrested for 'political activities' in 1944, which gave rise to a debate in Parliament.

Bob Paisley served in the Royal Artillery and fought in the North African and Italian campaigns, taking part in the liberation of Rome.

John Profumo served as a brigadier in the army and was mentioned in despatches. He also found the time to win Kettering in the 1940 by-election.

Robert Maxwell went from being a private in the Pioneer Corps to being a captain in the infantry. A marksman, he was awarded the Military Cross for storming an enemy pillbox in Brussels in 1945.

Jeff Chandler served in the army in the Pacific, rising from infantryman to First Lieutenant.

Raymond Baxter was an officer in the RAF flying Spitfires.

Rabbi Hugo Gryn was in Auschwitz extermination camp where he worked as a slave labourer.

George Bush was the US Navy's youngest ever fighter pilot. He flew 58 missions and was once shot down (and rescued). He won five medals.

Baroness Sue Ryder worked in the Special Operations Executive.

Sir Hardy Amies served in the Intelligence Corps and was head of the 1944 Special Forces Mission to Belgium. He rose to the rank of lieutenant-colonel.

Sir Fred Pontin worked for the Admiralty in catering and welfare.

Prince Philip served in the Royal Navy and captained a ship.

Anthony Powell served in the Welsh Regiment and the Intelligence Corps as a major.

Humphrey Lyttelton served with the Grenadier Guards.

Lorne Greene served in the Royal Canadian Air Force.

Martin Balsam served in the US Army Combat Engineers before transferring to the US Army Air Force.

George MacDonald Fraser served in the British army in Burma.

Robert Altman was a bomber pilot in the Pacific.

Johnny Carson served with the US Naval Reserve.

People who were evacuated in World War Two

Michael Aspel, Jack Rosenthal, Baroness Shirley Williams, Sir Michael Caine, The Beverley Sisters, Derek Jameson, Justin de Villeneuve, Sir Jonathan Miller, Jeremy Thorpe, Adam Faith, Harold Pinter, Bruce Forsyth, Barbara Windsor

THINGS SAID BY SIR WINSTON CHURCHILL

'I have never accepted what many people have kindly said, namely that I inspired the nation. It was the nation and the race dwelling all round the globe that had the lion heart. I had the luck to be called upon to give the roar.'

ANONYMOUS LABOUR MP: 'Must you fall asleep while I am speaking?'
WINSTON CHURCHILL: 'No, it is purely voluntary.'

BESSIE BRADDOCK: 'Winston, you're drunk!'
WINSTON CHURCHILL: 'Bessie, you're ugly. But tomorrow morning I shall be sober.'

GEORGE BERNARD SHAW: 'Am reserving two tickets for you for my première. Come and bring a friend – if you have one.'
WINSTON CHURCHILL: 'Impossible to be present for the first performance. Will attend the second – if there is one.'

'We are all worms but I do believe that I am a glow-worm.'

Winston, you're drunk!

'When I look back on all the worries, I remember the story of the old man who said on his deathbed that he had a lot of trouble in his life, most of which never happened.'

'Solitary trees, if they grow at all, grow strong.'

'Men stumble over the truth from time to time, but most pick themselves up and hurry off as if nothing happened.'

'History will be kind to me, for I intend to write it.'

'In my belief, you cannot deal with the most serious things in the world unless you also understand the most amusing.'

'We make a living by what we get. We make a life by what we give.'

'I am ready to meet my Maker. Whether my Maker is prepared for the great ordeal of meeting me is another matter.'

Bessie, you're ugly. But tomorrow morning I shall be sober.

SPORT

Jennifer Lopez was a high school star gymnast.

Jason Statham was a diver who represented Great Britain in the Seoul Olympics.

Kate Bosworth was a champion equestrian and played varsity soccer and lacrosse.

Suzanne Danielle represented her county at gymnastics while at school.

Joely Richardson attended a Florida tennis academy for two years.

Darren Day was a semi-professional snooker player.

Haydn Gwynne represented her county at tennis.

50 Cent was a talented boxer who nurtured ambitions to turn professional.

James Alexandrou swam for his county and was ranked in the national top ten.

A baseball hit by a bat travels as fast as 120 mph – almost precisely the same (maximum) speed as the puck in ice hockey.

Keira Knightley, Madonna and Uma Thurman are all keen fencers.

Joel Cadbury once scored a hole-in-one on a par 4 hole. Rarer still than the hole-in-one was his 3 under par albatross.

Sir Bobby Charlton also scored a hole-in-one.

Ricky Tomlinson was offered a football trial by Scunthorpe United but didn't take it up.

There are 108 stitches on a baseball.

Michael Parkinson was a good enough cricketer to play for Barnsley (with Dickie Bird and Geoffrey Boycott) and to have a trial for Yorkshire CCC.

Gary Lineker played second XI cricket for Leicestershire and once scored a century for the MCC playing at Lord's.

Terence Rattigan played cricket at Lord's, when he opened the batting for Harrow against Eton.

Eddie Charlton, the snooker star, appeared in the Australian surfing championship, played top-grade soccer, excelled at tennis and athletics, and carried the flag for Australia in the 1956 Melbourne Olympics.

Australian Rules Football was originally designed to give cricketers something to play during the off-season.

Johnny Mathis has scored a hole-in-one on no fewer than five occasions.

Sir Arthur Conan Doyle was a keen amateur cricketer who bowled the great W.G. Grace in 1900.

Lord Byron was an all-round sportsman who captained Harrow in their annual cricket match against Eton at Lord's.

It takes 3,000 cows to supply the US national football league (NFL) with enough leather for a year's supply of footballs.

Eminem is a keen darts player.

The average life span of a major league baseball is seven pitches.

The bullseye on a dartboard must be precisely 5 feet 8 inches off the ground.

A Costa Rican worker making baseballs earns around $3,000 per annum. The average American pro baseball player earns around $2,500,000 per annum.

At one stage in the 1920s Chelsea had three players who were medical students.

There are two sports in which the team has to move backwards to win: tug of war and rowing. (NB Backstroke is not a team sport.)

When Len Shackleton wrote his autobiography, he included a chapter entitled 'The Average Director's Knowledge of Football'. The chapter consisted of a blank page.

In 1972, an entire soccer team in Cordoba, Argentina, was jailed after the players kicked a linesman to death.

The Alexandra in Crewe Alexandra came from the name of the pub where meetings to set up the club were first held.

Dartboards are made out of horsehair.

WONDERFULLY PUNNY SPORTS STARS' AUTOBIOGRAPHIES

By George (George Foreman)

Life Swings (Nick Faldo)

Gray Matters (Andy Gray)

Biting Talk (Norman Hunter)

Opening Up (Mike Atherton)

It's Knott Cricket (Alan Knott)

Big Fry (Barry Fry)

Watt's My Name (Jim Watt)

Managing My Life (Alex Ferguson)

Heading For Victory (Steve Bruce)

Nine Lives (Matt Dawson)

It's All About A Ball (Alan Ball)

Right Back To The Beginning (Jimmy Armfield)

Hell Razor (Neil Ruddock)

Maine Man (Tony Book)

Banks of England (Gordon Banks)

The Real Mackay (Dave Mackay)

ALL THE BRITISH DRIVERS WHO HAVE WON THE BRITISH GRAND PRIX

1935 Richard Shuttleworth

1955 Stirling Moss

1957 Stirling Moss

1958 Peter Collins

1962 Jim Clark

1963 Jim Clark

1964 Jim Clark

1965 Jim Clark

1967 Jim Clark

1969 Jackie Stewart

1971 Jackie Stewart

1977 James Hunt

1981 John Watson

1986 Nigel Mansell

1987 Nigel Mansell

1991 Nigel Mansell

1992 Nigel Mansell

1994 Damon Hill

1995 Johnny Herbert

1999 David Coulthard

2000 David Coulthard

PEOPLE WHO HAVE RUN MARATHONS

(London except where stated.)

Richard Dunwoody

Adrian Moorhouse

Jeffrey Archer

Nell McAndrew

Sir Ranulph Fiennes

Beth Cordingly

Charlie Brooks

Richard Herring

Kate Garraway

Andrew Morton

Major Charles Ingram

Brough Scott

Iain Duncan Smith

Lorraine Kelly

Donal Macintyre

Sean 'P. Diddy' Combs (New York)

Will Ferrell (Boston)

Jorg Haider (NY)

Oprah Winfrey (Marine Corps)

Phil Selway (London)

KEEN SQUASH PLAYERS

Tom Cruise, Mary Archer, Richard Dunwoody, Richard Wilson, Mike Atherton, David Essex, Anton Mosimann, Ian Balding, Michael Palin, Trisha Goddard, Nicole Kidman, Ian McShane, Nicky Clarke, Damon Hill

KEEN TENNIS PLAYERS

Mariella Frostrup, Gabby Logan, Tamzin Outhwaite, Alistair McGowan, Sir Cliff Richard, Robert Duvall, Terry Wogan, Des Lynam, Prue Leith, Gordon Brown, Les Dennis, Sam Torrance, Angus Deayton, Tony Blair, Roger Black, Rory Bremner, Martin Amis, Raymond Blanc, Roger Lloyd Pack, Sir David Frost, Sir Richard Branson, Chris Patten, Geoffrey Boycott, Loyd Grossman, John Francome, Christopher Martin-Jenkins, Dermot Murnaghan, Jeff Lynne, James Fox, Jung Chang, Trevor Eve, Alan Hansen, Peter Snow, Simon MacCorkindale, Sir Jackie Stewart, Nicky Clarke, Ainsley Harriott, Anthea Turner, Rosanna Davidson, Michelle Trachtenberg

KEEN ON SAILING

Jonathan Dimbleby, John Major, Michael Grade, Robbie Coltrane, Annabel Croft, Jeremy Irons, Valerie Singleton, Peter Skellern, Elle MacPherson, Alan Titchmarsh, Kelsey Grammer, Chloe Sevigny, Russell Crowe

KEEN TABLE-TENNIS PLAYERS

Steve McFadden (won competitions as a child)

Kevin Spacey (requests a ping-pong table in his room whenever he's on location)

Lord Norman Lamont

Chief Rabbi Jonathan Sacks

Roger McGough

Paul Gascoigne

Julian Bream

Michael Owen

Matthew Broderick

WOMEN WHO ARE KEEN GOLFERS

Catherine Zeta-Jones, Claudia Schiffer, Teri Hatcher, Felicity Kendal, Carol Barnes, Dame Kiri Te Kanawa, Mary Parkinson, Jo Durie, Rachael Heyhoe Flint, Dame Naomi James, Celine Dion, Cindy Crawford, Hazel Irvine, Caryl Phillips, Nicole Kidman, Jodie Kidd, Michelle Trachtenberg

KEEN SNOOKER PLAYERS

Steve Cram, Don Black, Sir Alex Ferguson, Robert Harris, Gary Lineker, Nick Faldo, Noah Wyle (plays billiards like a pool shark at the Hollywood Athletic Club), Kelsey Grammer (billiards), Finley Quaye (was a snooker hustler as a boy), Lisa Kudrow (plays pool like a pool shark and can perform trick shots)

IF ...

If Holly Hunter married George W. Bush, she'd be Holly Bush.

If Iman married Gary Oldman, she'd be Iman Oldman.

If Cherie Blair married Oliver Stone, she'd be Cherie Stone.

If Ronni Ancona married Jason Biggs, she'd be Ronni Biggs.

If Minnie Driver married Alice Cooper, she'd be Minnie Cooper.

If Sandi Toksvig married Pauly Shore, she'd be Sandi Shore.

If Olivia Newton-John married Wayne Newton, then divorced him to marry Elton John, she'd be Olivia Newton-John Newton John.

JAMES BOND

'Who was the first person to play James Bond' is a famous trick question. No, it wasn't Sean Connery, even though he was the first movie James Bond (in *Dr No*). In 1954, James Bond was played by Barry Nelson in a one-hour US TV version of *Casino Royale*. Le Chiffre, the baddie, was played by Peter Lorre.

Since Barry Nelson, Bond has been played by Connery, George Lazenby, Roger Moore, Timothy Dalton and Pierce Brosnan (as well as by David Niven in the spoof *Casino Royale*).

Ian Fleming, the creator of Bond, took his hero's name from an ornithologist. Fleming was a keen birdwatcher and when he was looking for a name, he picked up a book by a distinguished American ornithologist named James Bond and decided to 'borrow' it.

Fleming also 'borrowed' the name of Bond's greatest enemy, Blofeld. Fleming had been pondering over a suitably nasty name for his villain when he chanced upon the name of Henry Blofeld, now a cricket commentator, in Boodles, the London gentlemen's club.

James Bond is renowned for his smooth talking. In *Diamonds Are Forever*, when Tiffany Case (Jill St John) asks him, 'Do you like redheads?', he replies, 'As long as the collars and cuffs match.'

For most people, Sean Connery is Bond, but Connery himself described the character as 'a Frankenstein monster I can't get rid of' and has said, 'I have always hated that damn James Bond: I'd like to kill him.'

James Bond has been going for so long that *Goldeneye* saw the first appearance by the daughter of a Bond girl. Eunice Grayson appeared in the first two Bond movies (indeed, it was to her that Bond first uttered the immortal words, 'The name's Bond, James Bond') and her daughter, Karen, 24, appeared in *Goldeneye*.

Bond's cars are almost as essential to the films' success as the villains and the girls. His most famous car is the Aston Martin DB5 with revolving numberplates, pop-up bulletproof shield and ejector-seat he drove in *Goldfinger*.

But if *Goldfinger* had the most memorable car, *Diamonds Are Forever* had the most memorable car stunt. That was the film when Connery (or his stunt man) two-wheeled a Ford Mustang down a narrow alleyway and then set it back on four wheels.

OTHER PEOPLE BORN ON CHRISTMAS DAY

1642 Sir Isaac Newton, English scientist

1899 Humphrey Bogart, American actor

1901 Princess Alice, British royal

1907 Andrew Cruickshank, British actor

1907 Cab Calloway, American musician

1908 Quentin Crisp, British writer and personality

1912 Tony Martin, American actor and singer

1918 Anwar Sadat, Egyptian politician

1923 Noele Gordon, British actress

1924 Rod Serling, American writer

1927 Alan King, American comedian

1934 Stuart Hall, British TV presenter

1936 Princess Alexandra, British royal

1936 Ismail Merchant, Indian film producer

1937 O'Kelly Isley, American singer

1941 Jim Bolger, British racehorse trainer

1942 Barbara Follett, British politician

1943 Hanna Schygulla, German actress

1944 Kenny Everett, British DJ

1944 Nigel Starmer-Smith, British rugby union commentator

1945 Noel Redding, British musician

1946 Jimmy Buffett, American singer

1946 Christopher Frayling, British playwright

1947 Kieran Prendiville, British writer and TV presenter

1948 Merry Clayton, American singer

1948 Barbara Mandrell, American country singer

1949 Sissy Spacek, American actress

1954 Robin Campbell, British musician

1954 Annie Lennox, British singer

1957 Shane MacGowan, British musician

1963 Ashley Metcalfe, British cricketer

1966 Stephen Twigg, British politician

1968 Helena Christensen, Danish model

1971 Lightning, British Gladiator

1971 Dido, British singer

1975 Marcus Trescothick, British cricketer

1978 Simon Jones, British cricketer

CHRISTMAS NOTES

Armenians celebrate Christmas on 19 January.

In the US state of Indiana, there is a town called Santa Claus where courses are held for department store Santas. Graduates become a BSc (Bachelor of Santa Clausing).

Christmas was officially abolished in England between 1642 and 1652 – thanks to the Puritans who hated the idea of anyone enjoying themselves.

Christmas cards had their origins in 15th-century Germany, and it wasn't until the mid-19th-century (and the advent of the postage stamp) that they were produced commercially in this country. Today, the most popular Christmas card is one depicting Santa Claus and his reindeer.

The *Mayflower* arrived at Plymouth Rock, Massachusetts on Christmas Day 1620.

THINGS SAID ABOUT CHRISTMAS

'Next to a circus there ain't nothing that packs up and tears out faster than the Christmas spirit.' (Kin Hubbard)

'Christmas is a holiday that persecutes the lonely, the frayed, and the rejected.' (Jimmy Cannon)

'What is Christmas? It is tenderness for the past, courage for the present, hope for the future. It is a fervent wish that every cup may overflow with blessings rich and eternal, and that every path may lead to peace.' (Agnes Pharo)

'There is no ideal Christmas; only the one Christmas you decide to make as a reflection of your values, desires, affections, traditions.' (Bill McKibben)

'Christmas waves a magic wand over this world, and behold, everything is softer and more beautiful.' (Norman Vincent Peale)

'Blessed is the season which engages the whole world in a conspiracy of love.' (Hamilton Wright Mabie)

'Christmas, children, is not a date. It is a state of mind.' (Mary Ellen Chase)

GENUINE PLACE NAMES FOR LOVERS OF DOUBLE ENTENDRE

Arsy (France)

Bald Knob (Arkansas, USA)

Balls Cross (West Sussex)

Bastardo (Italy)

Beaver (Pennsylvania, USA)

Bendery (Moldova)

Big Bone Lick (Kentucky, USA)

Blowing Rock (North Carolina, USA)

Bottom (North Carolina, USA)

Bra (Italy)

Broadbottom (Greater Manchester)

Burrumbuttock (Australia)

Buttock's Booth (Northamptonshire)

Climax (Michigan, USA)

Clit (Romania)

Cock Bank (Clwyd)

Cockermouth (Cumbria)

Comers (Grampian)

Condom (France)

Dildo (Canada)

Fertile (Minnesota, USA)

French Lick (Indiana, USA)

Fucking (Austria)

Hornytown (North Carolina, USA)

Humptulips (Washington, USA)

Intercourse (Pennsylvania, USA)

Knob Lick (Missouri, USA)

Knockin (Shropshire)

Lickey End (Worcestershire)

Loveladies (New Jersey, USA)

Lover (Wiltshire)

Muff (Northern Ireland)

Neck City (Missouri, USA)

Penistone (South Yorkshire)

Petting (Germany)

Phuket (Thailand)

Root (Switzerland)

Semen (Indonesia)

Shafton (Yorkshire)

Shag Harbour (Canada)

Thong (Kent)

Titz (Germany)

Twatt (Orkney)

Twin Humps Park (Australia)

Undy (Gwent)

Upper Dicker (East Sussex)

Wankers Corner (Oregon, USA)

Wide Open (Tyne and Wear)

Marriage etc.

Hugh Dennis met his wife Kate, a sound engineer, when Hugh was playing a talking fromage frais in a Soho voiceover studio.

Four of Mickey Rooney's weddings took place in Las Vegas.

Woody Harrelson married Neil Simon's daughter.

Baroness Ruth Rendell, Art Carney and Alexander Solzhenitsyn all remarried their spouses after divorce.

Couples who celebrated their Diamond Wedding Anniversary

Lord Longford & Elizabeth, Countess of Longford

Perry & Roselle Como

Sir Donald & Lady Jessie Bradman

Anthony & Lady Violet Powell

Bob & Dolores Hope

James & Frances Cagney

Sir Alec & Lady Merula Guinness

Karl & Mona Malden

Lord James & Audrey Callaghan

Fred Zinnemann & Renee Bartlett

Sir John Mills & Mary Hayley Bell

Michael Denison & Dulcie Gray

The Duke and Duchess of Devonshire

Lord Richard Attenborough & Sheila Sim

George & Barbara Bush

Charlton & Lydia Heston

COUPLES WHO CELEBRATED THEIR GOLDEN WEDDING ANNIVERSARY

Dame Catherine & Tom Cookson

Jack & Florence Haley

Dame Thora Hird & Jimmy Scott

Sir Matt & Lady Jean Busby

Ray & Gwendolyn Bolger

Lord & Lady Lew Grade

Hammond Innes & Dorothy Lang

Robin & Patricia Bailey

Walter & Ruth Pidgeon

Hume Cronyn & Jessica Tandy

Pat & Eloise O'Brien

Carl & Emma Jung

Queen Elizabeth II & Prince Philip

Dick & Mary Francis

Lord & Lady Yehudi Menuhin

The Rev. W. & Margaret Awdry

Sir Harry & Lady Myra Secombe

Googie Withers & John McCallum

Federico Fellini & Giulietta Masina

Marlene Dietrich & Rudolf Sieber

Eli & Anne Wallach

PEOPLE WHO WERE/ARE MARRIED TO THEIR MANAGERS

Cilla Black, Neneh Cherry, Joe Bugner, Clodagh Rodgers, Celine Dion, Pam Ayres, Charlotte Rampling, LaToya Jackson, Anthea Turner, Judy Garland, Randy Travis, Vanessa Williams, Victoria De Los Angeles, Ozzy Osbourne, Luke Goss, Caron Keating, Paula Radcliffe, Faith Evans, Susan Chilcott, Michael Barrymore, Anita Harris, Lynda Carter, Ronnie Spector, Rita Hayworth, Mary Black, Dolores O'Riordan

PEOPLE WHO MARRIED THEIR MINDERS

Roseanne Arnold, Patty Hearst, Princess Stephanie of Monaco

PEOPLE WITH SPOUSES IN COMMON

Sonny Bono & Greg Allman – Cher

Peter Sellers & Slim Jim McDonnell – Britt Ekland

Fiona Fullerton & Susan George – Simon MacCorkindale

Liam Gallagher & Jim Kerr – Patsy Kensit

Gary Oldman & Martin Scorsese – Isabella Rossellini

Dudley Moore & Pinchas Zukerman – Tuesday Weld

Gary Kemp & Jude Law – Sadie Frost

Mia Farrow & Ava Gardner – Frank Sinatra

Henry Fonda & William Wyler – Margaret Sullavan

Sir Rex Harrison & Richard Harris – Elizabeth Harris

Artie Shaw & Lex Barker – Lana Turner

Humphrey Bogart & Jason Robards – Lauren Bacall

Mimi Rogers & Nicole Kidman – Tom Cruise

Ursula Andress & Linda Evans – John Derek

Vivien Leigh & Joan Plowright – Sir Laurence Olivier

Catherine Deneuve & Marie Helvin – David Bailey

Brigitte Bardot & Jane Fonda – Roger Vadim

Peter Sellers & Sir David Frost – Lynne Frederick

Charlie Chaplin & Burgess Meredith – Paulette Goddard

Michael Jayston & André Previn – Heather Jayston

George Sanders & Ronald Colman – Benita Hume

Laurence Harvey & Michael Wilding – Margaret Leighton

Clark Gable & William Powell – Carole Lombard

Germaine Greer & Maya Angelou – Paul de Feu

Franchot Tone & Douglas Fairbanks Jnr. – Joan Crawford

Don Johnson & Antonio Banderas – Melanie Griffith

Dame Elizabeth Taylor & Joan Blondell – Mike Todd

Dame Elizabeth Taylor & Debbie Reynolds – Eddie Fisher

Rod Steiger & Philip Roth – Claire Bloom

Roger Vadim & Ted Turner – Jane Fonda

Gloria Swanson & Constance Bennett – Marquis de la Coudraye

Myrna Loy & Hedy Lamarr – Gene Markey

Lana Turner & Arlene Dahl – Lex Barker

Nancy Reagan & Jane Wyman – Ronald Reagan

Lana Turner & Evelyn Keyes – Artie Shaw

Mickey Rooney & Artie Shaw – Ava Gardner

John Huston & Artie Shaw – Evelyn Keyes

Gene Tierney & Hedy Lamarr – Howard Lee

Joan Fontaine & Ida Lupino – Collier Young

Joe DiMaggio & Arthur Miller – Marilyn Monroe

Jeanne Moreau & Lesley-Anne Down – William Friedkin

John F. Kennedy & Aristotle Onassis – Jacqueline Onassis

Rachel Roberts & Kay Kendall – Sir Rex Harrison

Jennie Churchill & Mrs Patrick Campbell – George Cornwallis-West

Donald Dewar & Lord Alexander Irvine – Alison McNair

Stavros Niarchos & Aristotle Onassis – Tina Livanos

James Hunt & Richard Burton – Suzy Hunt

Paulette Goddard & Oona O'Neill – Charlie Chaplin

PEOPLE WHO NEVER MARRIED

Irma Kurtz, Sir Edward Heath, Julie Christie, Sir Cliff Richard, Valerie Singleton, Selina Scott, Sir Jimmy Savile, Dame Mary Peters, Baroness Betty Boothroyd, Celia Imrie, Zandra Rhodes, Harold 'Dickie' Bird, Celia Hammond, Gloria Steinem, Ralph Nader, Lynsey De Paul, Michael Winner, Jean Alexander, Ann Widdecombe, Patricia Routledge, Sir Patrick Moore, Marcelle D'Argy Smith, Kate Adie, Eleanor Bron, Leonard Cohen, Lorraine Chase, Sir Cyril Smith

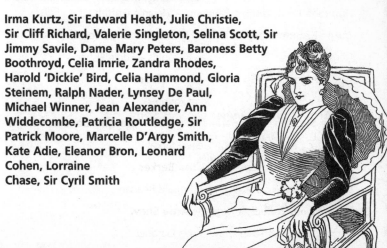

THINGS THAT SIMPLY DISAPPEARED

Deelybobbers

Pet Rocks

Clackers

Hai Karate After-Shave

Cabbage Patch Dolls

Broomball

Gonks

Paper Knickers

Hairstyles such as the Elephant's Trunk, Argentine Ducktail, Flat-Top, Conk, Spike-Top, Suedehead and Flop

WOMEN WHO DIED IN CHILDBIRTH

Jane Seymour (wife of Henry VIII, while giving birth to future Edward VI)

Two of Joseph Chamberlain's wives (one of whom was Neville Chamberlain's mother, and died when he was six)

James Watt's wife

Mary Shelley's mother (Mary Wollstonecraft)

Liz Smith's mother (when she was two)

Eric Sykes's mother

James Goldsmith's first wife

John Donne's wife

Charles Babbage's wife

Kenneth Grahame's mother (when he was five)

Fred Archer's wife (precipitating his suicide)

Princess Charlotte

Haing Ngor's wife (the Khmer Rouge's hatred of professionals meant he was unable to reveal that he was a gynaecologist and needed medical supplies to help her)

Al Jolson's mother (when he was eight)

Walter Pidgeon's first wife

Franz Liszt's daughter

Robert Johnson's first wife (aged 16)

Three of Jane Austen's sisters-in-law

Kim Il-Sung's first wife

Emperor Haile Selassie's daughter

Dan Maskell's mother (when he was 14)

Young Tom Morris's wife

Catherine Parr

MEN WHOSE PENIS WAS PRESERVED AFTER DEATH

Napoleon Bonaparte (it was eventually sold at auction where it fetched £2,500)

Grigori Rasputin (according to his biographer, 'it looked like a blackened overripe banana, about a foot long…')

People who died of lung cancer

Steve McQueen, Jacques Brel, Yul Brynner, Joe DiMaggio, Roy Castle, John Wayne, Buddy Adler, Duke Ellington, Roddy McDowall, Ray Harford, Stubby Kaye, Buster Keaton, Desi Arnaz, Tex Avery, Bruce Cabot, Art Blakey, Cantinflas, King George VI, Lon Chaney, Andy Kaufman, Alec Clunes, Chuck Connors, Frank Loesser, E.G. Marshall, Franchot Tone, Gary Cooper, Walt Disney, Dick Haymes, Fernandel, Harry Guardino, Moe Howard, Eddie Kendricks, Warren Zevon, Doug McClure, Ray Milland, Robert Mitchum, Forrest Tucker, Boris Pasternak, Lloyd Nolan, Jesse Owens, Robert Preston, Carl Wilson, Vincent Price, Eddie Rabbitt, Alan Jay Lerner, Nicholas Ray, Robert Taylor, Sir Stanley Baker, Michael Williams, Gilbert Becaud, Nat 'King' Cole, Albert Collins, Rosemary Clooney, Betty Grable, Melina Mercouri, Agnes Moorehead, Jennifer Paterson, Carmen Silvera, Jacqueline Susann, Sarah Vaughan, Nancy Walker

Celebrity bequests

Two days before her death in 1970, Janis Joplin amended her will to provide $2,500 'so my friends can get blasted after I'm gone'. She also left a guest list. The all-night party duly took place at a Californian tavern where she had often performed.

In 1964, Ian Fleming, the author of the James Bond novels, left £500 to each of four friends with the instruction that they should 'spend the same within twelve months of receipt on some extravagance'.

In 1962, Marilyn Monroe left all her 'personal effects and clothing' to Lee Strasberg, her acting coach, 'it being my desire that he distribute these, in his sole discretion, among my friends, colleagues and those to whom I am devoted'. She also left Strasberg most of her estate.

In 1998, author Hammond Innes left his London home to the actress Celia Imrie, whom he'd befriended towards the end of his life.

In 1986, Cary Grant bequeathed all of his 'wearing apparel,

ornaments and jewellery' to Stanley E. Fox on condition that Mr Fox shared everything out among 14 specified people – one of whom was Frank Sinatra.

W.C. Fields's last requests, as listed in his will, were ignored. He wanted his body cremated without any religious ceremony. However, both his estranged Roman Catholic wife and his mistress held separate religious ceremonies before his body was interred in a mausoleum in 1946. Nor did anything come of the provision he had made for a 'W.C. Fields College for orphan white boys and girls where no religion of any sort is to be preached'.

P.T. Barnum, the famous American showman, drew up a will in 1882 leaving his daughter Helen $1,500 a year for life. When she left her husband, Barnum wrote her out of the will. Then, in an 1889 codicil, he left her a property in Colorado, which he believed was worthless. Two years later, he died and Helen inherited this property, which turned out to have mineral deposits that made Helen wealthier than all the other beneficiaries of Barnum's will combined.

In 1964, Cole Porter bequeathed his diamond dress stud to Douglas Fairbanks Jnr.

In his will, Noah gave the whole world to his three sons.

PAIRS OF CELEBRITIES WHO DIED ON THE SAME DAY

John Adams (second US President) & Thomas Jefferson (third US President) – 4.7.1826

Charles Kingsley (author of The Water Babies) & Gustave Doré (painter) – 23.1.1883

Franz Liszt (classical composer) & Frank Holl (painter) – 31.7.1888

Wilkie Collins (novelist) & Eliza Cook (poet) – 23.9.1889

Charles Stewart Parnell (Irish leader) & William Henry Smith (founder of W.H. Smith) – 6.10.1891

John Ruskin (social reformer, artist and writer) & Richard Doddridge Blackmore (writer of Lorna Doone) – 20.1.1900

Carl Bechstein (maker of the famous Bechstein pianos) & Gottlieb Daimler (motor car manufacturer) – 6.3.1900

Marshal Henri Pétain (French soldier and leader of the wartime Vichy regime) & Robert Flaherty (film-maker and explorer) – 23.7.1951

Josef Stalin (Soviet dictator) and Sergei Prokofiev (composer who was persecuted by Stalin) – 5.3.1953

King Ibn Saud (of Saudi Arabia) and Dylan Thomas (poet) – 9.11.1953

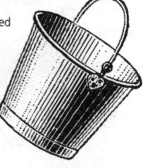

Ward Bond (actor) & Mack Sennett (film producer) – 5.11.1960

Michael Curtiz (film director) & Stu Sutcliffe (former member of The Beatles) – 10.4.1962

Jean Cocteau (playwright and film director) & Edith Piaf (singer) – 11.10.1963

Hedda Hopper (gossip columnist) & Buster Keaton (actor) – 1.2.1966

Billy Rose (Broadway producer) & Sophie Tucker (singer) – 10.2.1966

Che Guevara (revolutionary) & André Maurois (French author) – 9.10.1967

Mama Cass Elliot (singer) & Erich Kästner (author of *Emil And The Detectives*) – 29.7.1974

Steve Biko (anti-apartheid activist) & Robert Lowell (American poet) – 12.9.1977

Dame Gracie Fields (singer) & Jimmy McCullough (guitarist with Wings) – 27.9.1979

Joyce Grenfell (actress and writer) & Zeppo Marx (member of the Marx Brothers) – 30.11.1979

Thelonious Monk (musician) & Lee Strasberg (actor and drama teacher) – 17.2.1982

Muddy Waters (blues musician) & George Balanchine (choreographer) – 30.4.1983

William Powell (film star) & Tito Gobbi (opera singer) – 5.3.1984

Carl Foreman (film producer) & George Gallup (pollster) – 26.6.1984

Sam Spiegel (film producer) & Ricky Nelson (pop star) – 31.12.1985

Gordon Macrae (actor) & L. Ron Hubbard (creator of Scientology) & Vincente Minnelli (film director) – 24.1.1986

Wallis Simpson (Duchess of Windsor) & Bill Edrich (England cricketer) – 24.4.1986

Alan Jay Lerner (lyricist) & Jorge Luis Borges (writer) – 14.6.1986

Randolph Scott (actor) & Joan Greenwood (actress) – 2.3.1987

Mary Astor (actress) & Emlyn Williams (actor and playwright) – 25.9.1987

Arthur Marshall (writer and broadcaster) & Sir Thomas Sopwith (aviation pioneer) – 27.1.1989

Sugar Ray Robinson (boxer) & Abbie Hoffman (American activist and writer) – 12.4.1989

Tommy Trinder (comedian) & Mel Blanc (the voice of cartoon characters such as Bugs Bunny) – 10.7.1989

George Adamson (*Born Free* conservationist) & Diana Vreeland (fashion guru) – 21.8.1989

Graham Chapman (member of the Monty Pythons) & Norman Yardley (England cricketer) – 4.10.1989

Mel Appleby (of Mel and Kim) & Bhagwan Shree Rajneesh (guru) – 19.1.1990

Teddy Tinling (tennis dress designer) &
Rocky Graziano (boxer) – 23.5.1990

**Max Wall (actor and comedian) &
Major Pat Reid (Colditz escaper and
author) – 22.5.1990**

Serge Gainsbourg (French singer and
composer) & Edwin Land (inventor of the
Polaroid camera) – 3.3.1991

**Steve Marriott (rock star) & Don
Siegel (film director) – 20.4.1991**

Bernie Winters (comedian) & Jerzy
Kosinski (writer) – 4.5.1991

**Isaac Bashevis Singer (Nobel Prize-
winning writer) & Freddie Brown
(England cricketer) – 24.7.1991**

Robert Maxwell (businessman) & Fred
MacMurray (actor) – 5.11.1991

**Stella Adler (drama teacher) & Albert
King (blues singer) – 21.12.1992**

James Hunt (motor racing driver) & John
Connally (Former Texas governor and US
presidential candidate, who was riding in the same car as President
Kennedy when he was shot) – 15.6.1993

**Elizabeth Montgomery (actress) & Elisha Cook Jr (actor) –
18.5.1995**

Simon Cadell (actor) & Lord Douglas Jay (politician) – 6.3.1996

**Ray Lindwall (Australian cricketer) & Andreas Papandreou
(Greek Prime Minister) – 23.6.1996**

Alfred Marks (actor) & Margot Hemingway (model and actress) –
1.7.1996

Mother Teresa (aid worker) & Sir Georg Solti (orchestral conductor) – 5.9.1997

Carl Wilson (Beach Boy) & Falco (singer) – 6.2.1998

Benny Green (broadcaster) & Maureen O'Sullivan (actress) – 22.6.1998

Bettino Craxi (Italian politician) & Hedy Lamarr (actress) – 19.1.2000

Charles M. Schulz (*Peanuts* creator) & Screamin' Jay Hawkins (blues legend) – 12.2.2000

Sir John Gielgud (actor) & Dame Barbara Cartland (writer) – 21.5.2000

Perry Como (singer) & Didi (Brazilian footballer) & Simon Raven (memoirist) – 12.5.2001

John Lee Hooker (blues legend) & Carroll O'Connor – 21.6.2001

Chet Atkins (musician) & Joe Fagan (Liverpool FC manager) – 30.6.2001

Ken Tyrell (Formula 1 boss) & Aaliyah (singer) – 25.8.2001

Christiaan Barnard (heart surgery pioneer) & Troy Donahue (actor) – 2.9.2001

Milton Berle (comedian) & Dudley Moore (actor and pianist) – 27.3.2002

Chaim Potok (writer) & Leo McKern (actor) – 23.7.2002

Sir Paul Getty (philanthropist) & Dr Robert Atkins (diet guru) – 17.4.2003

Robert Stack (actor) & Dame Wendy Hiller (actress) – 14.5.2003

Strom Thurmond (US senator) & Sir Denis Thatcher (prime minister's husband) – 26.6.2003

Gregory Hines (actor and dancer) & Ray Harford (soccer boss) – 9.8.2003

Elia Kazan (film director) & Althea Gibson (tennis champion) – 28.9.2003

Alistair Cooke (broadcaster) & Hubert Gregg (performer and broadcaster) – 30.3.2004

Archibald Cox (Watergate prosecutor) & Jack Rosenthal (playwright) – 29.5.2004

Red Adair (firefighter) & Bernard Levin (newspaper columnist) – 7.8.2004

Hunter S. Thompson (writer) & Sandra Dee (film star) – 20.2.2005

PEOPLE WHO DIED IN POVERTY

Josephine Baker, William Blake, Mrs Patrick Campbell, Miguel de Cervantes, Christopher Columbus, Gustave Flaubert, Johann Gutenberg, William Hazlitt, Robert Johnson, Joe Louis, Herman Melville, Wolfgang Mozart, Thomas Paine, Edith Piaf, Rembrandt, Charles Rennie Mackintosh, Oskar Schindler, Gordon Selfridge (founder of the eponymous department store), Joan Sims, Anthony Steel, Laurence Sterne, Vincent Van Gogh, Vermeer, Oscar Wilde

FAMOUS PEOPLE BORN ON THE DAY OTHER FAMOUS PEOPLE DIED

Darren Gough – 18.9.1970 – Jimi Hendrix

Norah Jones – 30.3.1979 – Airey Neave

David Schwimmer – 2.11.1966 – Mississippi John Hurt

Lilian Thuram – 1.1.1972 – Maurice Chevalier

The Rock – 2.5.1972 – J. Edgar Hoover

Charles Wheeler – 26.3.1923 – Sarah Bernhardt

Pink – 8.9.1979 – Jean Seberg

Sophie, Countess of Wessex – 20.1.1965 – Alan Freed

Natalie Imbruglia – 4.2.1975 – Louis Jordan

Jim Dale – 15.8.1935 – Will Rogers

Derek Dougan – 20.1.1936 – King George V

Divine Brown – 9.8.1969 – Sharon Tate

Keith Vaz – 26.11.1956 – Tommy Dorsey

Barry Sheene – 11.9.1950 – Field Marshal Jan Christian Smuts

Suzanne Danielle – 14.1.1957 – Humphrey Bogart

Richard Littlejohn – 18.1.1954 – Sydney Greenstreet

Joe Haines – 29.1.1928 – Earl Haig

Charlotte Rampling – 5.2.1946 – George Arliss

Peter Purves – 10.2.1939 – Pope Pius XI

Helena Sukova – 23.2.1965 – Stan Laurel

Sinead O'Carroll – 14.5.1978 – Sir Robert Menzies

Ben Okri – 15.3.1959 – Lester Young

Ornette Coleman – 19.3.1930 – Arthur Balfour

Tim Yeo – 20.3.1945 – Lord Alfred Douglas

Teddy Sheringham – 2.4.1966 – C.S. Forester

John Hartson – 5.4.1975 – Chiang Kai-shek

Dennis Rodman – 13.5.1961 – Gary Cooper

Mary-Kate & Ashley Olsen – 13.6.1986 – Benny Goodman

Bill Withers – 4.7.1938 – Suzanne Lenglen

Oscar De La Renta – 22.7.1932 – Florenz Ziegfield

Louise Fletcher – 22.7.34 – John Dillinger

Ruthie Henshall 7.3.1967 – Alice B. Toklas

Monica Lewinsky – 23.7.1973 – Eddie Rickenbacker

Dino DeLaurentis – 8.8.1919 – Frank Winfield Woolworth

John Gorman – 16.8.1949 – Margaret Mitchell

Matt Aitken – 25.8.1956 – Alfred Kinsey

Derek Fowlds – 2.9.1937 – Baron Pierre de Coubertin

Savo Milosevic – 2.9.1973 – J.R.R. Tolkien

Michael Feinstein – 7.9.1956 – C.B. Fry

Karl Lagerfeld – 10.9.1938 – Charles Cruft

Stephen Gately – 17.3.1976 – Luchino Visconti

Holly Robinson – 18.9.1964 – Sean O'Casey

Eamonn Martin – 9.10.1958 – Pope Pius XII

Roger Taylor (the tennis player) – 14.10.1944 – Erwin Rommel

Melanie Blatt – 25.3.1975 – King Faisal of Saudi Arabia

Jenny McCarthy – 1.11.1972 – Ezra Pound

GENUINE I.T. HELPDESK EXCHANGE

CUSTOMER: My keyboard is not working.

HELPDESK: Are you sure it's plugged into the computer?

CUSTOMER: No. I can't get behind the computer.

HELPDESK: Pick up your keyboard and walk 10 paces back.

CUSTOMER: OK.

HELPDESK: Did the keyboard come with you?

CUSTOMER: Yes.

HELPDESK: That means the keyboard is not plugged in.

LASTS

The last letter George Harrison ever wrote was to Mike Myers asking for a Mini-Me doll.

19.11.1999 was the last date before 1.1.3111 when all the digits in the date were odd.

After Custer's Last Stand, Sioux Indian leader Chief Sitting Bull became an entertainer and toured the country with Buffalo Bill's Wild West Show.

The last time a First Division/Premier club had two players scoring more than 30 goals in a season was Sunderland in 1935–36 when Raich Carter and Bob Gurney each scored 31 goals.

EPIGRAPH

'If a little knowledge is dangerous, where is the man who has so much as to be out of danger?'
(Thomas Huxley)

ACKNOWLEDGEMENTS

The Other Book is the third – and (almost certainly) the last – in a series that started with *That Book* and continued with *This Book*.

As with the first two books, most of *The Other Book* is the product of fascinating facts I've collected over the past twenty years and, therefore, unique to this book (or, rather, not *This Book* but *The Other Book*, if you get my drift). Nevertheless, as with the first two books, I am happy to acknowledge material culled from the internet – especially in the sections insects etc, the human condition, fish etc., geography, birds etc., history, animals etc. and science – as well as fabulous contributions sent to me by friends and readers (sometimes by friends who are also readers or even by readers who have become friends). Once again, I would like to credit LexisNexis, the best and the most user-friendly search tool I've ever come across.

As always, I welcome your emails – yup, even when you write in with corrections (how else will I ever get it right?) – so please write to me at: thatbook@mail.com

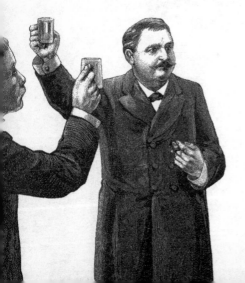

The Other Book was a team effort (even if I made damn sure that only my name appeared on the cover). So I'd like to thank (in reverse alphabetic order): Doug Young, Mari Roberts, Penny Chorlton, Luigi Bonomi, and Hugh Adams.

Since this is (almost certainly) the last in the series, I'd also like to thank the following people for their help, contributions and/or support (moral or otherwise): Gilly Adams, Alison Barrow, Jeremy Beadle, Marcus Berkmann, Chris Ewins, Jonathan Fingerhut, Jenny Garrison, Patrick Janson-Smith, Sam Jones, John Koski, Richard Littlejohn, Tricia Martin, Keiran Mellikof, Emanuel Mond, William Mulcahy, Nicholas Ridge, Charlie Symons, Jack Symons, Louise Symons, David Thomas, Katrina Whone and Rob Woolley.

As ever, if I've missed anyone out, then please know that – as with any mistakes in the book – it's entirely down to my own stupidity.